FIERCE HEART

Also by Stuart Holmes Coleman

Eddie Would Go

STUART HOLMES
COLEMAN

FIERCE HEART

The Story of Makaha
and the Soul of
Hawaiian Surfing

ST. MARTIN'S PRESS
NEW YORK

www.stmartins.com

Design by Kathryn Parise

Title page and chapter opener background photograph
by Phil Mislinski

LIBRARY OF CONGRESS CATALOGING-IN-PUBLICATION DATA

Coleman, Stuart Holmes.
    Fierce heart : the story of Makaha and the soul of Hawaiian
surfing / Stuart Holmes Coleman.
      p. cm.
    ISBN-13: 978-0-312-38451-7
    ISBN-10: 0-312-38451-3
    1. Surfing—Hawaii—Makaha. 2. Surfers—Hawaii—
Makaha. 3. Makaha, Hawaii—History. I. Title.
GV840.S8C57 2009
797.3'209693—dc22

2008046320

First Edition: May 2009

10 9 8 7 6 5 4 3 2 1

To my father and my mother,
Who taught me to love and to fight
For justice, peace, and the rights
Of all my sisters and brothers

Contents

❧

Contents ❧ x

List of Illustrations

※

Illustrations in Text

FIERCE HEART

◐◑ ◐◑ ◐◑ ◐◑ ◐◑ ◐◑ ◐◑ ◐◑ ◐◑ ◐◑ ◐◑ ◐◑

Introduction

Makaha Means "Fierce"

> *We the warriors born to live*
> *On what the land and sea can give*
> *Defend our birthright to be free—*
> *Give our children liberty.*
> —Israel "Iz" Kamakawiwoʻole

Makaha is a paradoxical place, a land of extremes. Driving along the Waiʻanae Coast of Oʻahu's Westside, I am always struck by its natural beauty. Yet in between the jagged cliffs of the Waiʻanae Mountains and the tranquil calm of the Pacific, there are burnt-out cars by the side of the road and makeshift camps of homeless Hawaiians in the beach parks. Infamous for its high rates of addiction, crime, and violence, the wild Westside instills a sense of fear and uneasiness in many who visit its shores. Yet it's also known for the generous aloha of its people who have shared their love of Hawaiian culture and water sports with the rest of the world. Even the waves at Makaha can be extreme, waist high and playful one day and then triple overhead and deadly the next. The slap-and-tickle spirit of the place can be summed up in a bumper sticker found on Rusty Keaulana's big blue truck: "Welcome to Makaha—Now Go Home!"

Locals in Makaha like to say, "There's only one road in and one road out." The phrase literally refers to Farrington Highway, the sole link between the Westside and the rest of O'ahu (and the world, for that matter), but it has other hidden meanings. The saying refers to how the road comes to a dead end a couple of miles before Ka'ena Point, the spear-shaped tip of the Island where Hawaiian mythology says the souls of the dead leap into the afterlife. But it's also a subtle way of saying, "Be careful what you do and say down here, because this is the end of the road and you have to go back the same way you came."

Wai'anae is a long way from the hordes of Waikiki, where millions of tourists visit every year. Ever since statehood in 1959, the number of American and foreign tourists has risen dramatically, but most come without ever experiencing authentic Hawaiian culture. By contrast, this part of the Island has the highest number of Native Hawaiians and settlements. Far fewer tourists venture down to the Westside, but the ones who do either fall in love with the place or retreat in fear.

One burly local named Melvin Pu'u told me that rental car companies used to draw a red line along the coast, telling customers they had to travel down there at their own risk. But like many others, I was willing to take that risk because of the potential rewards. With the fiftieth anniversary of statehood being celebrated in 2009, I began to realize that the hidden world of

Makaha still embodied the spirit of traditional Hawaiian culture in the Islands—that's why the people fought so hard to protect the place.

During my first visit to the Westside in 1995, I went with a group of friends on a camping trip to Makua, just down the road from Makaha. A few people had warned me that the locals didn't like haoles (Caucasians) from town encroaching on their territory, but I had just moved to Hawai'i and wanted to explore this undeveloped part of the Island. When we arrived, there were groups of Hawaiian families camped near the trees and we set up our tents down the beach from theirs. That night, I remember sitting around a fire and listening to stories about how other campers had been robbed and beaten up by big local guys. I looked at the pale faces gathered around the fire, not knowing if these stories were rumors or reality. In the distance, I could hear the soft yet powerful voice of Israel Kamakawiwo'ole singing from somebody's CD player. I didn't know then that this was his favorite beach, where he and his family often camped. Staring at the stars later that evening, I fell asleep to the sound of waves crashing on the sand.

The next morning, I remember waking up and seeing pods of spinner dolphins swimming off the coast. Some of the sleek, playful creatures would jump and spin in the air. A group of us stumbled out of our tents in the early morning light, grabbed our snorkeling gear, and swam out to meet them. The dolphins cavorted around us and let us swim in their domain before gliding away and disappearing into the depths. It was a magical morning. The local families down the beach were also swimming, fishing, and enjoying the ocean, our differences dissolving in the salt water and morning light. Watching the sun rise over the mountains and glisten on the clean, green water, I could see why the people here were so attached to the land and the sea. The more I learned about the history of Hawai'i's people and how their land had been taken away from them, the more I understood why they were so protective of it.

Looking for a window into Hawaiian culture, I started writing about surfing. For my first big article, I interviewed Rusty Keaulana, who had just won his third longboard world championship title. Capitalizing on his rising fame, he had worked with Quiksilver to start up a new surf shop called Russ K Makaha. At the grand opening, I was stoked to see some of Hawai'i's greatest surfers mingling in the crowd: old beach boys like Rabbit Kekai, big-wave pioneers like Peter Cole, and modern pros like Bonga Perkins. The elegant and spacious store was filled with racks of expensive new Russ K longboards and stacks of Quiksilver surfwear and accessories.

Seeing Rusty's parents, I introduced myself to Buffalo and Momi Keaulana. Surrounded by fans, Buffalo seemed distracted, but his wife was as open and lovely as the orchid in her thick brown hair. While I mentioned my hometown to Auntie Momi, she lit up and told me that one of her ancestors had been a sea captain from my hometown of Charleston, South Carolina. Joking that we might be distant cousins, she laughed and said her heritage was a "chop suey mix" of Hawaiian, Portuguese, Chinese, and a touch of haole! Her warm smile and hearty laughter made me and the other guests feel at ease as she welcomed us to the opening. She then helped gather everyone into a circle and asked the *kahu*, priest, to bless the store and all of us.

Wandering around the shop that day, I saw old black-and-white photos of Buffalo surfing at Makaha and recent color shots of Rusty and his older brother, Brian, riding waves around the world. In one corner, there was a sort of shrine to Eddie Aikau, the legendary Hawaiian surfer and lifeguard who had disappeared at sea. Inside the glass case the artist had mounted pictures of Eddie surfing, standing with his family, or sailing on a double-hulled canoe. The artist also had placed silver surfing trophies and koa canoe paddles inside, along with tiki figures and posters. After seeing that shrine, I started reading articles about Eddie and decided to write a book about his life. As part of my research for *Ed-*

die Would Go, I talked to scores of people who had known him and his family. That was when I decided to drive out to Makaha and interview Rusty's brother Brian, who had known Eddie and was also a big-wave rider and lifeguard.

Brian's *'ohana* (family) was intricately connected to Eddie's. Although the Aikau brothers were older, they surfed and paddled with the Keaulanas. Brian's father, Buffalo, had been like a mentor to Eddie, training with him on the voyaging canoe *Hokule'a*. Surfing is a tribal sport, and both families had produced generations of champions. When they were younger, Eddie and his brother Clyde had looked up to Buffalo and watched him perform in the Makaha International Surfing Championship in the sixties. Likewise, Brian and his brother Rusty had grown up watching Eddie and Clyde surf at the Duke Contests in the seventies and at their father's contest, the Buffalo Big Board Classic. Years later, the Keaulana brothers began competing with Clyde in the Quiksilver Big Wave Invitational in Memory of Eddie Aikau Contest at Waimea Bay in the eighties and nineties.

On New Year's Day 1999, I joined thousands of other spectators at the Bay to watch the best big-wave riders in the world compete at the "Eddie." Standing on the cliffs above the beach, I saw Brian and Rusty paddle into waves so big they looked like mountains of rushing water. As a kid, I used to have nightmares about tidal waves washing away my hometown, and staring at those massive waves revived those old fears of drowning. At one point in the contest, Brian suffered a nasty wipeout on a massive wave. Lifeguards on Jet Skis zoomed in to make sure he was okay, and I later learned he was the one who had pioneered this rescue technique after he almost died at the first Eddie Contest in 1986. After being thrashed by the waves and pinned under the churning water, he climbed back on his board and continued surfing.

After seeing that contest in 1999, I called Brian to set up an interview. We talked about Eddie, and Brian invited me down to Makaha to "talk story." Although I had surfed down there before and camped at nearby Makua, I kept hearing stories of stabbings and shootings on the Westside. Friends warned me to get out of there before dark because once the local boys started drinking all hell could break loose. I had seen the news stories about the rising rates of crime, drug addiction, and murder on the Waiʻanae Coast. But this was also the home of Rell Sunn, the Queen of Makaha, who was known for her warmth and aloha. Besides, I knew I would be in good hands. After all, the Keaulanas were one of the most powerful local families in Hawaiʻi, a respected surfing tribe like the Aikaus.

Known as the "Mayor of Makaha," Buffalo Keaulana worked with his sons to help keep order on the wild Westside. A pure Native Hawaiian with a thick, powerful build and shaggy hair, Buffalo was a rare breed. Like the Native Americans, the Hawaiian people had once numbered in the hundreds of thousands, until the white man arrived. Within a century of Western contact, most had been destroyed by foreign diseases, and the survivors intermarried with other races. But more than just surviving, Buffalo and his family had thrived in Makaha and created a strong Hawaiian community.

I was a little intimidated about meeting Brian because of his reputation as one of the "world's best watermen," which was what several magazines had called him. I had seen him surf in films like *In God's Hands,* being towed by Jet Skis into massive waves at Jaws on Maui, and I had read about him in books that compared him to a modern-day Duke Kahanamoku, the father of Hawaiian surfing. In spite of all the media hype, though, I was surprised by how friendly and down-to-earth Brian had been on the phone. Now it was time to meet him face-to-face.

After passing through Hawaiian homestead settlements in Nanakuli and Waiʻanae, I finally arrived in Makaha. Walking down the beach, I could see a posse of six or seven local boys gathered around picnic tables under the palm trees. One was huge and looked like Israel Kamakawiwoʻole, the sumo-sized Hawaiian singer who had been Makaha's most famous son. The others were heavy, dark, and muscular, and they clearly ruled the roost. As Greg Noll once said, these guys were big enough to "pop my head like a pimple." A "Jawaiian" mix of Jamaican reggae and Hawaiian music was drifting out of one of the big four-wheel-drive trucks parked beside them as they sat drinking beers and surveying their beach domain. I had been told that the Westside boys were die-hard divers, and I could see spearfishing equipment in the trucks. Walking down the beach, I felt like a fish trying to avoid their spearlike stares.

I looked around for Brian and then spotted him walking toward me from the orange lifeguard tower. Wearing a white tank top and black shorts, he had black hair, brown skin, and a surfer's build, lean and muscular. He looked serious behind his black shades, but then he smiled and said, "Howzit?" After we clasped hands, Brian embraced me like an old friend. He then spread out a blanket on the beach, offering me drinks and food from the cooler he had brought. As we began talking, I mostly listened, because it soon became clear that I had a lot to learn from this man.

Looking into the deep brown eyes of Brian Keaulana is like seeing the soul of Makaha. The history of the place is etched in the lines on his face, just as the Keaulana name is tattooed across his brothers' backs. Sitting on the crescent-shaped beach, I looked at the placid blue ocean and tried to imagine what it would be like to grow up here. Small waves rolled in like distant memories as Brian told me about his past and why this place is so unique. "Makaha is the heart of Hawai'i, because everybody from around the world comes here when they really want to find the true essence of what Hawai'i is. It really comes down to here, right on this beach, from these people, the waters, the ocean, and the mountains."

Born and raised on this dry patch of land between the ocean and the mountains on O'ahu's Westside, Brian is well versed in its history and culture. *Makaha* literally means "fierce" in Hawaiian, he told me, but the Westside's reputation for fierce localism is often misunderstood. "People on the Wai'anae Coast are really extreme people. If you come with respect and treat people good, they treat you extremely good. But if you treat them bad, they're going to treat you real bad. They are emotionally extreme people over here."

Known as a sort of peacemaker, Brian has helped resolve many disputes in Makaha. But when pushed, he can push back, hard. After winning the state paddling championships years ago, Brian, his best friend, Melvin Pu'u, and the Makaha team were confronted by some guys from the other canoe clubs. The "townies" were making fun of the "country boys" and looking for a fight. "Brian and Melvin were right there," Brian's haole friend Keoni Watson recalls. "It turned into this huge fight, more like a riot. At the end of it all, the Makaha guys went home in police cars. Everyone else went home in ambulances."

Brian explained that *makaha* also refers to the opening of a fishpond, or a gateway. "If you climb up on this mountain over here and you look down, you see this huge channel," he said. "This is one of the few places that has a huge channel where the waves hardly close out. It's like a gateway to the ocean." And a channel to distant destinations. Brian spent most of his childhood on this small beach and, under the guidance of his father and *hanai* (adopted) uncles such as George Downing and Greg Noll, became one of the most talented watermen in Hawai'i. As a boy, Brian often dreamed of traveling to distant places, and the ocean became his gateway into the worlds of professional surfing and water safety.

In his roles as surfer, lifeguard, and Hollywood stuntman, Brian would eventually travel around the globe, but in the end, he always came back to Makaha. As an ambassador of Hawaiian culture, he has met all kinds of interesting people at surf festivals in France and lifeguard demonstrations in Japan and Australia, but he prefers being at home with his family. Brian credits much of his ocean smarts to his father's common sense and wisdom. Although Buffalo never graduated from high school, oceanography scholar and big-wave rider Ricky Grigg says he is "a man of great Hawaiian wisdom." Grigg learned a lot about fishing and coral reef formation on their dives together. "He inherited a thousand years of what the Hawaiians learned, and he made me realize all of that when he taught me about the ocean."

Although his father is pure Hawaiian, Brian says he never learned to speak the language because it was forbidden when he was growing up. After the missionaries came and converted the people, their descendants went into business and politics and eventually took control of Hawai'i. As the old saying goes, "The missionaries came to do good, and they ended up doing very well." Once in power, they banned the native language and cultural practices such as the hula, surfing, and chanting, which they felt were un-Christian. "In any culture, if you destroy their language, they cannot communicate, and if they cannot communicate, they lose all their knowledge," Brian says. "That's what happened to the Hawaiians. It was lucky that Hawaiian culture survived through key families. It was never lost, but it was in limbo."

The Keaulanas held on tightly to their cultural traditions even while the rest of the world seemed to shun them. Brian says his father was a descendant of high chiefs, yet he had grown up in grinding poverty. At a young age, Buffalo began living off the land and finding food and comfort in the ocean like his ancestors. Many Hawaiians were pressured to assimilate into mainstream American society and made to feel ashamed of their own culture. Yet they knew their ancestors had once been fierce warriors, and they occasionally lashed out against haoles who came down to Makaha and acted like they owned the place. But in some ways, they were just fighting to protect their culture.

Brian explained how Buffalo rediscovered his ancestral roots after sailing on a sixty-foot canoe called the *Hokule'a*. Created in 1975, this double-hulled voyaging canoe was a re-creation of the ancient vessels that brought the first Polynesians to the Hawaiian Islands more than a thousand years ago. For Native

Hawaiians like Buffalo, seeing the sixty-foot canoe sail on its maiden inter-island voyages was like reawakening an intense pride in their culture, and it helped launch a movement called the Hawaiian Renaissance.

After the *Hokuleʻa* voyage, the Keaulanas worked with a group of friends to start the Buffalo Big Board Classic at Makaha. Brian said the purpose of the event was to celebrate Hawaiian culture, have fun, and unify the local community. The contest emphasized traditional cultural practices such as longboarding, tandem surfing, and canoe paddling. At one point, the Buffalo Big Board Classic also hosted a music festival, attracting throngs of spectators and some of Hawaiʻi's best performers, such as Israel, or Iz, as he came to be known, and the Makaha Sons. As Brian described the scene, I looked down the sparsely populated beach and tried to imagine Iz's voice hovering over the huge crowds.

Brian also talked about how Rell Sunn began her annual Menehune Contest to get local kids off the streets and into the ocean. Rell had learned to dive, fish, and lifeguard under Buffalo's tutelage. Together they saved hundreds of people from the fierce waves and currents of Makaha. Likewise, Rell was like a sister to Brian and his brother Rusty, both of whom marveled at her surfing and diving skills. A graceful surfer and talented waterwoman, she helped start the first women's pro tour and became Hawaiʻi's first female lifeguard. When she was at the top of her game, Rell was diagnosed with breast cancer, yet she never stopped surfing. She said being in the ocean had helped her survive.

Following in the footsteps of his father and Rell, Brian also took up lifeguarding and eventually rose to the rank of captain. After working with the military, the Coast Guard, and the film industry, he would later revolutionize the field of water safety. "A true lifeguard has to be super-knowledgeable," Brian told me, looking toward the surf occasionally for any signs of trouble. "In order to prevent something from happening, he has to have the foresight to see something before it happens." Whereas most traditional lifeguards were reactive, he emphasized the need to be more proactive. Yet he says modern guards have a lot to learn from Hawaiian wisdom about the ocean. "Old school, new school—it's a combination of knowing your past and your history and how the Hawaiians used to read the ocean or the color of the sky, telling you what storms may be coming in. Lifeguarding now is combining scientific schooling with ancient knowledge."

As a lifeguard, Brian had rescued countless people from drowning, but in spite of all his skills and courage, he couldn't save those who were closest to him. Bruddah Iz became morbidly obese and struggled with drugs, high blood pressure, and heart disease. While Iz put on more weight and grew to more than eight hundred pounds, Sistah Rell was slowly wasting away to nothing due to the cancer. Brian's two closest friends were dying, and there was nothing he could do. Yet even in the midst of their suffering, he could feel the deep aloha they shared with him, his family, the community, and the world.

"When people come to Hawai'i, they hear people say, 'Aloha,' " Brian says. "But they don't really understand the *kauna,* which is like the meaning." He explained that *alo* is like the leaf of the taro plant and signifies the human face, and *ha* is like the breath of life. "The Hawaiians used to put their heads together and exchange breaths. So *ha* is like Chinese *chi* or Japanese *ki*." When greeting each other or departing, they would touch foreheads and exchange breaths. "Aloha is enveloping someone with your whole essence or aura. It's understanding the true essence of yourself and giving it to others." Rell once defined aloha as "giving and giving until you have nothing left to give," and she said this was the fate of the Hawaiian people.

❧❦

After almost three hours of talking on the beach, Brian invited me to his brother Rusty's house for a lu'au with their new corporate sponsors from Japan. He and his family had just started a surfwear company called Real B Voice, the *B* standing for "Buffalo," and they were having a party to celebrate. Brian introduced me to everyone. Buffalo sat at a picnic table "talking story" with his Japanese guests, whose faces were red from too much sun and too many beers. He was telling a funny anecdote about surfing with legendary actor James Arness. "You know da guy from *Gunsmoke*," he said in his thick pidgin, drawing an imaginary pistol on his Japanese guests. They seemed to be having trouble understanding everything he was saying, but they got the gist and laughed, happy to be in his presence.

Brian's mother, Momi, was making sure everyone had plenty of *poke* (raw fish), poi (pounded taro root), and smoked fish to eat, while his younger brother Jimmy doled out beers to everyone. Looking out over the endless blue sea from his yard, Rusty tended his fishing lines and began reeling in fish for the grill. There were large *ulua* heads stuck on spikes and hanging from coconut trees around his yard like trophies. After much eating and drinking, Buff broke out his 'ukulele and the family started singing old Hawaiian songs. Not knowing all the lyrics, the Japanese businessmen and I hummed along as we swayed to the music.

Looking around during the party, I was amazed to see this local Hawaiian family genuinely bonding with these Japanese businessmen. Just fifty-eight years before, Japanese warplanes had bombed Pearl Harbor and launched America into one of the most fierce wars in history. Yet here they were arm in arm, drinking and singing Hawaiian songs. Their aloha had overcome any racial animosity, and they shared a common love of the ocean.

At one point, I went looking for the bathroom and found a stack of more than thirty surfboards in a storage room, all with Rusty's surf company logo emblazoned on the front: "Russ K Makaha." There were trophies on the shelves from his three-year reign as the world champion longboarder. On the wall there was a Budweiser poster with Buffalo, Brian, Rusty, and some of the local boys, standing on the beach next to their surfboards. And below Buffalo the caption says: "Chairman of the Board."

A few hours later, I reluctantly said my good-byes and headed back to town while I could still drive. I was still reeling from the beers and excitement of meeting the entire Keaulana clan. During that one day in Makaha, I learned more about aloha and Hawaiian culture than during my previous six years in Honolulu. From that point on, I knew I'd be going back to Makaha to learn more about the Keaulanas. I was also curious about Sistah Rell and Bruddah Iz, their adopted family members who had become international icons in the worlds of surfing and music.

On the drive home, I remembered talking to Brian about his friendship with Rell, who had passed away the year before. He had told me how they used to go out surfing each New Year's Eve, from 11:45 P.M. till 12:15 A.M., to catch the last wave of the old year and the first wave of the new one. But now Rell was gone, and so was Iz. On New Year's Eve 1999, on the edge of the new millennium, Brian paddled out into the darkness and could feel the presence of both friends. Driving back toward the bright lights of Honolulu, I realized that the timeless spirits of Rell and Iz lived on in Brian, the Keaulanas, and their extended family in Makaha. I hoped their stories would provide a window into Hawai'i's past and a glimpse of her future.

CHAPTER 1

🐦 🐦 🐦 🐦 🐦 🐦 🐦 🐦 🐦 🐦 🐦

When Worlds Collide

Ua mau ke ea o ka'aina i ka pono.
The life of the land is perpetuated in righteousness.
—King Kamehameha III

The highest peak on Oʻahu, Mount Kaʻala rises up like a god at the head of the Makaha and Waiʻanae Valleys and watches over the entire Westside. Ancient Hawaiian kahuna (priests) considered it one of the most sacred sites on the Island and built *heiau* (temples) at its base. They believed the mountain wore the golden robes of Kane, heavenly father of all living things, who was associated with the sun. Like the clouds that envelop Mount Kaʻala, the history of the Waiʻanae Coast and its people is shrouded in myth and mystery.

Local legends say that Wakea, Sky Father, and Papa, Earth Mother, first mated on the coast of Makua, which means "parent." Their children were born in a womblike lava tube nearby called Kaneana. It was here that the Polynesian demigod Maui landed his canoe, learned to make fire, and gave the gift of light to the people. Farther down the coast at the northwestern corner of the island, Kaena Point juts out into the ocean like the long, rocky finger of Mount Kaʻala, pointing toward the endless sea of eternity. Here the souls of the dead would leap from this world to the next. Though poor and isolated, this part of the Island offers rich mythical stories about the supernatural origins of life and the final destination beyond death.

At the base of Mount Kaʻala and along the Waiʻanae Coast, there are the remains of old *heiau*. The people of the land once gathered at these stone temple sites to celebrate and make offerings to their gods: Kane, Ku, Lono, and Kanaloa. Wandering among these crumbling ruins, a boy like Richard "Buffalo" Keaulana probably wondered what solemn chants and ceremonies his ancestors had performed at these sacred sites. Touching the lava rocks must have sparked his imagination and given him a glimpse of Hawaiʻi's ancient past, before the arrival of the white men and their tall ships.

A pure Hawaiian, Buffalo came from a long line of leaders, including some of Hawaiʻi's great chiefs and ancient explorers. Like most Hawaiians, he revered his ancestors and probably felt like they were watching over him as *ʻaumakua,* spirits that could take the form of sharks, lizards, sea turtles, or any element of nature. Buffalo knew of kahuna who could recite genealogies going back to the gods and the first humans who walked this land. There were familiar stories from the Kumulipo, the Hawaiian creation story that traced their ancestry back to the origins of creation. The spirit of his ancestors was in the sea, the forests, and the mountains because they were all part of nature and eternally present. Though Buffalo grew up in an increasingly Westernized world, he never forgot the proud origins of his people.

According to the ancient chants in the Kumulipo, Wakea's first child, Haloa (long stalk), was stillborn and buried in the earth. He returned in the form of taro, the sacred plant also known as *kalo* that became a central source of food in Hawai'i. His brother was born soon after and also named Haloa. His mission was to nurture his brother, *kalo,* who would in turn provide nourishment for all their people. Like most Hawaiians, Buffalo grew up eating poi, the purple paste made from pounded *kalo.* This staple was part of their daily diet, and the stories of Haloa fed their spiritual hunger and love of the land.

These beliefs about their interdependence on nature also helped sustain Hawai'i's people for centuries, ever since the first Polynesian voyagers sailed here in their double-hulled canoes and settled the Islands more than twelve hundred years ago. As a boy, Buffalo would have heard stories about the legendary navigators who guided their canoes all the way across the Pacific. But staring at the seemingly endless sea, he must have wondered if these were just made-up stories, childhood myths. Only later in his life, Buffalo would sail on the *Hokule'a,* a modern replica of these voyaging canoes, and retrace the journeys of his ancestors all the way back to Tahiti.

Living on the most isolated island chain on earth, ancient Hawaiians had to be innovative and completely self-sufficient to survive. The people in Wai'anae had an even greater challenge in that they lived on the driest part of O'ahu. To conserve their natural resources, they developed a sophisticated plan to divide the land into wedge-shaped districts called *ahupua'a* that stretched from the mountains to the sea. Instead of having individual ownership, each district was communally managed by the *ali'i* (chiefs). The people worked hard and played hard, and many of their activities revolved around the sea.

The name Wai'anae may have originated from the fact that fishing became their main source of food, *wai* meaning "water" and *'anae* being the large mullet so abundant in the area. Besides being talented fishermen, the people on the Leeward Coast felt at home in the ocean and excelled at sailing, surfing, and paddling canoes. When the surf was up, almost all work came to a standstill as people rushed to the shore to ride the waves. The commoners generally rode shorter wooden boards on their stomachs, while the chiefs stood up to ride their long, heavy boards. During the Makahiki season, they held festivals on the beach. The chiefs would compete against each other, and people would gamble on who would win. A similar festival would later be resurrected in the form of the Makaha International Surfing Championship during the 1950s and '60s, and Buffalo would become one of its early champions.

The past is interwoven into the present, and the Makahiki season is still celebrated today in Hawai'i. Sponsored by Quiksilver, the annual Makahiki surf contest in Makaha features longboard surfing, canoe paddling, and tandem surfing, where couples perform balletlike poses while riding the waves. But the origin of the Makahiki season came from the fact that war was taboo from mid-October to January because it was prophesied that Lono would return during this time and bring peace. But when the season was over, old conflicts would often resume, and warriors would fight for control over the land and freshwater streams. The people developed their own form of martial art called *lua,* and bandits who lived in Makaha would swoop down from the hills to beat up and rob travelers along the coast. Theft would continue to be a serious issue on the Westside even in modern times, though later it was less about tribal conflicts and more about a lack of economic opportunities.

For centuries, Mount Ka'ala and the Wai'anae Mountains have

served as a kind of defensive wall guarding the small Hawaiian villages of the Leeward Coast of O'ahu. Cutting across the sky like the serrated edge of a stone spearhead, these mountains have kept the people of Wai'anae isolated from the rest of the world, and its fierce warriors fought to maintain their independence. Yet this isolation could not last. "A gap in the Wai'anae Range where one can cross over is called Kolekole Pass," writes Bob Krauss in *Historic Wai'anae,* "because it was here that the warriors of Wahiawa (the other side) and those of Wai'anae met in battles that left their flesh *kolekole* (raw) with wounds." One Wai'anae kahuna prophesied that "big fish" would arrive one day in the form of foreigners and eat up the natives like little fish.

When the British ships under the command of Captain James Cook first sailed to Hawai'i in 1778, the local fishermen thought that Cook was the god Lono returning for the Makahiki festival. Sailing, paddling, and swimming, thousands of natives greeted the three ships with a mixture of curiosity, fear, and awe. On the Big Island of Hawai'i, they feted the visitors with huge feasts and gifts before they departed. Although there were several thousand *kanaka maole* (Native Hawaiians) living in Wai'anae at the time, Cook and his officers passed them by, thinking the land was barren, rocky, and barely inhabited. In fact, there was a thriving local culture, where *kalo* and other crops grew in the mountains and fishponds flourished on the coast.

Later that year, the captain and his men returned to the Big Island after the Makahiki season was over. After trading and interacting with the foreigners, the chiefs no longer considered them benevolent gods or peaceful guests. When one of his small boats was stolen, Captain Cook ordered his men to take a local chief hostage until it was returned. A skirmish broke out, and the warriors killed Cook and four of his men on the beach. This event began the long and contentious relationship between Hawaiians and the endless waves of foreigners who would land upon their shores and gradually take over the Islands.

With the aid of Western guns and ships, a young chief named

Kamehameha waged battles against his rivals on the Big Island, Maui, and Oʻahu. After driving the last warriors off the steep cliffs of the Nuʻuanu Pali, he conquered Oʻahu in 1795 and united the Islands. A great warrior and natural leader, Kamehameha became the first king of Hawaiʻi, but none of his royal descendants would ever achieve the same level of power and leadership. Many of the conquered chiefs fled to the isolated area of Waiʻanae, where they formed a school at Pokaʻi Bay to preserve the old ways. Their kahuna taught the history, culture, and chants of the ancient chiefs of Oʻahu, instilling in their students a sense of pride and a resistance to change. Growing up on the Westside, Hawaiian boys would inherit a fierce pride in their culture and a suspicion of outsiders.

During his reign, Kamehameha embraced the new technology, ideas, and goods of the West without sacrificing the independence or culture of the Hawaiian kingdom. But after he died, Kaʻahumanu, his favorite wife and royal regent of the Islands, gradually came under the increasing influence of Western advisors. After seeing that the foreigners had broken many of their traditional taboos without consequence, she and Kamehameha's son Liholiho even commanded the kahuna to destroy the ancient temples. Six months later, in 1820, the first Protestant missionaries arrived, bringing with them a new God to fill the spiritual void.

The cultural and religious transformation of the Hawaiian people was compounded when Kaʻahumanu converted to Christianity. She then dismissed most of the remaining *kapu* (taboos) and insisted that her people study the Bible. The people wavered between their traditional ways and beliefs and the new faith and rules of the foreigners, whom they called haoles, which literally means "no breath," because they seemed to lack the spirit of joy in their lives. Coming from such different worlds, these cultures continued to clash like waves against a rocky shore. And like their ancestors, the Hawaiians found comfort in the ocean, whether they were fishing, swimming, or surfing.

When the first Western sailors and traders arrived in the Islands and saw surfing for the first time, they marveled at the Hawaiians' ability to "walk on water." But the missionaries were frightened and offended by the Hawaiians' near nakedness. They condemned the "savage" sport and banned traditional practices such as the hula because they thought these acts led to promiscuity and depravity. Surfing and the hula suffered a serious decline for decades and were looked down upon by the white establishment. Along with denigrating Hawai'i's culture and traditions, the haoles introduced deadly illnesses that would almost destroy its people.

Just as the Native Americans had been infected by foreign diseases, Hawaiians began to fall victim to the same kinds of mass epidemics. When this was coupled with a profound cultural and spiritual depression, their health as a people declined dramatically. Strong warriors succumbed to common diseases such as chicken pox and influenza, which struck them down in vast numbers. Because of their isolation from the rest of the world, they had no natural defenses to protect themselves from these foreign illnesses. Within forty years of Western contact, the Hawaiian population had gone from an estimated four hundred thousand to about forty thousand. Nine out of ten had died, and the rest were physically weak and spiritually broken. Most of their religious services consisted of funerals, and survivors spent much of their time burying and mourning for the dead.

In the face of such devastation, Wai'anae remained a fiercely independent region under the command of Chief Boki. A powerful Hawaiian leader, Boki distrusted the haole and resented their Western diseases, business practices, and alien beliefs. But he knew he would have to work with them to stay in power. Eventually, many Hawaiian families like the Keaulanas became dedicated Christians while also maintaining the spiritual beliefs of their ancestors.

Influenced by the haole merchants and traders, most of the local chiefs or ali'i fell under the spell of alcohol and Western goods. The merchants in turn wanted the sweet-smelling sandalwood that was so abundant in Wai'anae and highly sought after in the Orient. So the chiefs forced most of their followers to harvest as much sandalwood as possible to fuel their greed. Gradually, the taro fields grew fallow and the fishponds deteriorated, and the people began to starve. The chiefs continued their collaboration with the haole businessmen who decided that the land should be divided and sold in order to promote private ownership. The missionaries also supported this movement because they thought it would encourage Hawaiians to become small, independent farmers.

Starting in 1848, the king and the legislature enacted what came to be known as the "Great Mahele," which legalized landownership and divided the land into parcels. According to author Bob Krauss, the missionaries argued that "the Mahele provided that a commoner had only to file a claim in order to receive title to his *kuleana,* the parcel of land his family had worked for generations." But complicated legal procedures and title claims were used to intimidate the commoners from filling out the forms. Besides, the idea of buying and selling land was inconceivable to Hawaiians. They didn't believe that humans could own any part of nature because the land was considered sacred, a gift to be shared by the community and preserved for their descendants. Coming from a communal way of life, they rejected the idea that land could be bought and sold or taken away from the people. They must have wondered if these foreigners would even try to claim the rights to the streams, the ocean, or even the sky.

Only a few commoners signed up for the land, and the ruling chiefs claimed the title to the rest. After Chief Boki passed away, his wife, Liliha, gave her claim to Makaha to High Chief Abner Paki, who continued Boki's resistance against the ways of the Western missionaries. Like many *ali'i,* Paki liked to surf, drink, and gamble, activities that were condemned by Ka'ahumanu's missionary advisors.

Encouraged by sea captains and traders who also resented

the Puritanical influence of the religious leaders, supporters of Liliha and Paki attempted to overthrow Ka'ahumanu and the Kamehameha Dynasty. But the plot failed, and government soldiers came in to establish control. Liliha was stripped of her title as Governor of O'ahu, and Paki converted to Christianity. He probably realized it was futile to fight against the growing influence of the Western missionaries and politicians, but he never gave up his love of surfing or drinking. Nor did his people. Dependence on alcohol, drugs, and *pakalolo* (marijuana) is still common in Wai'anae, and some would say it's a way to numb the pain they feel over the loss of their land and culture.

With their newfound desire for imported goods from Europe, Paki and other *ali'i* began selling off their vast parcels of land to Western businessmen who were buying up everything they could. "The chiefs were selling their rights to foreigners," historian Samuel Kamakau wrote, "and those who were thus turned out [of their homes] became wanderers without any property and had to become contract laborers and serve like slaves." Many Hawaiians made their way into the city to find work, while a small number survived on subsistence farming and fishing. Wai'anae's once-thriving villages were all but abandoned, and the people became homeless in their own homeland. And to this day, thousands of itinerant Hawaiians can be found camping on the beach grounds in Wai'anae. Then and now, the people of the land needed a new leader to guide them.

Eventually, foreign companies and businessmen bought up huge tracts of land that were turned into profitable sugar plantations. Because the Hawaiian population had been decimated by disease, alcohol, and despair, the landowners brought in waves of immigrants from Portugal, Japan, China, Korea, and the Philippines to work the fields. With the rise of the big plantation owners, they began to assert increasing control over the Hawaiian monarchs. In 1893, a group of haole businessmen collaborated with American marines to overthrow Hawai'i's last ruler, Queen Lili'uokalani. They established their own republic and then, in 1898, convinced President McKinley and the Congress to annex Hawai'i and make it an American territory despite fierce opposition from many Hawaiians.

The new territorial government took over most of the royal land, which was ceded to the United States on behalf of the Hawaiian people. Control and ownership of that land was a controversial issue and is still disputed to this day. Much of the best land was leased out to plantation owners and non-Hawaiians for farming and development. In 1920, more than two hundred thousand acres of the least arable land were turned into Hawaiian homesteads in places such as Nanakuli, where many present-day Hawaiians' parents settled as tenants. A little more than a century after the first Westerners touched these shores, they now had almost total control of the Islands. But this version of history was never taught in school, and it was only years later that most Hawaiians would learn about the overthrow of the Hawaiian kingdom.

After annexation, Hawai'i became an important part of America's growth as an economic and military power. Endowed with some of the deepest and safest harbors in the world, the port of Honolulu grew into a busy trading post in the Pacific, while farther up the coast Pearl Harbor was being built up as an important military base. The Islands also began to attract wealthy Americans who wanted to explore this exotic outpost in the middle of the Pacific. In order to entertain these tourists, local Hawaiian watermen began teaching them the ancient art of *he'e nalu* (wave-sliding or surfing), along with sailing and paddling outrigger canoes.

Early explorers and journalists such as Mark Twain were intrigued by surfing but didn't have much luck with the sport. "I tried surf-bathing once, subsequently, but made a failure of it," he wrote. "I got the board placed right, and at the right moment, too; but missed the connection myself. The board struck the shore in three-quarters of a second, without any cargo, and I struck the bottom about the same time, with a couple of gallons of water in me." After nearly drowning, Twain concluded, "None but the natives ever master the art of surf-bathing thoroughly."

Yet by the turn of the century surfing was enjoying a revival in Waikiki. With the help of Hawaiian beach boys who instructed him, American writer Jack London tried surfing and had more success with it. Writing lavishly about what he called "a royal sport of the natural kings of earth," London described the Hawaiians' agility in the waves. He wrote that many of the best surfers were often descendants of *ali'i* or at least treated like royalty for their regal grace in the ocean. More and more tourists picked up the sport from Hawaiians during their stays in Waikiki.

With the growing popularity of surfing in the Islands, Hawaiian watermen such as George Freeth and Duke Kahanamoku traveled to America and performed surfing demonstrations on the West and East Coasts. After setting new world records in swimming at the 1912 Olympics in Stockholm, Duke surfed in Southern California and New Jersey, where a group of bystanders watched in awe. Fans formed small surf clubs and dreamed of surfing in Hawai'i one day, but outside of the Islands the sport remained the refuge of only a few dedicated groups of "beach bums" on the fringes of American society.

The American people never liked their nation being called an empire, but their government began establishing colonial control over Hawai'i, the Philippines, Guam, and other Pacific "territories." The sugar plantations flourished in Wai'anae, and wealthy land barons ruled the area like feudal lords. Hawai'i was basically run by the "Big Five," a wealthy group of Hawaiian corporations owned by the descendants of business and missionary families.

These powerful dynasties started out as plantation owners who controlled the Republican political machine and then diversified into banks, businesses, real estate, and transportation. The elite landlords kept their immigrant workers in plantation camps, which were divided by race. The plantation owners encouraged tension between the Japanese, Chinese, Filipino, and other ethnic groups to keep them from uniting and organizing into labor unions. Meanwhile, Hawaiian families like the Keaulanas continued to eke out a living through fishing and farming the dry homestead lands in Nanakuli. Although Buffalo's family came from a noble line of chiefs and warriors, he was conceived during a time of great poverty, when his people had very little power. Yet even while forming in his mother's womb, he had royal blood and salt water running through his veins.

Like many Hawaiians, Buffalo's father, Abraham "Red" Keaulana, found work down at the docks in Honolulu Harbor. As the father of a boy and three girls and with another baby on the way, he had to work hard to support his growing family. But one day at the docks, Abraham was killed in a tragic accident while saving two co-workers from being struck by a wrecking ball. His last act was to sacrifice himself to help his co-workers, and he died just one month before Buffalo was born.

Buffalo's mother was devastated, but Mary Phoebe Mahi Keaulana had to remain strong for her daughters and the child to come. During her pregnancy, an old Hawaiian-Japanese woman told Mary something that would later turn out to be very prophetic: "If you have a girl, she'll be just like everyone else. But if you have a boy, he'll be famous the world over, but not a penny in his pocket." After hearing this story from Buffalo's mother years later, his wife, Momi, would say, "Boy, did she say true words!"

Born on September 2, 1934, Richard "Buffalo" Kaloloʻokalani Keaulana became the fifth child and second son of Abraham and Mary Keaulana. In spite of the humble circumstances of Buffalo's birth, he could trace his lineage back to King Kamehameha and the ruling *aliʻi* of Hawaiʻi. Part of a rare and vanishing race, Buffalo and his four older siblings were pure Hawaiians and heirs to a vanished kingdom. Raised in a poor and fatherless household, they were forced to fend for themselves from an early age.

But they must have believed that their ancestors were watching over them and their spirits were part of the land.

During his early years, Buffalo's family moved several times, and he went to three schools before they settled on homestead land in Nanakuli. His family had roots in this area before the streets even had names. When the construction workers were building the roads, his mother had befriended many of them and given them food, even though the Keaulanas didn't have much to share. "To honor my dad's family, they would name that street Keaulana Avenue," Brian says. "The nearby break in Nanakuli became known as Keaulanas."

Life was a struggle, because Buffalo's mother had five kids to support and they needed a father figure in their lives. Unfortunately, she found a man who resented her son and was not kind to her kids. "When we first moved here, my mother remarried a Filipino guy," Buffalo says, recalling the time in his life when everything changed. "Every time I came home, he would lick [beat] my mother because he never liked me. So I would stay away from the house. I would come by only when he was away from the house."

Buffalo often slept at the houses of friends or on the beach, because he didn't want to see his mom get hurt. "His stepfather was very, very mean to him," his wife, Momi, says. "He went from family to family at a young age and fended for himself. He had a rough childhood . . . He knows how homeless people feel and what it's like not to have anything in your stomach." Even as a boy, he would often have to sleep on the beach and go spearfishing in the ocean for food. "I know how it is to starve," he says. "Because I didn't have a spear, I'd get me a clothes hanger and then make the hanger into a spear. I would get my goggles and just float around on the reef and just shoot *manini*. I would catch 'em and make good soup out of those small fish. I always eat seafood."

With this crash course in survival, he would go on to become one of the best divers in the Islands, famous for his fishing and bodysurfing skills. He spent so much time in the ocean that his mother said he was like a "water buffalo," and the nickname stuck. It was reinforced by the fact that he had a thick frame, a large head, and a shaggy mane of light brown hair. As a restless boy with no father, Buffalo wandered among the endless sugarcane fields and camps in search of food and to make friends by helping out. But he soon found a group of men who would become like mentors to him and introduce him to his life's calling.

Buffalo was a young boy when the first haole surfers ventured down to the Westside. Big-wave surfing pioneers John Kelly and Wally Froiseth discovered the pristine beauty of Makaha in the late thirties. They were born on the mainland, but their parents moved to Hawai'i when John and Wally were young children. Both boys had started surfing the gently rolling waves in Waikiki on the long, square-tailed wooden boards that Hawaiians had been surfing on for hundreds of years. But as the boys grew older, they developed a hunger for bigger waves and better equipment.

Sick of sliding out on the big redwood boards that had no fins on the bottom to guide them, these two innovators cut down the backs of the boards into narrow tail sections that would hold in bigger waves. Wally said the new design could "really get you in the hot curl" of the wave, and the name stuck. The new "Hot Curl" boards would later evolve to include a narrower nose and tail and a long, sharklike fin on the bottom. This became the template for the modern surfboard and big-wave gun.

Ready to test their new equipment, Wally and John would drive out to Makaha in a beat-up old Ford with their boards strapped to the top. They would bounce down the dirt road, past the Wai'anae Sugar Plantation until they came to the wide white beach at the end. The two muscular men would lug their heavy wooden boards down to the beach, and theirs were often the only footprints in the sand. Smiling at their good fortune, they would surf the big blue waves for hours all by themselves as local kids gathered on the beach to watch. Wally and John gradually began sharing their skills and knowledge with young Hawaiian surfers such as George Downing, who became like a son to Wally. After the war, George would go on to become a fearless big-wave rider and a mentor to many up-and-coming surfers like Buffalo.

While this new breed of surfers enjoyed their carefree days playing in the glassy waves with the local kids, fascist regimes in the East and West began to assert their racial and military superiority over the rest of the world. With the rise of Germany's Third Reich and Japan's Empire of the Sun, the United States began building up its military presence in the region, yet Americans were reluctant to get involved in a worldwide conflict. The sleeping giant had yet to be awakened.

As a young boy, Buffalo had lived in Honolulu for a time, but now it was just a distant world beyond the Wai'anae Mountains, a glowing city whose lights he could see at night. And countries like Japan and Germany seemed like abstract images over the horizon. Asia and Europe were places that he had only heard about in school or from the children of plantation workers who would talk with strange accents about the distant homelands their parents had left behind. Even when war broke out in Europe, those living on the Westside were not terribly affected by the Allied forces fighting the German and Axis powers. But on the clear blue morning of December 7, 1941, the course of world history was irrevocably altered when Japanese planes bearing the symbol of the Rising Sun descended on Hawai'i. Suddenly the most isolated chain of islands on earth became the battleground of two competing world powers.

Buffalo Keaulana was seven years old when the first planes came flying low across the central valleys of O'ahu and began bombing Pearl Harbor and air bases on O'ahu. The explosions shook the Island like an earthquake and created ominous clouds of black smoke that darkened the skies. Although it must have seemed like the end of the world, that "day of infamy" would be the beginning of a new era for Buffalo, Hawai'i, and the world.

When the ships stopped burning and the air finally cleared, Pearl Harbor had become an underwater graveyard. Thousands of sailors were entombed in the sunken ships.

Six decades later, Buffalo's son Brian would work as a stuntman on the film *Pearl Harbor,* which attempted to re-create the pandemonium of that fiery morning. In one scene, Brian and other stuntmen were consumed in flames as explosions tossed them from the lurching deck of a sinking battleship. But not even Hollywood's best special effects could capture the blood, smoke, and carnage of that attack.

Transformed by the war, Hawai'i came under martial law, and the military took control of the government and almost every aspect of life in the Islands. The people endured years of food and fuel rationing and nightly blackouts. Many beaches were closed and cordoned off with barbed-wire fences. Government officials worried about Japanese spies and rounded up many nationals, who were later imprisoned or deported. The people of the Westside watched as federal authorities closed down the Japanese-language school in Wai'anae and transformed it into a venue for the USO to entertain the thousands of servicemen training on the Wai'anae Coast. There was talk of forming internment camps like Manzanar and others on the West Coast. But there were too many Japanese living in Hawai'i at the time, and local legislators insisted that the Japanese were loyal to the United States.

To prove their loyalty, a large group of nisei (second-generation) Japanese petitioned to join the army, and some came from the Wai'anae Sugar Plantation. They later formed the famous 442nd Regimental Combat Team and fought in the European Theater. Their motto was "Go for Broke," and the people read newspaper reports about how the 442nd charged into fierce battles, sustaining some of the heaviest losses of the war. While their own relatives were held in internment camps in the California desert, these soldiers later helped liberate the skeletal survivors held in frozen German concentration camps such as Dachau. The 442nd became one of the most decorated military units in American history.

Although Hawaiians had fought valiantly in the war, many did not like the massive military buildup on Oʻahu and the fact that their land was still being used for target practice. They resented the destructive bombing of Kahoʻolawe, the island off Maui, and the live-fire training in Makua, just west of Makaha. Native Hawaiians would always remember the attack on Pearl Harbor, but they also resented the continued bombing and destruction of their own land by the U.S. military during and after the war. The explosions left enduring scars on the land and in their hearts. Many locals witnessed American planes and helicopters dropping bombs on the neighboring valley. They could hear the explosions and smell the burning smoke from the fires that consumed the lush fields and forests where their ancestors once lived and farmed.

Hundreds of thousands of soldiers from all over the United States had been sent to Hawaiʻi on their way to deadly battles in the Pacific Theater. Many of them stayed after the war to work at the many military bases that had been built on Oʻahu. Buffalo and his friends could only watch as the government took over Pokaʻi Bay and turned what was once a school for Hawaiian culture into a beach recreation center just for soldiers. The military also seized a big part of Waiʻanae and used it as a storage facility called Lualualei, building an enormous underground ammunition depot. Next to the Waiʻanae Sugar Plantation, the U.S. military became the largest landowner on the Leeward Coast, to the frustration and anger of the locals.

After the war, the plantation shut down due to rising labor costs and the declining price of sugar. Most of the workers left for the city. Meanwhile, soldiers who had taken up surfing in Waikiki began making the trek down the coast to Makaha. When they moved back to their homes in the continental United States, many took their love of surfing with them. But like MacArthur, many vowed that they would return. The sport started to take off in California because it combined a mixture of exotic Hawaiian adventure with rugged American individualism.

Hearing about the growing popularity of surfing on the West Coast, Wally Froiseth, George Downing, and another big-wave pioneer named Russ Takaki sailed to California and surfed up and down the coast. The three men bonded with local surfers and told them of the extraordinary surf in Makaha. Soon California surfers such as Buzzy Trent, Woody Brown, and the Hoffman brothers moved to Hawai'i and began making pilgrimages to the Westside.

In 1953, newspapers across the country published an Associated Press photo of Downing, Trent, and Brown streaking down the glassy face of a large Makaha wave. The grainy black-and-white image struck most Americans as strange and exotic, because surfing was still such a new sport. But for wide-eyed California surfers it captured the essence of what they loved, inspiring a small group of diehards to migrate to this remote region of O'ahu. These daring watermen and big-wave pioneers helped introduce Makaha to the surfing world while also being an inspiration to locals like Buffalo, who studied their every move on the waves.

Wanting to capitalize on the growing popularity of surfing in Makaha and the cheap land on the Westside, an enterprising Chinese-American man named Chinn Ho formed a *hui* (group) of businessmen to buy the former plantation lands. Overnight he became one of the Island's first Asian developers to break into the white power establishment. He wanted to turn the area into small communities and sell inexpensive plots of land to the former plantation workers, surfers, and Hawaiians who wanted to return and live on the Westside. While the cane fields withered, Buffalo watched as bulldozers began clearing roads and plots of land for future houses.

Under the GI Bill, many veteran Japanese-American soldiers went back to school and joined the ranks of the growing Democratic Party. War hero Dan Inouye, who lost his arm and many of his closest friends in the fighting, became one of Hawai'i's most powerful leaders. Inouye and other rising politicians started campaigning for statehood because they believed in the American Dream of unlimited growth and profit. Hawaiians were torn between their loyalty to the United States and its ideals of democracy and their resentment of its military, economic, and political policies in the Islands. After all, they were still the poorest segment of the population. Many locals like Buffalo had no place to call their own and camped along the coast. "I know what it means to be homeless," he says, "sleeping in a cardboard box down on the beach."

Staying with friends or living on the beach, Buffalo learned to provide his own food. "In order to survive with other families, you had to stay outside in the dark or shadows for a while," Buffalo says. "Then, your friend would help you get your foot in the door. There was lots of work to do. In the early morning, we'd gather eggs. Next, we'd go diving for fish. And the rule was, 'Don't come home until a whole *pakini* [washtub] is full.'"

Buffalo's reputation as a talented diver and fisherman began to grow among his peers, but his teachers thought he was just a wild child. Not having enough money for lunch, he would go fishing during recess and bring his catch back to the school cooks, who would feed him. But he was often late to class or absent for days at a time, and he didn't like all the school rules. He once spent a week picking *kiawe* bean pods so he could buy decent clothes and a pair of slippers to wear to school. When he came to Waipahu High School in his new slippers, the teacher turned him away, saying he couldn't come to class without "proper" shoes. Angry and frustrated, Buffalo says, "I had a few words for her that probably I shouldn't have said. But that was it. I didn't have money for shoes."

After dropping out of high school, Buffalo would spend his days fishing, diving, and surfing at Makaha. This isolated beach at the western end of O'ahu was slowly emerging as a testing ground for some of the best surfers in Hawai'i and California.

Chinn Ho would continue trying to develop the Westside and years later would work with the Wai'anae Lion's Club and the Waikiki Surf Club to sponsor an annual surfing contest that would bring crowds of surfers and spectators out to the Westside each December. With the rise of the Makaha International Surfing Championships in 1954, thousands of people began visiting this isolated beach for two weekends of surfing, concerts, and parties. Occasional conflicts arose between Hawaiian and haole surfers, but most were united in their common love of the ocean.

Though terribly shy and suspicious of haoles, Buffalo eventually became friends with many of the visiting surfers. He earned their respect by winning the Makaha International's bodysurfing competition during the first year. In the next two decades, he would win many awards and honors as a surfer, lifeguard, and community leader. True to the prophecy of the old Hawaiian-Japanese lady, this poor high school dropout from the Westside would become famous as one of the world's great watermen.

Years later, in 1980, he would preside over his own contest called the Buffalo Big Board Classic, where the people honored him like a high chief. Modern kahuna chanted in Hawaiian, and a herald blew the conch shell to start the royal procession. During the opening ceremony, young, muscular men dressed as traditional Hawaiian warriors carried him on a platform to the stage. Watching the proceedings, State Senator Fred Hemmings described Buffalo as the *ka mo'i,* or king, whose face "reflects the glory and dignity of all his people." The people of the Westside had finally found a new leader.

CHAPTER 2

Buffalo, Henry, and Da Bull

The haoles say "charisma" and the Hawaiians say "mana."...
It's not something you can learn; no one's going to teach
you that. You're just born with it.

—Kimo Hollinger

Watching surfers such as John Kelly, Wally Froiseth, and George Downing ride the big waves at Mahaka, Buffalo was hooked and tried to find a way to get his own board. "We'd give anything to try their surfboards," he says. "In fact, as soon as one of them wiped out, one of us would get to their board first and take a few rides on the inside before giving it back."

Too poor to buy his own surfboard, Buffalo tried to make his own by ripping up wooden ties from the old railroad tracks, gluing them together, and shaping them into a crude board with a saw and machete. Yet even with his makeshift equipment, he had a natural understanding of the powerful waves. Like a seasoned cowboy on an untamed horse, he was thrown a few times before he learned how to ride them. But as he improved, Buffalo caught the eye of some of the visiting California surfers, especially a skinny haole kid named Greg Noll.

Only seventeen at the time, Greg had somehow convinced his parents to let him move to Hawai'i for a year to finish high school there. He told them that an older surfer named Billy Ming would be his guardian and look after him, and they allowed him to go on his big adventure. Living on the beach in an old tin Quonset hut with a group of older surfers, the scrappy teenager attended classes at Waipahu High School and got his friend Billy to write excuses for him whenever the surf was good. Stepping on the sharp reef, Greg's feet often got cut and later infected, so the school nurse gave him permits to wear slippers or flip-flops to class. The other kids resented the hell out of him because he was the only student in school who didn't have to wear shoes and could get excuses to cut class anytime he wanted. Greg was also one of the only haoles in the entire school, and he often had to fight for respect from the locals.

While camping at Makaha Beach, Greg met a big-shouldered Hawaiian bodysurfer from Nanakuli. "When we started surfing, there was just a handful of guys surfing Makaha," Noll recalls, and most were haoles. But there was this one local guy who was "really an outstanding waterman, and his name was Buffalo Keaulana." After sizing each other up and exchanging nods, the talkative haole and the quiet Hawaiian gradually began to gravitate toward each other. "Pretty soon, I'd come in, and he'd ask if he could borrow the board. For the first couple of months, we became better and better friends." Each curious about the other's culture, they began surfing together and hanging out at the beach.

One day, Greg invited Buffalo to go to the Aloha Days festival in Waikiki, where they were holding paddling races and other sporting events. Needing to escape the isolation of Makaha for a while, Greg and another California transplant named Mike Bright were looking forward to competing in front of the crowds and checking out the scene at Hawaiʻi's most famous beach. "Buff, you wanna go with me and Mike into Waikiki and paddle in some of the races?" Greg asked. But Buffalo refused. "So I pestered him a little bit. He didn't like the idea of having to fill out the bullshit forms and everything. . . . Buffalo was a really, really shy guy. You could hardly get two words out of him. He was very, very quiet, typical country Nanakuli boy."

Greg found out that Buffalo had barely traveled beyond the Westside, and that made him more determined to take Buffalo to town. "I finally talked him into it. We got into the car; we drove to Waikiki." The two haoles and the Hawaiian competed in many events, and each won an award. They also enjoyed just watching all the tourists and locals gathered on the beach. "What we did wasn't as important as the relationship we built up," Greg says. "Mike won something; I won something. I had filled out all of Buffalo's forms for him, and he ended up winning something.

"We got back in the car and were heading back to Makaha. Everybody's hungry, so I stopped," Greg continues. "Buff didn't have any money, and I bought him some hamburgers and fries and we kept driving. All the way in, he never said one word; all the way back, he grunted a couple of times. Finally, we get to Nanakuli, and the first word out of his mouth on that whole trip was, 'My auntie stay over here; turn.' So we turn. 'Turn over here again.' We turn; we stop. He gets out of the car; he never looks back; he never says no thank-yous, no nothing. He just walks away. So Mike and I are driving back from Nanakuli to Makaha, and I go, 'Jesus Christ, man, have you ever seen anybody with less to say than that in your life?' We both agreed that Buff won the No-Talking Championship!"

A couple of days later, Greg and Mike were sitting in their old Quonset hut with their two other roommates when they heard some cars pull up to Makaha Point. "I look out and there's four trucks, carloads of Hawaiian guys," Greg recalls. He shakes his head and laughs, remembering the sick sense of foreboding he felt. " 'Oh, fuck, we're in trouble now! What did we do?' Man, I look out, and there's Buff, and he gets out of the car, and he's got a case of beer on his head. The next guy's got a case of beer and some pineapples, pupus (snacks), all *kine* stuff. They came in; we had a great time, ate. You know, I mean we're starved-out haoles out there, trying to poke fish and eat oatmeal for our sustenance. So we finally got a chance to eat and drink big-time."

After partying all day and into the night, the Hawaiian brud-dahs and the California haoles finally said their good-byes. "I mean that's really the beginning of my friendship with Buffalo. The lesson for me was that Buffalo is not a guy who does a lot of chest-thumping and talking. Buffalo does things by his actions and his deeds. Over a period of fifty years, we've been friends ever since 1954, when we first came over," Greg says. "That was the beginning of our long relationship. The next fifty years we've ended up going all over the world together. The guy has become an ambassador for Hawai'i." For a man who had never left the Westside until that first trip to Waikiki, Buffalo would go on to make a name for himself in surf towns around the world.

When Greg took off for the mainland later that year, he left his surfboard with Buffalo. Up to that point, Buff could surf well, but his real strength was as a bodysurfer. Without using flippers, he would just swim into the waves and ride them on his stomach all the way to shore. "He looked so natural streaking across the waves like a seal. I actually expected him to turn and swim out to sea when he was done," Greg says. "He was one of the best bodysurfers on the face of the earth. If you've ever watched guys get right in the pocket [curl of the wave] and do the roll deal, Buffalo was the guy who invented that. So I left him my board that year and that was the first board that he ever owned, and I'm very proud of that. But at the same time, it was kind of a double-edged sword, because on the next trips to Hawai'i, every time I left, I had to give him my board!"

With no high school diploma and few job prospects, Buffalo says he flirted with crime for a few years, hanging out with guys who were robbing stores and stealing cars. After a few brushes with the law, he had a long talk with surf pioneer Russ Takaki, who was working for the state as a court-appointed counselor for troubled youth. Having met Buffalo in the surf, Russ saw he was headed for trouble and advised him to join the army and learn some discipline. The Korean War was still raging, and they were always looking for new recruits. "I wanted to go in the service," Buff says. "I never liked staying out and hanging with the wrong crowd."

At the recruiting office at Schofield, he met with a group of colonels, majors, and sergeants. "They just wanted anybody who had a good finger to pull the trigger," he says. "They asked me a question about my bad record. 'Give us a good reason why we should let you into the military.' I said I liked to learn 'discipline.' They looked around and started giggling to themselves. They said, 'Do you know the meaning of discipline?' I told 'em no. 'How do you know the word?' 'Because this guy told me to ask you guys to teach me discipline.' So one sergeant said, 'Bring 'em, I want him in my company.' So I went into his company—sixteen weeks of basic training," Buff says, shaking his head. "When I came out of basic training, I learned how to say, 'Yes, sir! No, sir!'"

Not sure what to do with this burly Hawaiian who hardly ever spoke, his commanders learned about his impressive ocean skills and sent him to work as a lifeguard at the local recreation center on the North Shore. Not bad duty for a soldier, especially when some of his friends were being shipped off to war. "I was appointed to go to Army Beach at Hale'iwa," Buffalo recalls.

"Everybody went to Korea, and only me stayed back in Hawai'i. I met a lot of good people."

Working as a lifeguard, Buffalo became a favorite of the colonels and generals because he would catch lobster and fish for them and watch over their kids in the ocean. He often had to rescue officers and their family members from the big waves and treacherous currents. "Because I saved their lives, they wanted to recommend me for another stripe or something. Colonel O'Malley was one of the guys who had two sons that surfed. When they were kids, I would take them out diving, surfing, and swimming. The colonel said, 'Teach my kids how to catch fish, Buff.'" Under Buffalo's guidance, they went on to become respected fishermen, surfers, and lifeguards.

Meanwhile, Greg Noll had returned to Hawai'i and begun exploring the North Shore with a group of California and local surfers who were determined to find new surf spots and bigger waves. At that point, the North Shore was a wild and remote territory, barely inhabited by a small number of farmers, fishermen, and local families. The area was so isolated and unknown to modern surfers that they began naming some of the places. John Kelly said the waves were so big at one surf break that he called it Himalayas. After Greg took a group of his friends to a new break, they dubbed the spot Noll's Reef in his honor. He had a voracious appetite for food, drink, and adventure, and the once-skinny haole had bulked up considerably since his last visit to the Islands. His friends nicknamed him Da Bull because of his hulking frame and the fearless way he charged into big waves.

In 1957, Greg Noll became one of the first surfers to ride the huge swells at Waimea Bay. The place was thought to be too dangerous and deadly after a surfer named Dickie Cross had drowned there during a massive swell in 1943. But fourteen years later, Greg and a courageous group of Californians paddled out and rode the towering waves. Filming from the rocky cliffs on the shore, Bruce Brown caught the action in his movie

The Big Surf. Waimea Bay and the North Shore soon became the center of the surfing world, and pictures of the place appeared in surfing mags and mainstream publications such as *Life* and *The Saturday Evening Post.*

One day after surfing Sunset, Greg was driving over the Haleiwa Bridge when he caught a glimpse of a lone surfer at an unknown beach break. Greg turned down a dirt road and came upon a large field of thorny *kiawe* bushes. He and his friends made their way down a cow trail and discovered a pristine beach with perfect waves. The Hawaiian surfer waved for them to come and join him, and they surfed all day in this new spot. Afterward, he invited them to the little shack he had built on the beach and cooked them his specialty: rice cooked with seawater, *moi* fish, and all kinds of spices. This began Greg's friendship with a man named Henry "Hanale" Preece, an old friend of Buffalo's from Makaha.

"Henry was the kindest and most generous Hawaiian I ever met," Greg says. He was also a handsome Hawaiian who had a way with the ladies, but his charming ways eventually caught up with him. "Henry had knocked up this girl from Nanakuli, and she had six of the meanest Hawaiian brothers, who were after him." According to Greg, Henry moved to the North Shore to start a new life and put the Wai'anae Mountain Range between him and her six brothers. Hanale and Da Bull reconnected with Buffalo, who was working down the beach as a lifeguard, and the three became lifelong friends and troublemakers. They would usually hang out at Henry's shack on the beach and throw wild parties on the weekends. "I lived at the beach there for three or four years," Henry says with his thick pidgin accent. "While I was doing that, I was teaching the girls how to surf, and they'd bring me food and all that. I never need too much money. Oh yeah, it was a good life."

As more and more surfers started exploring the waves on the North Shore, Henry's shack became a central place to "talk story" and party. Chun's Store was just up the road from Army Beach, and Buff would go in there to buy food and cases of Primo beer. When the owner asked him to pay, Buffalo would ask him to put it on his bill. At the end of the month, he would basically hand over his paycheck to the store owner. "When we had money, we'd buy beer at three dollars or something a case; when there was no money, we'd make swipe with pineapple juice," Henry remembers. Swipe was a delicious but deadly mixture of fresh pineapple, yeast, sugar, and a few secret ingredients. After letting it ferment for a few days, he says, they would put "maybe half a quart of vodka or gin to give a kick to it."

At one party, Henry invited Greg and fellow big-wave riders Peter Cole and Jose Angel down to the shack. In honor of these well-known surfers who had moved over from the mainland, they prepared a big batch of swipe. Henry served it up in chilled, hollowed-out pineapples that he had stolen from the nearby fields. The two haoles thought swipe was just a type of juice with a little vodka, and they drank up the lethal concoction. According to Henry, "Greg and all those guys said, 'Hey, what is this? It's pretty good juice.' Peter Cole said, 'That's the best I ever drank!' I don't think Peter ever forgot that." Especially when he woke up in the bathtub the next morning. "It was a great party," Peter recalls. "The pineapple swipe went down real easy, but boy, the bottom part of your mouth would get numb after about three glasses of it. Pretty soon, you would be one of the bodies on the rocks," Peter says with a laugh. "It looked like Sherman's troops had come through the South on Sunday morning, with bodies all over the place!"

Following in the footsteps of other California surf zealots like Buzzy Trent and Fred Van Dyke, Peter had made the pilgrimage to Hawai'i in late August of 1958. He soon became part of a diverse band of brothers who had known each other for years and were respected as some of the best watermen of their time. Peter had been a lifeguard with Buzzy in Santa Monica as a kid and surfed with Fred at Steamer Lane in Santa Cruz. While studying at Stanford, Peter became an All-American swimmer and just missed making the Olympic team. This group of haole transplants formed a tight circle on the North Shore and jokingly referred to themselves as the Knights of the Round Table, even naming their old beach house Meade Hall. Armed only with their spearlike boards and sense of adventure, they charged into the North Shore's ominous waves, which roared like gigantic sea dragons.

On the surface, the Meade Hall gang was a diverse lot of wave warriors who seemed to have very little in common. Unlike Henry and Buffalo, who never finished high school, Peter and Fred had college degrees. The two haoles taught at Punahou School, one of the largest, wealthiest, and oldest private schools in the country. Though they enjoyed teaching at the prestigious school in the heart of Honolulu, they envied the fact that Buffalo and Henry lived near the beach and got to surf so much. In fact, both teachers could not resist playing hooky every now and then when the waves were really big.

In spite of their educational and social differences, guys such as Peter and Fred loved Hawaiian culture and were in turn welcomed by many of the Hawaiian surfers. They eventually bought homes on the North Shore and raised their families there. "I think the haoles and the Hawaiians intermingled in a good way in those days," Peter says. A lively sense of humor and a love of pranks helped ease any racial tension. "I always felt real good vibes and there were a lot of laughs. There was always a practical joke or something going on."

Decades before you could call a surf report or read about wave heights on the Internet, surfers used to call friends who lived or worked near the beach to get the lowdown on the wave conditions. One time, Peter called Buffalo at Army Beach to find out if there was any surf before making the hour-long drive from town to the North Shore. "Oh, it's really good out here. It's overhead; it's beautiful; you should come out," Peter remembers Buffalo telling him. "I get in the car and drive out, and it's just as flat as a lake." Peter saw Buff just sitting in a chair and drinking a beer at Aliʻi Beach, looking at the glassy ocean and smiling. "I said, 'Buffalo, what's the deal?' He said, 'Well, I was getting lonely and wanted some company. Have a beer!' " After talking story and having a few beers with him, Peter began to realize that Buff didn't want people calling him all the time about the surf. "He knew that if he gave a false report, we wouldn't bug him."

Buffalo, Henry, and Greg loved playing practical jokes on each other. Once, after surfing all morning, the three amigos went to Jerry's, the local Japanese burger joint, to stuff their faces. The haole and two Hawaiians plowed through piles of food, grunting and belching their satisfaction. Greg and Buffalo then decided to play a little version of "dine and dash" on Henry. After eating, Greg slowly stood up and walked outside without saying a word, winking at Buffalo as he left. Then, Buff got up and casually walked out as well. Before Henry realized what was going on, the Japanese owner came up to the table and gave him the bill. "He said, 'You guys ate about eight dollars' worth, you know.' I say, 'What guys? I don't know those guys.' "

As he coughed up the money for their lunch, Henry looked up to see Greg and Buffalo looking in the window and laughing. But what comes around goes around, and Henry would later get his revenge. "Buff and I pull the same thing, too. Eat fast, and I get up first, and Buffalo eats fast and leaves Greg. Me and Buff come out, and we watchin' Greg, wondering how he going to pay the Japanee guy for the meal. It was so damn funny . . . Greg would say he only had one dollah, and I say, 'You the only haole I know who only get one dollah.' "

Of course, the dine-and-dash trick didn't always work so well for Greg, especially when he stepped outside and encountered a group of hostile locals. "Once Buff and me was drinkin'," Henry recalls, "and this guy said, 'Eh, you guys betta go outside—your haole friend getting lickings.' We go outside and four or five Filipino guys are trying to mob him." Never missing a good fight,

Buff and Henry immediately jumped into the brawl to defend Greg. Being big Hawaiians, they gave the Filipino guys a run for their money. Afterward, Henry says, "We bring him inside and tell him, 'When you go outside, haole, no go outside without us.' "

Fight first and ask questions later—that was how many local disputes were resolved and friendships were formed. "We was brothers," Henry adds. "Nobody would touch him and we take care of him." Later, Greg and Henry sealed their friendship over beers and blood. "We had recently watched an old movie where a cowboy and an Indian had cut their wrists and become blood brothers," Noll writes in his memoir, *Da Bull*. Henry grabbed a pointed beer car opener and sliced his hand. Greg did the same, and they clasped hands. "We ended up becoming haole and Hawaiian blood brothers. Twenty years later, we still have the scars to prove it."

According to Henry, "there was always fistfights at that time" in Hawai'i. Fights would flare up between different ethnic groups due to the old plantation rivalries. There was also lingering resentment toward the haole *luna* (overseers) and owners who had fanned the flames of racial prejudice between the different races so they wouldn't unionize. But whereas most haoles were scared witless by these racial brawls, many Hawaiians like Henry and Buff actually enjoyed them. "Those days was fun," Henry sighs. "You fight up, and when you done, you shake hands . . . and tomorrow you drinkin' with the same guy and you got a black eye."

Greg became popular with the locals because he wasn't afraid to scrap with them. In fact, many of his high school classmates thought Greg had a permanently discolored eye, because he was always getting into fights. At a surfboard auction in 2005, an old Filipino man walked up to Noll, who was surrounded by fans, and showed him a copy of their old yearbook from Waipahu High School. And sure enough, he had a black eye in the photo. Noll said when he left the Islands he had a black eye and when he came back he had another one, so people thought it was a birthmark or something. As Greg stared at this younger version of himself, he chuckled over how he had changed. The crowd was also amazed to see how the skinny kid in the yearbook had evolved into this burly, heavyset surfing legend.

"When I came to Hawai'i, there was just a handful of my guys and a handful of Hawaiian guys," Greg says, looking back on the delicate racial balance they maintained. "I gravitated more toward the Hawaiians than the haoles because they did stuff I liked more. They had the neat parties; they played the neat music." Greg and Peter loved the 'ukulele and the slack-key music that Hawaiians had invented, using a different system of tuning on the guitar. But when the alcohol began to flow, old resentments would occasionally rise up like a rogue wave and come crashing down on the haoles. Drunken arguments would suddenly erupt into fistfights.

"If you had to pay the price of a black eye once in a while," Greg says, "I figured that was small enough payment. Most of the other guys didn't like the black eyes, so they sort of stayed away." But Buffalo and Henry were always protective of their haole friends and even fought fellow Hawaiians to protect them. "Henry has probably saved my ass on so many occasions I couldn't even count. I was staying at his house one time, and they were having a party. I had the flu, and I was crapped out in the front room on the couch. . . . The party dwindles down and there were these two guys from town. The room kind of goes quiet, and some guy says, 'Hey, you guys, let's go kick the haole's ass.' I'm sitting there listening to this. Henry comes back and says, 'That's my haole. You like fight, you gotta go through me and fight me first.'"

An honest fight might earn respect in places like Makaha and the North Shore, but it earned no points in the army. Buffalo kowtowed to no man and sometimes resolved arguments with his fists. He was also considered undisciplined by some of his superiors. One day at Hale'iwa beach, Henry remembers sitting with Buff when the general walked by with a sergeant named

Maddox. "We was sitting there at the table, and here comes the general. And the general says, 'Hi, Buffalo.' " Without standing up or saluting, Buff just said, "Hi, General." While the general liked the burly Hawaiian and found him funny, the colonel resented him and fumed over this blatant lack of protocol in front of superior officers.

Sergeant Maddox tried to make Buff's life miserable by forcing him to do extra kitchen duty, but the general was often there to rescue him. One night while drinking too much, Buff and his friends busted all the windows inside the Army Beach hut. Afterward, Buff went to see the general, who covered up the episode for him and sent some soldiers down there to fix all the windows. "Why do you think the general loved him so much?" Henry says with a smile. Because when the general wanted fresh lobster or fish for his parties, "Buff was right there to get 'em for him. In those days, lobsters was gold."

"Buffalo had it pretty good because he was Special Services, and he was at Army Beach for a lot of the time," says Peter Cole, who would later work for the military as a civilian planner. "That's not bad army duty." Besides, Buff also represented the army well in the Makaha International. Many guys in the military surfed, and they often had a surf club that would enter the contest, representing the army. A lot of the competitors were soldiers stationed at Schofield, which meant they could come right over the army-controlled Kolekole Pass to the Makaha side without having to drive an hour through cane fields and on bumpy, congested roads. Just like today's Pipeline Masters, the Makaha contests were becoming so popular that lines of traffic would back up for miles.

Competing against the best watermen from Hawai'i, California, Peru, and Australia, Buffalo won every bodysurfing meet except one from 1954 to 1958. These titles earned him respect in some military circles, but the Hawaiian knew his time in the army was coming to an end. So he moved back to Makaha and started surfing back at his old home break. In 1958, Peter Cole won the surfing division and Buffalo came in second. When the big Hawaiian stood onstage to receive his trophy, he shyly nodded and waved at all the people on the beach who were clapping and yelling. Greg was astounded to see how far his quiet friend had come in the surfing world since the first time they competed in Waikiki. But Greg knew that part of Buffalo's success came from the new Styrofoam surfboards they were riding. Ten years before, the long redwood planks that Wally Froiseth and John Kelly first rode at Makaha had been replaced by lighter balsawood boards. Now the Styrofoam boards were even lighter, more maneuverable, and less expensive to make. As the popularity of surfing exploded, demand for new surfboards skyrocketed.

Though Greg was often broke in Hawai'i, he had an entrepreneurial streak and quickly found a way to make money off the growing popularity of surfing. Tapping into the rising demand for new surfboards, he set up a factory in Southern California. Greg hired some of the best shapers and fiberglass experts in the business, and Greg Noll Surfboards started producing some of the most popular equipment in the industry. After all, he was one of the top big-wave riders and his name carried plenty of clout. "Da Bull" was as aggressive in the water as he was in business. But Buffalo and Henry knew Greg's soft side, and they would prod him to share his newfound success with his old Hawaiian buddies.

"Oh yeah, we had a free board every year," Henry laughs, remembering how they used to play "drink and dial" with their haole friend. "Every time Greg forgets, we would drink and then call him up and reverse the charge. We talked long time, too. He not home, we talk to his wife. He had a shop at that time, and we call him up again." When Greg complained that the calls were costing him a lot of money, Henry says, "I tell him, 'Eh, buddy, you betta send the surfboards or we going to keep callin' and reverse the charge.' It didn't take long before two surfboards came in. He was a good brother, you know."

Years later, after wiping out on one of the largest waves ever ridden, Greg quit the surfing scene and became a commercial fisherman in Alaska. But he would return to Hawai'i periodically to see his old friends. A few years ago, Greg came to Makaha with two boxes of Dungeness crab. "Henry would call Buff, and Buff would come over with twenty guys and then Henry's got his twenty guys," Greg says. "We've got fifty people and all the picnic tables lined up. I'm sitting in the middle of Buff and Henry, and we're eating crab, drinking beer, and having a good time. Henry's feeling pretty good, and he looks over at me and says, 'I love you, bruddah!' and he pours his beer over my head. And all of the gangstas on both sides of the table go, 'Oh, oh, here we go!' All I can see is dark eyes this way and dark eyes that way. Henry had a small *puka* [hole] in his T-shirt, and I reached over and shredded his goddamn shirt. And, man, you could have heard a pin drop at that table."

Watching this whole episode, Buffalo just laughed, but the other locals were preparing for a fight between the haole and Hawaiian. "And then Henry reached over and gave me a big kiss and started laughing," Greg says. "He's sitting there with his tit hanging out, laughing, and Buff is laughing. The table is still not getting it, and pretty soon, they all started to laugh. It was like 'hey, this is proof that a haole and a Hawaiian can still drink, get drunk, and have a good time without kicking the crap out of each other.' But it was hard for them to get it at first. Those guys were expecting the shit to fly. When they laughed, they laughed hysterically like it was the funniest goddamn thing they had ever seen."

Bridging any racial tension between haoles and Hawaiians, Buffalo, Henry, and Da Bull managed to stay best friends for over forty years. Looking back over his life, Greg says that he was proud to be the first surfer to ride the massive waves at Waimea Bay and take off on one of the biggest swells ever ridden at Makaha. He was also proud to be a legendary surfboard shaper and the father of a son who is carrying on that tradition.

"But at the very top of that list, I'm also as proud as I can be of both Henry Preece and Buffalo and that I will go to my grave with these guys being my best friends," Greg says, his voice choking. "I'm honored that they would allow me into their culture."

CHAPTER 3

🜨 🜨 🜨 🜨 🜨 🜨 🜨 🜨 🜨 🜨 🜨

The Makaha International

*The Makaha International Surfing Championship
was actually a water sports carnival . . . that laid the
foundation for international competition.*
—Fred Hemmings

Just as Wally Froiseth was one of the first modern surfers to
ride the waves of Makaha in the 1930s, he also became a pioneer in establishing the first international surf contest there.
Wally and an entrepreneurial surfer named John Lind had

founded the Waikiki Surf Club, and they competed against a growing number of other sports clubs in surfing, swimming, and outrigger canoe paddling. But the small waves and crowded conditions of Waikiki didn't always make for exciting contests, especially with its many distractions. Looking for a new venue that would capture the spirit of surfing, they chose Makaha. On the surface, this seemed like a ludicrous plan, because it was the most remote spot on the Island, with hardly any infrastructure or paved roads. Would international contestants actually travel to Makaha for a contest and would fans drive an hour out of town along bumpy plantation roads just to watch?

Wally and John gambled that Makaha's reputation as a famous surf spot and an exotic destination would be a big draw for surfers and spectators alike. Besides, they knew this was not going to be an ordinary contest but a new, world-class event and cultural celebration. They wanted to give surfing more respectability and share its spirit of adventure, while also paying homage to Hawaiian culture. "In those days, we were looked down on as bums and nobody respected surfing," Wally recalls. But he figured that if people could just come down for a weekend and see surfers competing and racing across the faces of big, beautiful waves they, too, would understand the allure of this ancient sport, Hawai'i's gift to the world.

Like the traditional contests held during the Makahiki season, the new Makaha International would feature unique events like tandem surfing and canoe surfing. Dating back to *ali'i* couples who used to surf together, tandem surfing events brought men and women together on the same board, challenging them to do all kinds of acrobatic maneuvers that looked like ballet on the water. Racing six-man outrigger canoes had always been a popular part of local culture, but now paddlers were taking them out into bigger and bigger waves to surf them as well. It was a dangerous sport, and only the best watermen could guide the canoe down the face of the wave without tipping over, breaking the canoe, or hurting themselves.

To pull off this kind of event, Wally and John knew they needed help from different sectors. They contacted Chinn Ho, the owner of the land, about holding the event in Makaha. They thought Ho would reject the idea of hordes of surfers descending on his land, but he enthusiastically embraced it. The shrewd real estate developer knew that this would be the perfect way to expose people from town to the inexpensive beachfront properties that were for sale. With real estate prices in Honolulu rapidly rising, land in Makaha became a bargain, especially for surfers, immigrants, and Hawaiian families.

"I believe that surfing was part of the initiative to invest a lot of money in Makaha," says Hawai'i state senator Fred Hemmings, who competed in the event as a young boy and went on to become a world champion. According to Hemmings, the visionary Chinese businessman saw beautiful beaches, undeveloped land, and the rising glamour of surfing as a winning combination for the future of Makaha. "Chinn Ho definitely recognized surfing as a major draw to his location and made a huge commitment to the development of the area." Once Ho was on board, they began working with the Wai'anae Lion's Club to bring in local businesses and community leaders who were also eager to develop the area.

After all the planning, Wally and John finally held their inaugural contest in December of 1953, and hundreds of people attended. Unfortunately, the waves never showed up. They went ahead and held paddling and swimming events, but the competition was marred by underlying racial tensions. Faced with a frustrating lack of surf and an abundance of alcohol, arguments arose between the Makaha and Waikiki surfers about how to cook the pig, the centerpiece of the big luau. Then the conflicts expanded to include some of the Californian haoles and local Hawaiians, erupting into a few fistfights.

Knowing they needed a local leader to maintain order at the event, Wally says, "We asked Buffalo to be in charge of the 'lifeguards.' So he'd have his own group, and they'd keep the guys out of the surfing area during that time because they all knew and respected him. He's a big guy, too!" Although Wally says that Buffalo never abused his power, he and his posse did have to rough up some guys who were drunk or unruly. "The guys that he had trouble with deserved it. He was really helpful in kind of controlling the beach so that the ordinary guy wouldn't be hassled."

In spite of a rough start, the idea of the Makaha International took root, and the event grew bigger the next year. In 1954, the waves came up and scores of top surfers flew over from Southern California, including a group of surfers from San Diego who called themselves the Windansea gang. For the first time, the best competitors from Australia also began migrating to Makaha, making the event truly international. Some surfers spent their life savings to fly to Hawai'i and take part in the event. Too young and poor to afford a ticket, Bob McTavish, a scrappy surfer from Down Under, stowed away on a cruise ship just to compete in the contest.

Fred Hemmings started going out to the Makaha International with his family when he was just a kid. Fred would always remember the long drives out to the Westside. "Driving to Makaha was a journey. Basically, the only freeway was a segment in town, and you got off that segment in downtown Honolulu, and you took Farrington Highway," Hemmings recalls. "It was a two-lane asphalt road that basically weaved its way through the cane fields of the 'Ewa Plain and around Barbers Point, and then you went to the sleepy little town of Nanakuli, with pretty much nothing in it but an old movie theater and a little store . . . And then we'd spend the night in Makaha Beach, and they would have bonfires. Those were the carefree days of youth, and there were none of the socioeconomic problems that Makaha seems to be challenged by now." Fred competed in the Junior Men's event when he was twelve, but before then he mostly went to watch his older sister and brother compete in the women's, men's, and tandem events.

Makaha could be a challenging place to surf because the waves could be really small or really big, and the break had four distinct sections. The biggest waves rose up at the Point, about one hundred yards from shore, and they would suddenly wall up and break into a long, curving section called the Bowl; they would then re-form at the Boil and go screaming toward a final inside section that often crashed into the outgoing backwash from the beach, launching surfers into the air. Only the most versatile surfers could figure out the waves' natural patterns and match them to the changing conditions of the wind and swell direction. But for those who figured it out, the wave was magic. "Makaha is one of the best-kept secrets in the surfing world," Fred says fondly. "In my estimation, it's still one of the best waves in Hawai'i. It's the most versatile surfing site maybe in the world. You can surf a two-foot wave there in a tandem event. You can also surf a twenty-foot wave, the biggest wave you can paddle into."

Wally had asked his old friend Russ Takaki to help judge the events, and they set up three stands on the beach. Surfers were judged on the height of the waves they rode, the length of their rides, the maneuvers they performed, and their overall sportsmanship. Competitors would wear T-shirts with numbers stenciled onto them, and they would paddle out in heats of as many as twenty-four surfers. Riding a long redwood board that weighed almost one hundred pounds, George Downing outmaneuvered the others and won the first men's surfing event by using his intimate knowledge of the break and expert wave choice. Buffalo won the first bodysurfing division, using his muscular six-foot frame and 190-pound body to ride the waves.

Although surfing was becoming more glamorous, bodysurfing was still revered as the purest and most original form of wave-riding. Whereas most people could only catch the breaking wave and ride the white water straight toward the beach, bodysurfers like Buffalo learned to catch the rising swells and ride them at an angle. Positioning himself right in the front of the curl of the wave, he was the first to be able to get fully barreled in the tube, then roll up the wave's face upside down, come down with the lip, and continue riding. Nobody had ever seen maneuvers like that, and the wide-eyed crowds on the beach would whistle, clap, and yell.

While thousands of spectators drove from town to watch the different events during the day, many stayed for the evening entertainment as well. One event included night surfing, and people camped on the beach and watched in amazement as the surfers paddled out into the darkness. As the Makaha International brochure described it, "A highlight of the annual international surfing championships is the nighttime searchlight and torchlight events." The military had become involved in the event and provided the searchlights, adding a surreal effect to the festivities. Once used to scour the night skies for enemy planes, their beams now swept over the waters like a lighthouse, tracking surfers as they glided across the waves.

"The searchlights play over the pounding and rolling surf while the surfers try and pick up the best waves and ride shoreward," the program read. "As they slide across the crest of the giant Makaha combers, the searchlights pick up and follow them until they hit the shoreline or cut out of the waves. The phosphorescent Makaha waters add a spectacular touch not seen any place but Hawai'i. While the surfers ride the giant waves, bonfires blaze on the beach."

Over the next two years, the Makaha International continued to grow in size and stature. What had started as a seat-of-the-pants surf contest had grown into a full-fledged cultural phenomenon perfectly suited for the time. People ate and drank on the beach as they watched the events, and they continued partying into the night. "It got out of control, and it was like Woodstock for a while," says surf historian Mark Fragale. "The first phase was starting the contest and developing an infrastructure, and the second phase was its universal acceptance."

Contestants started coming in from all over the surfing

strongholds around the world: Peru, South Africa, Australia, the mainland United States, and Hawaiʻi. "To participate or to win this contest had huge ramifications," Fragale says, referring to the fact that the Makaha International connected surfing's past with its future. "So it brings surfing competition from the ancient Hawaiians right to the modern Hawaiian people, not only Hawaiian by race but residents of Hawaiʻi that are full of aloha." For Buff, competing on his home territory and winning at sports that his ancestors had been doing for centuries gave him a newfound sense of pride. He went on to win the bodysurfing events for several years, and he kept rising through the ranks of the surfing contests each year, placing third in 1957 and second in 1958.

Once Buffalo got a taste of fame and surfing's growing popularity, he seemed to want more of it. He loved being in Makaha for the International, but when the contest ended, everyone left. The international competitors went back to their home countries, and the crowds went back to town, taking all the beautiful, young women with them. For the first few years of the event, he had been busy working in the army, shuttling back and forth between the North Shore and the Westside. But when he got out of the service and returned to Makaha, he found the place to be too slow and isolated. As a handsome Hawaiian and talented surfer in his prime, Buffalo knew that he could probably get a job working as a beach boy in Waikiki, where the rich and famous came to play.

The beach boys were a tight-knit and talented group of watermen who taught tourists how to surf, sail, and paddle outrigger canoes. But their greatest skill consisted of showing guests the laid-back Hawaiian lifestyle and their way of having fun. After being in the ocean all day, they would hang out on the beach with tourists all night. Strumming their ʻukuleles, they would sing Hawaiian songs and drink away the evening. Wealthy women from the mainland who were looking for a little adventure would often fall for the seductive charm of these beach boys. Hearing stories about making good money and having romantic flings, surfers like Buffalo decided it was time to move to Waikiki and get in on the action. There was a strict pecking order among the beach boys, and new recruits had to put in their time helping the older, established guys. Although Buff was from the country and new to the game, his victories at the Makaha International carried a lot of weight.

Walking through Waikiki in the late fifties, Buffalo would have seen wealthy tourists, visiting celebrities, and legendary watermen. They generally gathered in front of the two oldest and most prominent hotels on the beach: the elegant white dame known as the Moana Surfrider and the posh "Pink Lady" known as the Royal Hawaiian. Both hotels were built where Hawaiian royalty once lived. In 1934, the Outrigger Canoe Club formed the Waikiki Beach Club to organize and oversee the beach boys. The most famous beach boys were the Kahanamokus, whose oldest brother, Duke, had put Hawai'i on the map as an Olympic swimming champion and world-class waterman. The tall, handsome surfer had introduced surfing to parts of the mainland United States and Australia, where it went on to become a national pastime.

Duke and his five brothers mingled easily with movie stars like Bing Crosby and Carole Lombard and often took them for canoe rides and taught them how to surf. Duke's brother Sam was an intimate friend of the tobacco heiress Doris Duke, the world's wealthiest woman at the time, and she became an avid surfer and waterwoman under his tutelage. While most tourists would leave an envelope full of cash for the beach boys on their departure, Doris decided to stay in Hawai'i and later bought Sam a house near her mansion on Diamond Head.

By the time Buffalo arrived on the scene in 1958, the beach boys had established themselves as a beloved yet occasionally controversial part of the local culture. They all had colorful nicknames like "Panama Dave" Baptiste, "Chick" Daniels, "Steamboat" Mokuahi, "Turkey" Love, and "Rabbit" Kekai, so Buffalo fit in well with this menagerie of party animals. While some would play 'ukulele and guitars for the crowds at Moana Pier each night, others would engage in all kinds of crazy antics, like dressing up in costumes and women's clothing to parade along the beach.

Most tourists and locals loved these easygoing, athletic watermen, but some businessmen and religious folks felt like they were just lazy gigolos who hustled visitors and divorcées from the mainland. Although they indulged in many romantic and silly escapades, the beach boys took ocean safety seriously and saved many lives in the process. Buff was already recognized as an accomplished waterman, but he was not the type to make a living out of sweet-talking the tourists and seducing strangers. Still, he managed to get by as a beach boy and enjoyed the parade of wealthy tourists cruising back and forth across the Pacific.

The year 1959 was a turning point for Waikiki, the Islands, and the surfing world. Hawai'i became the fiftieth state, and the first jumbo jets started flying to Honolulu. Statehood had been a heated issue, but the referendum showed that the majority of people were in favor of joining the Union. Many Hawaiians had fought for America in the war and dreamed of taking part in its post-war growth and prosperity. Torn between their Hawaiian roots and American dreams, most locals cast their lot with the latter. They were betting that statehood would bring more tourism, jobs, and money to the Islands. Yet they resented the military's ownership of much of the land.

Politicians and businessmen organized big parties and parades in Waikiki and throughout the state, as if celebrating the marriage of the two cultures. Yet some Hawaiian activists looked on the proceedings as the final seduction of their native culture as they exchanged their political sovereignty for economic security. As a territory, Hawai'i had been like an exotic South Seas mistress for decades. Now the United States was ready to formalize their relationship and deepen their military and economic ties. With the evolution in transportation, the distance between them had become less and less of an obstacle. What had started out as a rolling five-day deep-sea cruise to Hawai'i in the thirties had gradually turned into a bumpy fifteen-hour flight during the late forties. But the new jumbo jets shortened the time even more, and Pan Am and other airlines could now reach the Islands in just seven hours. While the world was shrinking, America was expanding its hold on the Pacific.

As more and more tourists started coming to Waikiki, they returned to the "mainland" United States with tales of surfing, hula, and Hawaiian music. The sales of surfboards, grass skirts, and 'ukulele soared on the mainland, but tiki culture still remained an exotic twist to the traditional backyard barbecue. But when *Gidget* hit the big screen in '59, the movie became a box-office hit and a cultural phenomenon. The film was based on the book by Frederick Kohner, who had written about his daughter Kathy's surfing exploits in Malibu. The movie about the cute "girl-midget" brought the suburbs to the beach, spawned a series of sequels, and helped transform a fringe water sport into a national frenzy. Soon after, the Beach Boys exploded onto the music scene with hits such as "Catch a Wave" and "Surfin' USA."

Surfing was suddenly Hollywood hip, and people flocked to the coast to get in on the scene. Hard-core watermen found themselves surrounded by so-called posers, hodads, and kooks who strutted up and down the beach with their new boards. But for Buffalo and the beach boys, this meant a big increase in their business and social activity. With the popularity of *Gidget* and hit songs like "Surfer Girl," the number of women in the water greatly increased while the size of their bikinis continued to decrease. Life was good for the beach boys, and Buff began looking for his own surfer girl.

One day while surfing in Waikiki, Buffalo saw a local woman riding the waves, and he was struck by her beauty and grace on the water. After asking around, he found out that her name was Leimomi Whaley. She was a pretty Hawaiian-Portuguese woman whose sweet smile and big laugh were balanced by a sharp eye and a short temper. She worked at a beach concession stand called the Hale Auʻau, where she rented surfboards to tourists. Momi was the sister of a beach boy named Ed "Blackout" Whaley, a talented surfer with a reputation as a ladies' man. He had won the tandem surfing events at the Makaha International in 1955 and again in '59, making him a local celebrity.

"Blackout Whaley was a classic, a real good-looking Hawaiian, and these haole girls would come over and fall in love with him," Peter Cole says. "He didn't chase the girls; the girls chased him. The beach boys were very popular in those days." Unlike the haole women who pursued her brother, Momi didn't play that game and wasn't going to chase after any man. Buff began hanging around the beach stand where Momi worked, hoping to meet her. But he didn't have Blackout's way with the ladies, and she was wise to the ways of the beach boys.

As Buffalo pursued Momi, she held him at arm's length. "He'd come every day and play his ʻukulele where I used to work at the Hale Auʻau," Momi recalls. "He'd sit over there, and I'm renting these surfboards, and he's playing the uke all the time. He did this for almost two months straight. One day, he wasn't there, and I thought something must be wrong. I got so used to seeing him there," Momi says. Feeling shy and awkward on land, Buffalo decided to try approaching her in the ocean. So while surfing that day, he purposely bumped his board into hers. But according to Momi, his plan backfired.

"I used to love to surf; so every time we used to have a lunch or dinner break, I'm with my surfboard out there," Momi recalls. "So this one day I was outside there, and I had this spotted bikini thing on, and he bumped his board into my board, and my top went Pop! I went underwater like this and lost my top. I was going crazy. I turned around, and he just went away. What am I gonna do now? So I see one of the beach boys and I said, 'Hui, gimme your shirt!'" When he asked why, she explained that she had lost her top. "He said, 'I like see 'em,' and he wouldn't give me his shirt. By then, I'm pissed. So I walk up the beach [arms crossed], fit to kill, and he looks at me and goes, 'Ooh, are you pissed!' By then, I was so pissed I didn't care who saw me! And I said, 'Where is that SOB? I wanted to find him and whack 'em with my surfboard.' He didn't come by for a while. Then, finally, he came up and said, 'I apologize. I'm sorry.' I gave him a very bad time for about a year."

Sitting in their kitchen forty-five years later, Momi and Buff share the story of how they began dating. He says it was a done deal from the beginning, but she counters that it took a while for her to come around! "One of the guys at the beach told me, 'Hey, this guy Buffalo says he can go out with you,'" Momi recalls, and that made her even more determined to resist his advances. Later, Buffalo came by and worked up enough courage to ask her out. "So one day he comes and he plays his 'ukulele, and he says, 'Hey, you like go out?' And I looked at him and said, 'Excuse me, are you talking to me?'"

"I don't see anybody else around here," Buffalo said.

"Excuse me?" she said. "Do you know who Emily Post is? Have you ever heard of etiquette? Let me clue you in. If you ask a girl out, you ask nice. 'Would you like to go to the movies,' or whatever."

"Okay, I play your game," Buffalo said. "Are you doing anything tonight?"

"No," she said.

"You want to go to the show?"

Momi looked sweetly at him and said, "No."

"Then why the f—— don't you tell me in the first place?" he snapped back.

Momi recited her first real conversation with Buff at his retirement party thirty-five years later, and the crowd at the party roared with laughter. Despite his initial rejection, Buffalo continued pursuing Momi. One night he took her drinking with the beach boys at a local diner and he ended up passing out in his plate. "I was all drunk already," Buff says, shaking his head, "and I crashed right into the food."

"I turned around, got up, and walked out, and one of the guys says, 'Momi, you've got to take care of him.' I said, 'I'm not,' and walked out. And then he tells me, 'You left me,' and I said, 'When you're all in your food, brah, good-bye!'"

"All I remember is we went to the restaurant," Buffalo confesses, "and the rest is blank."

On their next date, they went to a party at the Elks Club in Waikiki. "We were over there having a good time, dancing on the table," Momi says with a laugh. "All of a sudden, he comes up and grabs me by the arm and says, 'Tell everybody good night.' One of the boys says, 'He told everybody he's your boyfriend.' I go, 'What?!' I turned around and said, 'Who the hell do you think you are?!'" Momi said that she made him take her home, but Buffalo says they were "walking toward the bushes!" Momi corrects him, saying, "No bushes. I made him take me straight home and drop me off. I was so mad!" She had seen him running around town with the haole girls and she wasn't going to be like the "fast and easy" tourists he used to pick up in Waikiki. But Momi couldn't stay angry for long, and Buff always found a way to win her back.

"Buffalo was always the rascal, but he met his match with that one," says Anthony "Ants" Guerrero. Ants was Momi's first cousin, but they were more like brother and sister. After her mom died and her father moved away, she had gone to live with the Guerrero 'ohana. "Momi and I are about five years apart, and I was always tagging along with all her boyfriends." Ants began hanging around with the beach boys in Waikiki, while Momi would often stay at home with her uncle. "My dad was a mechanic and a machinist, and he could fix anything," Ants says, remembering how she became interested in cars and engines. "I couldn't be bothered with that jazz. I would sneak off and go surfing. I would come home and somebody's under the car with oil all over. There's Momi and my dad! Even today, when we need to fix things, we call Momi."

Along with being able to fix cars, she also learned how to heal people. "She was very culturally inspired, especially in *kahuna lapa'au* (herbal medicine)," Ants says. "Momi's a healer. She started with her mother and knowledge about different plants. Buff's mom was also excellent in that, so Momi's pretty good with herbs.

"I was very fortunate in having Momi as a sister," Ants continues, remembering how she set him straight when he thought about becoming a beach boy instead of going to college. "I was working on the beach, making one hundred dollars a day and all that jazz. I also played ball for St. Louis, and I had all these free rides to play ball, but I turned them all down." Momi helped convince him to go away to college on the mainland. During his last years, though, Ants started thinking about dropping out. "But then Momi told me this: 'Brother, you better make us real proud and graduate, but don't come home until you do.' I guess that was a calling for me, because then the bank picked me up."

Ants would eventually become vice president of First Hawaiian Bank, with a corner office on the top floor of Honolulu's tallest building. Standing at the window, the bald-headed executive looks down the coast toward the Westside and says, "I love this corporate world because I'm able to help out a lot of people, but at the same time, you gotta get away from it." That's why he still has a home in Makaha.

Just as Momi helped straighten out Ants, she had the same effect on Buffalo. He was growing tired of the beach boys' constant partying, drinking, and sleeping around. Missing the laid-back lifestyle in Makaha, he was ready to settle down, get married, and start a family.

Wanting to be a husband and a father, Buff proposed to Momi, and she accepted. The next few months flew by in a blur of wedding plans, invitations, job searches, and tense conversations about where to live and what to do. Unable to afford any kind of expensive wedding, they planned a simple service at a local Catholic church in Waikiki with a reception to follow at the Guerrero home. Ants says his father was glad to help because he liked Buff and loved Momi like his own daughter. "Buffalo and my dad were close because of the kind of person my dad was. He came from poor beginnings, too, so he could understand."

Leimomi Whaley and Richard "Buffalo" Keaulana were married at St. Augustine Church on November 5, 1960, in front of a large gathering of friends and family from all over the Island. The service at the church went as planned, but the reception at the house grew bigger and bigger until it spilled out into the streets and turned into a block party. Henry Preece was the best man, and he rented a limo so he could take Buffalo and Momi and one of the bridesmaids around town. The party continued on without them, but the different factions of locals from the Westside and town started drinking too much and staring each other down. "It was crazy at the wedding because we had Nanakuli versus Waikiki," Ants remembers. "A lot of swipe was going back and forth. The whole street was a great party."

Kimo Hollinger remembers how all the guests were just swimming in alcohol and getting along fine until the very end of the party, when the tide suddenly turned. "The country guys and the town guys started looking mean at each other," he recalls. "This one guy, Big John from Makaha, I remember him saying, 'When Makaha guys roll, we roll like the tide.' It was like they were just going to charge." Kimo was a strong, tall lifeguard working in Waikiki at the time, but at that point he just wanted to save himself. "My friend dove out the window. I was just cowering in the corner. And this guy Rona came up and started yelling at them, 'The cops are coming! The cops are coming!' I don't know if Rona had called the cops, but he was just a smart guy." Everyone scattered before any fights broke out, and the reception ended peacefully.

After a brief honeymoon, Buffalo and Momi packed up their

gifts and belongings and drove down to the Westside. Knowing he had a wife to support, Buff had secured a job as the first park keeper at Makaha. The couple moved into a newly constructed two-story bathhouse on the beach. The first floor consisted of public restrooms and a storage facility, and the second floor was a small apartment, which Momi transformed into a home. The bathhouse soon became a gathering place for local surfers, stray pets, and anyone who didn't have a home. The Keaulanas soon had scores of kids and adults hanging around the house. When Momi complained that it was too much, Buffalo reminded her that he had once been homeless and just wanted to help these stragglers get on their feet and find a place to live.

Shortly after moving into their new home, the young couple began preparing themselves for the onslaught of crowds that would be driving down in droves for the upcoming Makaha International. As the contest continued to grow each year, a diverse array of corporate sponsors jumped on board, including Aloha Airlines, the Wai'anae Businessman's Association, Honolulu Paper Company, and Canadian-Pacific Airlines. "Remember, this wasn't just a thing for surfers," Mark Fragale observes. "It became very political." As the park keeper of Makaha, Buffalo had to deal with city planners, military officials, and reps from the Department of Parks and Recreation, who were working together to coordinate how they were going to handle this annual influx of thousands of people. Surfing was becoming a fruitful, commercial business in the sixties, and everyone wanted a piece of the pie.

Since its inception in 1954, the Makaha International had become the launching pad for a rapidly growing and rapidly changing industry. "To put this in perspective, the surfboards were made of wood, and Hawai'i was a territory when the contest began," Mark Fragale observes. Soon after Hawai'i became a state in 1959, the nature of the event changed dramatically, and so did the equipment. The new boards were shaped out of polyurethane foam and covered in fiberglass resin, with a skeg or fin on the bottom to help guide the board and keep it from sliding out in big waves. A burgeoning surfboard industry developed to meet the rising demand, and shop owners like Greg Noll were starting to make good money selling boards, bathing suits, and surf fashion. "Surfing was in its infancy as far as the commercial aspect," Fragale says, "and here's a gathering of people with all kinds of commercial possibilities."

As a newly married man and the first caretaker of Makaha Beach, Buffalo felt like this was his year to win the senior men's surfing event. He had an intimate knowledge of the surf spot and had developed a new trick, which would give him an edge over the others. Unfortunately, for the first two weekends of the contest the waves were fairly small, so they had to postpone the event and run the paddling and swimming heats. On the third weekend, a winter swell finally came through, producing solid, six- to eight-foot waves, and the contest went into high gear.

Makaha's waves can be challenging to ride because they start out breaking toward the right out at the Point and then they can begin breaking to the left farther in at the Bowl before swinging back around to the right at the Blowhole for the final inside section. Being a "goofy foot," Buffalo naturally stood with his right leg forward on the board, meaning that he would have his back toward the wave instead of facing it when he went right. Since Makaha generally breaks to the right, this was a minor handicap in transitioning from one section of the wave to another. It would be like a left-footed soccer player having to play on the far right side of the field. In order to deal with this, Buffalo learned to "switch stance" on his board, and this ambidextrous maneuver would become his secret weapon.

Buffalo had learned the move from California surfer Butch Van Artsdalen, who had been one of the first surfers to pioneer and master the technique. Butch had been a talented baseball player, and this maneuver was comparable to world-class switch-hitting. "I'd been watching Butch switch stance a lot and figured that's what I needed on the turn at Makaha," Buffalo says.

After months of practicing and falling down, he finally smoothed out all the kinks before the contest. During the first round, Buff used the trick against the master himself and ended up winning his heat. Having beaten Butch at his own game, Buffalo says that the California surfer just gave him a funny look and said, "Hey, I saw that move."

During the finals, the rains came down, and only the most loyal fans remained on the beach. Buffalo's intimate knowledge of the break helped him choose the biggest waves and make the longest rides. Using his new maneuver, he glided down the waves and then would switch his stance on the inside section so seamlessly that the judges just shook their heads in amazement. When they announced the scores, no one was surprised that Buffalo had won the Makaha International. He had competed against five former winners, including mentors such as George Downing and Wally Froiseth. Now, Buff was considered the new world champion. Although there were no cash awards, he was given a waterproof watch donated by Security Diamond and a plaque from the Waikiki Surf Club. But the real prize was the respect he gained in the surfing world and the knowledge that he was going to be a father soon.

Six months later, Momi gave birth to a baby boy named Brian, and Buff wasted no time baptizing him in the surf at Makaha. Brian was bound to become a surfer, because his father took him surfing literally before he could walk. At first, Buff just wanted to paddle around with his three-month-old baby, but then a wave came, and Buff couldn't resist. He stood up and held Brian in his arms as he glided down the face of the wave. Momi was not pleased with Buffalo's little surfing adventure, but she realized it was important to get the baby "waterproofed" because they lived right beside the ocean. Over the next few years, the couple would have two daughters, Lehua and Jodie. Each year, Momi would gather her growing brood and take them to watch their father compete in the Makaha International.

As the contest grew, the organizers brought in grandstands,

announcers, and more media. ABC's *Wide World of Sports* got involved in the early sixties, and suddenly the event gained worldwide recognition. People across the country could watch the highlights of the competition on their TV sets. With helicopters hovering above, ABC really brought home the excitement of surfing and validated the rising stature of the sport. Each year, the event was held in the middle of winter. "When it was on television on the mainland, half of the place is covered in snow," Fragale says. "Here you see blue water, palm trees, and people surfing in the dead of winter." Watching the big waves rise up at the Point, they would see the surfers race across the big Bowl and into the inside section, where the backwash from the previous waves would meet the incoming wave and often launch surfers high into the air. "It's like Shakespearean theater," Fragale says, "and all the action is right in front of you."

To highlight the drama, a former British pro wrestler named Lord James "Tally Ho" Blears would emcee the event. With his booming voice, immense stature, and love of language, he would narrate each contest heat as if it were a battle scene. Blears had served in the merchant marine in the Second World War, and his ship had been torpedoed and sunken by Japanese Zeros. After he survived in the ocean for three days, an American ship picked him up, and he ended up moving to Hawai'i. He became a champion wrestler and later produced and emceed wrestling events all across the country. Along with wrestling, Lord James and his family loved to surf, and they eventually joined the migration of people moving to Makaha. They befriended the Keaulanas, and Lord James's children competed in the Makaha International. His son Jimmy and his daughter Laura eventually became champions. Hearing Lord Tally Ho Blears's booming voice describe each heat brought a certain grandeur and dramatic flair to the event. Gradually, Hollywood celebrities and millionaires from the mainland joined the hordes of fans coming out to Makaha, where sooner or later they would have to meet the man called Buffalo.

CHAPTER 4

✺✺ ✺✺ ✺✺ ✺✺ ✺✺ ✺✺ ✺✺ ✺✺ ✺✺ ✺✺

The Wild West

Like a true nature child, he was born, born to be wild.

—Steppenwolf

As the park keeper at Makaha, Buffalo Keaulana would often ride a friend's horse along the beach like an Indian chief watching over his domain. Buffalo's official duties included taking care of the bathhouse and keeping the beach clean, but he was also the unofficial lifeguard, beach boy, and guardian of Makaha. As in his days in Waikiki, he looked after the tourists and young kids and taught them how to surf. Occasionally he would have to rescue the frightened city folks who were swept under by the large waves that galloped across the bay like wild horses. Buffalo knew fear and panic were the biggest obstacles to safety, so he pushed his children and the local kids to confront their fears and ride bigger and more powerful waves. If they wiped out or got bucked off their boards in the backwash, he would always encourage them to climb back on and try again.

When not working, Buffalo was usually surfing, fishing, or diving for dinner to feed his growing family. They still lived in the upstairs apartment of the two-story bathhouse, and the bottom half consisted of public restrooms on one side and a storage area for all his surfboards, diving equipment, and tools on the other side. Momi and Buffalo had had four kids in seven years, and they all lived snugly in this little A-frame house by the sea. After Brian, Jodie and Lehua, they had Rusty, who was named after Russ Takaki, the Japanese surfer who had encouraged Buffalo to join the army.

The family often went to sleep with the sound of the ocean murmuring in the distance and woke up to the sound of thunderous waves crashing below their windows in the dawn light. Buffalo was usually the first one out in the lineup, and he would sit on his board like a cowboy watching the waves roll by like wild horses. Then he would catch one, jump up, and ride it all the way to the shore. As word of the new swell spread, other local surfers and friends from town would drive out to join him. All of his children loved playing in the ocean after school and on the weekends, but as Brian grew older he began to join his father for early surf sessions before having to shower and get ready for school.

For eleven and a half months out of the year, Makaha was a relatively quiet country town. A growing number of homes were sprouting up along the arid coastline, along with a new grocery store and gas station on the main road. In the fertile valley, big ranchers began raising horses, pigs, and chickens and small farmers grew taro, vegetables, and marijuana, which locals called *pakalolo*. But for two weeks each winter this quiet community was transformed into a boisterous carnival atmosphere when the Makaha International Surfing Championship arrived.

During that time, Wally Froiseth and the contest organizers treated Buffalo more like the local sheriff than a park keeper. They would basically deputize his posse of friends to help keep the peace among the rival factions during this mass annual migration of surfers and fans from around the world. After the box-office success of the *Gidget* films, ABC's *Wild World of Sports* continued covering the Mahaka International for a few years. Soon millions of Americans became enamored with surfing and Hawai'i, and surfers suddenly became minor celebrities. Not only was Hawai'i a popular tourist destination, but also many visitors ended up moving to the Islands. The lure of cheap land and beautiful beaches began to draw more and more people to the Westside.

For an ever-expanding culture that loved its Western TV shows and movies, surfers in America came to be seen as a new kind of cowboy, free-spirited icons exploring the ocean frontier. They lived by their own code, referred to their big-wave surfboards as "guns," and rode the galloping surf into the sunset. Always pushing westward, more and more of these Southern California pioneers began moving to the Islands, trying to escape the conformity of mainstream American culture. Sometimes these haole surfers came into conflict with the local Hawaiians, but as Greg Noll can attest, it was worth the occasional black eye. But unlike the violent clashes between the so-called cowboys and Indians in the popular Wild West movies of the time, most of these transplants eventually embraced the indigenous culture and bonded with the locals over their love of surfing and Hawaiian culture.

After hearing about life in the Islands, waves of other surfers began landing on Hawai'i's shores, the birthplace of surfing and America's final frontier. Although Hawaiians were not pushed onto reservations, most of them gradually moved to homestead lands on the far eastern and western corners of the Islands. There they struggled to eke out a living and maintain their cultural identity in an increasingly Western society. Full-blooded Native Hawaiians were hard to find, but Buffalo was an even rarer breed because he still practiced the culture of his ancestors and also shared it with many haole surfers who made Makaha their home.

Just as surfers represented a new kind of cowboy, some of Hollywood's most famous cowboys were also surfers. Known as the Duke, John Wayne had been a bodysurfer in Southern California until he injured his shoulder while surfing one day and was forced to give it up. (Later, the Duke starred in a film with Duke Kahanamoku, who played a Polynesian chief, and they became friends.) James Arness took up surfing when he moved to California and became an avid surfer while pursuing his acting career and playing small parts in a few of Wayne's films. Then, in 1955, Arness was offered the leading role in the new TV show *Gunsmoke.* He didn't know whether to take the part at first because television was still an unproved medium, but Wayne encouraged him to go for it. After a few seasons, Arness became one of the most beloved actors in America, immortalized for his role as Marshal Matt Dillon.

Before becoming a big TV star, James Arness had spent time in Hawai'i when he was a soldier in World War II and had always longed to return. So after achieving fame and fortune in the hit series *Gunsmoke,* he started making trips to Hawai'i to surf with his son, Rolf. Overwhelmed by the crowds in Waikiki and hearing about the pristine waves on the Westside, Arness began driving out to Makaha. He had seen pictures of Buffalo in the surf magazines, heard he was a champion surfer, and knew he was the local authority at the beach. But when he actually saw Buffalo surfing at Makaha, Arness was amazed by his understanding and intimacy with the surf break. Buffalo knew exactly where to catch the biggest swells and how to navigate each section of the wave, from the outside Point to the Bowl to the Inner Reef. Although Arness was a big Hollywood star and a fairly good surfer, he was impressed with Buffalo's surfing skills, his low-key demeanor, and his unspoken authority at the beach. After they had surfed a few times together and nodded at each other from across the water, Arness decided to meet the Hawaiian waterman.

Buffalo was sitting in front of the bathhouse one day eating lunch with a group of friends when the tall TV star ambled toward him. He and the others immediately recognized the six-foot-seven haole man with the rugged good looks as the one and only Marshal Matt Dillon, but they just smiled and nodded, not knowing what to say. They didn't know if Arness was going to be a cocky Hollywood actor or just a regular guy, and Jim didn't know how these local Hawaiians felt about his coming down to their part of the Island uninvited. Recalling the moment forty years later, Buffalo says there was a brief pause as they sized each other up, the Hollywood cowboy and the Hawaiian Sitting Bull. Arness then broke the silence and introduced himself.

"What are you guys eating?" Jim asked.

"Oh, fish and poi," Buffalo said, gesturing for him to take some of the freshly grilled fish and the pounded taro root, which was a staple of the Hawaiian diet. Jim asked if he could try the fish, and they began eating and talking. When Buffalo offered Jim some poi, he joked that he couldn't stand the stuff but would love to try the chili water they were drinking. Buff warned him that it was extremely hot. Jim boasted that he could handle it, saying, "I eat chili peppers in Mexico." He took the jug of chili water and began chugging it, and suddenly his face turned red and tears started pouring from his eyes.

Barely able to speak, Jim gasped, "Hot! How do you turn this thing off?!"

"Da poi," Buffalo said, pointing to the thick purple paste. Although he hated poi, Jim scooped up the gluelike substance in his hand and just started devouring it. "He ate that whole thing!

He was shoveling it in, trying to put the fire out," Buffalo recalls with a laugh. "He said, 'Goddamn, that's hot! No wonder you guys eat poi.' " The chili water incident served as the perfect icebreaker, and afterward Jim and Buffalo started hanging out together at the beach.

Jim and his son, Rolf, rented a house right on the beach at Makaha, and Jim used to invite Buffalo and Momi over for dinner. During their long conversations, Jim would tell them about coming to Hawai'i for basic training during the Second World War and how he was harassed by a haole sergeant until a big Hawaiian sergeant stepped in and took him under his wing. Jim was later shipped to the European Theater. He explained that the slight limp in his right leg came from when he was wounded by machine-gun fire during the 1944 invasion of Anzio. A humble man, he never mentioned that he was awarded a Purple Heart.

After the war, Jim had gone to Hollywood to try his luck as an actor. He took some bizarre roles as a monster in *The Thing* and a shipwrecked sailor in *Two Lost Worlds,* where he was forced to fight dinosaurs on a volcanic island. Then, in 1955, he was recommended for the leading role in *Gunsmoke,* which went on to become one of the longest-running dramatic series in TV history. "He went from being a nobody in the service," Momi says, "to all of a sudden being a big somebody!"

Because James Arness was such a popular TV actor, star-crazed fans and paparazzi used to accost him all the time, with little regard for his privacy or personal space. That's why he stopped going to Waikiki and started spending his time in Makaha. Yet even in this remote beachside town, wide-eyed locals and tourists still approached him all too often. "Every other place he went, people just hounded him," Momi remembers. "That's why they like to come to this side, because Waikiki was such a madhouse. Everybody and their uncle would say, 'Can I have your autograph? Hey, Mr. Dillon!' " Occasionally teenagers on the Westside would walk up and do the quick draw in front of Jim, but Buffalo and Momi would usually clear the way and keep people at a distance so he and his son could enjoy their vacation. "When he came down with us, we would just say, 'Knock it off! Over here, they're just like anybody else; they just want to relax. So if you're thinking of rushing him, guess who you got to pass by!' " As a feared and respected local leader, Buffalo would just have to give people a stern look and they would stay away.

Along with being Jim's informal bodyguard on land, Momi says, "Buff was like his personal lifeguard when he would come out to Makaha." Buff kept an eye out for Jim in the big outside waves and also watched over his son in the smaller surf near the shore. Named after his grandfather, Rolf Aurness (the original spelling of the family name) was a curly-haired, lanky kid who loved to surf. Treating the young haole boy like one of his own children, Buffalo taught Rolf about how the wind, currents, tides, and underlying reefs helped form the waves and showed him how to avoid being pounded by incoming surf by paddling out in the deep channel or diving like a duck underneath the waves.

As a kid, Rolf had fallen out of a tree and busted his head wide open, so Jim made him wear a helmet for a while and asked Buffalo to make sure he kept it on in the surf. "The father was very watchful over him, very protective of Rolf," Momi explains. Buffalo took water safety seriously, but he also had a mischievous side and loved playing jokes on Jim. "Buff was like the recreational director," she adds. "Buff took a coconut leaf and made a horn out of it." Rolf was running around and blowing it all over the place, driving Jim crazy, so he took it away. "Uncle Buff, my father took away my horn," Rolf said. So Buff would tell him, "Come here; I'll show you how to make another one." Hearing his son making all that noise, Jim would just look at the big Hawaiian, shake his head, and laugh.

Returning several times each year, Jim became a regular fixture in the Makaha community because he enjoyed its carefree spirit and generosity. "Jim used to love to come to this side because Buff and all our friends would get together, play

Hawaiian music, and just sit down and enjoy," Momi says. Talking about his life in Hollywood, Jim would tell her, "It's a frickin' rat race. People come at you like paparazzi all the time . . . It's like living in an hourglass—you're in a glass looking out and everybody's just looking at you."

After a day of surfing, swimming, and fishing, Buffalo would gather his friends and family for an evening of good food, beers, and music on the beach. "We would get together, and everybody would bring potluck," Momi says, adding that Jim would always insist on buying everything they might need. "What we do over here is 'dollah, dollah,' " she would tell him. "You put a dollah in, I put a dollah in, he puts a dollah in—we all going to share. We don't care if you got fifty dollars or one thousand dollars—it makes no never-mind to us—but everybody shares in the pot. That's what we do, and that's why we get along fine, because nobody's higher than anybody else." But realizing the millionaire actor wanted to pay the Keaulanas back for their hospitality, she would wink and say, "But if you want to throw in a couple hundred dollars, that's okay!"

Along with teaching Rolf how to surf and dive at Makaha, Buffalo used to take him, Buff's kids, and the Sunn sisters, Rell, Martha, and Anella, out in his nine-foot Glasshopper, a small catamaran-shaped motorboat with a Plexiglas hull. Buffalo would point out all kinds of sea life through the bottom and then chase schools of fish through the blue-green water. They would see lionfish, spotted eels, sea turtles, needlefish, and prickly puffer fish. The kids loved being on the boat and learning about all the colorful creatures and the world beneath the waves. Buffalo would also take Jim out fishing, and sometimes they would surf the little boat through the small waves on the way back.

One day after Jim and Rolf returned to California, Buffalo anchored the motorboat in the channel, and overnight the waves grew to over twenty feet. The huge waves smashed the little Glasshopper into a hundred pieces. After hearing about the accident on his return to the Islands, Jim took Buffalo down to the local boat dealer and bought him a thirteen-foot Boston Whaler with a 33-horsepower Johnson motor on the back. On one of their first voyages, they took out the Whaler to see if they could ride it in bigger surf. "Now, instead of catching five- to six-foot waves," Buff says, "we're catchin' fifteen- to twenty-foot waves in the boat!" *but no glass bottom ?*

During the Makaha International, Buffalo would take magazine photographers and cameramen out in his motorboat to help them take the best pictures of the competition. Because he was such a knowledgeable waterman, he knew exactly how close to get to the waves without endangering the people in his boat. He also provided water safety during the contests and would often use his Whaler to zoom in from the channel and rescue surfers who had suffered bad wipeouts or injured themselves before the next set of waves came through the impact zone.

Watching from the shore or later from inside the boat, Brian would study his father's every move during these dramatic rescues. Twenty years later, Brian would pioneer his own water safety procedures in big waves and during contests. Starting in 1965, Buffalo also began working with the newly formed Duke Classic. Named after Duke Kahanamoku, who was known as "the father of modern surfing," the contest was held each winter on the North Shore. Unlike the Makaha International, which was an amateur contest with hundreds of competitors, the Duke Classic was an invitational event only for the top twenty-four surfers in the world.

During this time, there was a shift in the surfing scene away from the laid-back atmosphere and smaller waves of Makaha to the more seriously competitive arena of the North Shore, with its generally larger and more powerful waves. California surfers like Dewey Weber also complained that the mostly Hawaiian judges at the Makaha International favored local, Hawaiian surfers over haoles.

Although Weber was considered one of the best young "hotdoggers" of the day, the Californian felt stifled in the crowded waves of the International, which had as many as twenty-four surfers competing in a thirty-minute heat. He also felt the judges didn't appreciate the Californians' radical new style, which included more sharp turns and cutbacks, as opposed to the Hawaiians' more graceful and fluid style. He and others like Ricky Grigg and Mike Doyle excelled in the bigger and less crowded waves of the Duke Contest, which consisted mostly of young haole surfers competing in six-man heats.

Many Hawaiians resented the vocal criticism of the Makaha International by Californian surfers like Weber. Buffalo and others also felt slighted when they were not invited to the Duke Classic. But the Westside waterman had one more chance to prove himself in the newly formed World Surfing Championships, which were held every two years in various locations around the globe.

In 1965, Buffalo was invited to compete in the World Surfing Championships held in Lima, Peru. He had never traveled beyond the island of O'ahu, much less to a foreign country in another hemisphere, so this was a big trip. His teammates Fred Hemmings and Paul Strauch took him to Reyn's, an upscale clothing store that was providing the Hawai'i team with shirts, pants, and blazers with a Hawaiian logo on them. Buffalo rarely wore shoes, but his young teammates urged him to go buy some, because surfers in Peru came from the upper class and were very formal. Not one to be intimidated by wealth and class, Buffalo bought some high-top Keds to go with his outfit and brought along his 'ukulele to play at the cocktail parties.

After their long flight, all of the competitors were invited to a lavish reception hosted by the Peruvian president. That reception kicked off a week of partying. The aristocratic Peruvian surfers loved Buffalo's homespun sense of humor and carefree ways. Although they came from different worlds, Fred Hemmings says, "there was great camaraderie between the Hawaiians and the Peruvians in surfing." Class and politics didn't matter out in the ocean, where no amount of money could buy character or ability, and the Peruvians recognized that Buffalo had plenty of both.

The World Championships were held at a surf spot called Punta Roca, thirty miles below Lima. During the contest, Buffalo did well in the early rounds, because the waves were big and he and the other Hawaiians knew how to ride them. Unfortunately, during the preliminaries he sliced his foot open on a sharp mussel shell. "My toe was just dangling," Buffalo says. "I couldn't surf no more." Felipe Pomar of Peru went on to win the contest, barely beating Australia's Nat Young and Hawai'i's Paul Strauch.

While some of his friends tried bullfighting, Buffalo restlessly limped from party to party, drinking to numb the pain in his foot. "I was still young and a wild man," says Hemmings, "and certainly Buffalo has never been shy about having a cold beer . . . So we really had a good time—we were the Young and the Restless."

Back in Hawai'i, Buffalo, Momi, and the crew from the World Championships reunited at Fred's engagement party. Fred brought out a Peruvian surfing magazine to show everyone pictures of their trip, but he didn't think about how the spouses would react to some of the revealing photographs. In one photo, Buffalo is standing with his arms around two lovely Peruvian ladies in skimpy bathing suits, waving his hands and wearing a big smile. Without missing a beat, he told his wife, "Honey, see my hands—I was waving hi at you." Momi then replied, "Lucky your two hands are this way. Any place else, and you would be six feet under!"

After that contest, Buffalo continued competing in the Makaha International, but he gave up on the professional contest scene because he didn't like the growing commercialism and competition of the sport. As the Duke Contest and other pro events became more popular, the crowds and camera crews moved over to the North Shore. Like an athlete who continues competing past his prime, the Makaha International struggled to retain its former glory but gradually faded out of the limelight. A new generation of younger surfers was taking the stage when the equipment began to change in 1968 to adapt to the bigger and more powerful waves on the North Shore. Just as the heavy wooden planks had been replaced by long Styrofoam and fiberglass boards a decade before, now shorter and skinnier surfboards were becoming the rage because they were lighter and more maneuverable.

With the shortboard revolution of '68, the art of surfing reflected the changes in pop culture. The anti-war movement had gathered strength, and legions of disillusioned young people and angry vets began protesting the government's "unofficial war" in Vietnam. The two bikers in Dennis Hopper's film *Easy Rider* captured the counterculture lifestyle of this freewheeling generation by hitting the road and taking a psychedelic trip across the country. Likewise, surfing became a free-flowing and adventurous way to drop out of modern society and into something more timeless and pure. Riding waves allowed surfers to tune into the ocean's natural rhythms and tap into its endless energy. For a "true nature child" who was "born to be wild," surfing was more natural than riding a motorcycle along a winding highway, but the sense of freedom was the same.

As their boards and bathing suits got shorter, young surfers grew their hair longer and started experimenting with drugs and more radical maneuvers. Instead of a stylized, formal dance with the wave, the new breed of surfers switched to a faster-paced, freestyle form that was more in sync with the spirit of drugs and rock and roll. But Buffalo was more of a traditionalist, and he didn't like the radical new style of surfing or the hallucinogenic drugs that often went with it. Although the acrid scent of burning *pakalolo* often hovered over the beach at Makaha, the local posse didn't like the wild-eyed breed of acid trippers who used to come down to the beach.

Fred Hemmings remembers the time when a well-known surfer was going on and on about the magical effects of LSD and

Buffalo grew increasingly agitated. At one point, the acid guru began talking about how reality is just an illusion and that they could all be just imagining their existence. "Well, Buff had enough," Fred recalls. "He calmly looked at our LSD friend and said, 'How 'bout I punch your head? You goin' imagine dat?' Needless to say, our loquacious friend was snapped back to reality by Buffalo's wise and few well-chosen words."

Wanting to keep his son away from drugs, James Arness began grooming Rolf for competition at an early age. James bought him the best equipment and took him to every contest in California and Hawai'i. Rolf was starting to make headway on the amateur surfing circuit and exploded onto the contest scene in 1968 when he was only sixteen. That year, he was the youngest Californian to compete in the World Championships in Puerto Rico, but he was eliminated by former champ Felipe Pomar. Fred Hemmings managed to win the event, though his styles of surfing and clothing were increasingly out of sync with the younger, psychedelic surfers.

While most of the surfers had long hair and wore Nehru jackets, flowered shirts, and beads, Fred had short hair and was dressed in slacks, tie, and a sports coat. Surrounded by the scent of marijuana smoke, he would later joke, "I felt like an IBM salesman at a Cheech and Chong convention." Rolf was only a teenager and was influenced by the party atmosphere of the time, but his dad kept a close eye on him and pushed him to channel his energy into healthy competition. It would be two more years before Rolf would have a chance to win the world title again. During a break in the contest series, he decided to join his dad in the Transpacific Yacht Race from California to Hawai'i.

James Arness was not only a dedicated surfer, but he was also a competitive sailor. During the summer of '68, Jim and his son sailed their fifty-eight-foot ultra-light catamaran called the *Seasmoke* to the Islands in just nine days, winning the race and setting a new record. To celebrate, Jim invited Buffalo and

Momi to join him at the awards ceremony in Waikiki. Momi was pregnant with her fifth child, so she was not drinking, but Buffalo was imbibing enough for both of them. "Buff was about two sheets to the wind when he picked us up, and here I am about eight months pregnant," Momi says. "We're driving into town, and Buff's laughing. Jim gets Buff out, and all of a sudden, he starts meandering around. So Jim hangs on to me like he's my escort, and I said, 'Watch out; they're going to blame you for this!'" She pointed to her swollen belly, and they both started laughing as onlookers stared and snapped photos of them together. "Most of the movie guys would come by," Momi recalls, "and he would turn around and say, 'This is Buffalo and Momi . . . and this is my future baby.' My young son Jimmy was named after James Arness."

Meanwhile, Buffalo had stumbled off into the party and was chatting with a nice-looking blonde in a black outfit. Momi spotted the jealous husband walking toward him, so she sent James to waylay the man and rescue Buffalo. "So all of a sudden, I go, 'Jim!' and he runs over there and goes, 'How do you do? I'm James Arness.'" Starstruck, the man muttered, "Oh, the guy from *Gunsmoke*." As Jim shook the guy's hand and tried to distract him, he motioned with his other hand to get Buff out of there. Jim would later joke about how he had "saved his ass again."

On the way home later that evening, Buffalo wanted to take Jim out to a diner, but Momi said she was tired and wanted to go straight home. By the time they reached Makaha, Buffalo was passed out in the backseat of the car. Instead of trying to wake him, Jim just picked up the big Hawaiian and carried him upstairs. Holding him over his shoulder, Jim asked Momi, "Where do you want me to put this?" Still peeved from Buffalo's behavior at the party, she turned and said, "Just drop 'im."

Loaded with stories from his wild times in Makaha, James Arness began sharing them with his fellow actors in Hollywood. Word spread about Buffalo and his family, and soon other Western TV actors began showing up on Hawai'i's Westside. One day, Momi saw this tall, handsome man outside her door who looked exactly like the star of the show *Lawman*. "This guy came up the steps, and I looked at him and said, 'Aren't you John Russell?' And he said, 'Are you Momi?'" Buffalo had met Russell at Makaha and wanted to surprise his wife by sending the handsome actor to pick her up for a party on the beach.

On another occasion, Momi recalls, "I hear a knock on the door, and there's Chuck Conners, the Rifleman. All these guys are coming over because Jim tells them about Buffalo." The Keaulanas would share their home, food, and culture, showing the actors how to do an authentic Hawaiian *hukilau*. After gathering their friends and guests, the Keaulanas would wade out into the ocean with a big net to corral schools of fish for dinner. Afterward, they would cook their catch and sit around the fire, eating fish, drinking beers, and singing Hawaiian songs for the rest of the evening. Afterward, Chuck Conners told Momi, "No wonder James Arness comes down to this side of the Island. You guys have a ball down here, and you don't tell people about it."

When Jim and his son returned to Makaha in the winter of 1969, Rolf had just won a trifecta of surfing contests in California. These victories earned him a spot on the U.S. team for the upcoming World Championships in Victoria, Australia. Competing against mentors like Buffalo, Rolf placed fourth at the Makaha International that year. One of only twenty-four surfers in the world invited to the Duke Classic, the seventeen-year-old placed fourth in that event as well. After surfing big waves in Hawai'i that winter, Rolf was primed and ready to compete in the World Championships in 1970. He flew to Australia with his father weeks before the event to surf and get in shape for the contest. His childhood friends Anella Sunn and her sister Martha also flew down for the championships, representing Hawai'i and a new generation of female competitors. Rell would have been there, too, but she had just gotten married and had a baby.

Wayne "Rabbit" Bartholomew will never forget when Anella

and Martha came down to his home break of Snapper Rocks in Rainbow Bay to prepare for the world contest. Rabbit would go on to become a future world champion and head of the Association of Surfing Professionals, but at the time he was just a skinny Aussie teenager who was in awe of these beautiful Hawaiian women who embodied "this image of Polynesian grace on a wave." With the freezing air and water temperatures, the Sunn sisters provided a warm welcome to Rolf and the other Hawaiian competitors when they flew Down Under for the World Championships.

Along with the usual tension between the Aussies and Hawaiians, there seemed to be a new animosity toward the contest and competition in general. The contest got off to a rough start due to the lack of waves and an abundance of drinking, drugs, and fights. Former U.S. champ Corky Carroll had been temporarily suspended from the competition after calling the championships a fiasco and starting a fight in the hotel bar. Narcotics agents found drugs in some of the competitors' rooms, but they weren't arrested and were still allowed to compete. After a flat spell at Bells Beach and a subsequent search for bigger surf, the men's event was finally moved to a remote beach break called Johanna, where hollow six-foot waves peeled across the sandbar. Although the water was cold and he had to wear a wet suit, Rolf was on fire during the contest. His unique blend of Californian hotdogging and Hawaiian power-styling worked perfectly in the mid-sized surf, and the judges unanimously declared him the winner.

With his boyish good looks and sweet smile, Rolf was a popular champion. Yet he resented headlines like "Son of *Gunsmoke* Wins Title" that always emphasized his father's fame over his own accomplishments. After returning to the United States, Rolf began appearing in surf magazines and even on TV programs like *The Merv Griffin Show* in an effort to establish his own identity. Tired of traveling with his father on the contest circuit, Rolf quit surfing competitively and started hanging out with his mom and sister. Unfortunately, both women had become deeply mired in the Malibu party scene and tried to pull Rolf away from his father's influence. Yet just as he was emerging out of his father's shadow, the shy, lanky teenager began experimenting with LSD. After dropping acid, Rolf dropped out of society, descending into a tunnel of addiction, depression, and isolation.

"Rolf—disturbed by his parents' conflict, let down after his surfing success, confused by fame, and split open by LSD—was spiraling out of control," surf journalist Drew Kampion later wrote. Rolf's wake-up call came a few years later when his sister overdosed and his mother died of alcoholism later that year. Like a bad acid trip, his life seemed to lose all meaning. "The whole psychedelic movement was coming to a close," Rolf says. "Fortunately, my dad kind of rescued me before then and got me into rehab." He eventually dropped out of the surfing scene almost completely. The carefree days of surfing in Hawai'i and around the world were over. James Arness retired and settled down in Los Angeles, but he stayed in touch with the Keaulanas over the years and often talked about getting together again.

When Buffalo was inducted into the Surfing Hall of Fame in 2005 in Huntington Beach, Jim sent a limo to pick them up and bring them to his home in Brentwood for a reunion. "We were so tickled when we got to see him in Brentwood. Poor thing's got arthritis now, so his back is all bent," Momi says. "As soon as we got out of the limousine, he ran right up to Buff and just grabbed him."

Although his hair was white and his back bent, Jim wore the same big smile on his gaunt face and still had a larger-than-life personality, just like when he first introduced himself to Buffalo. They laughed about Jim's drinking chili water that day at the beach and all the wild parties they attended. Sitting in Jim's living room surrounded by memorabilia from his stints as a surfer in Hawai'i and an actor in Hollywood, they reminisced about the old days in Makaha. They recalled memorable surf sessions together with just a handful of friends, each taking turns riding the pristine waves on the Westside, when they were still young and wild.

CHAPTER 5

What It Means to Be a Waterman

*Generally used to describe the surfer who is comfortable
in a wide variety of ocean conditions and has a broad store of oceanic
knowledge; more specifically applied to those who are accomplished
at a particular set of surfing-related activities, including diving,
swimming, sailing, bodysurfing, fishing, spearfishing,
surf canoeing, and oceangoing rescue work.*

—Matt Warshaw,

The Encyclopedia of Surfing

After buying the Waiʻanae Sugar Plantation and dividing the land into smaller plots, Chinn Ho began selling the area piece by piece over the next few decades. In the process, he became one of the biggest real estate developers in the state and opened up a region that had been previously dominated by Hawaiian chiefs, private ranchers, plantation owners, and the U.S. military. Now it was available to anyone who wanted to escape from the city and live in the country near the ocean.

In spite of its dry terrain, lack of water, and poor infrastructure, the Westside became a hot spot for Japanese developers, haole tourists, hapa (mixed-race) homeowners, and small farmers whose families had come from all over Asia to work on the plantations. Native Hawaiians continued moving back to the area, hoping to live on homestead land and reclaim some of their lost culture. They resented the influx of so many foreigners, especially those who wanted to develop the area. Racial tension grew between the locals who had lived on the land for generations, including Native Hawaiians and the former plantation families, and those Japanese and haole developers who were driving up land prices in their quest to transform the place into a resort area—a kind of Waikiki on the Westside.

Protected by its majestic wall of mountains, the Waiʻanae Coast offered seclusion and beauty for those who wanted to escape mainstream society. Its rugged coastline appealed to watermen, who loved the sea and felt at home in her moody embrace. Wealthy and powerful men who loved surfing began moving their families to the Leeward Coast, including commanders from Pearl Harbor and rich oilmen from Texas. Yet these newcomers soon realized that wealth and power held little sway over the poor locals who valued strength and character over titles and material possessions. Sensing the growing antagonism and fierce localism of the Westside, they sought out the friendship of Buffalo and the Keaulana clan, who were like the gatekeepers to the Makaha community.

On the eastern end of Makaha, the army had built a recreation center on the beach where the royal school for Hawaiian chiefs had once been. Known as "Rest Camp," the pristine beach attracted many surfers in the military who loved the secluded spot on the Westside. Stationed at Pearl Harbor in the mid-fifties, Captain Fred Bakutis used to surf at Rest Camp, where he ran into Buffalo on occasion. The captain had first seen Buffalo competing at the Makaha International. Sitting on the beach, which was packed with people and tents, Fred and his young son Robert "Bunky" Bakutis felt Buffalo was unique among the competitors because he seemed to be having fun while performing these incredible maneuvers. "Everybody would applaud when he would surf because he was just such an amazing figure to watch," Bunky recalls with a measure of childhood awe almost fifty years later. "He was unusually graceful and knowledgeable."

Fred and Buffalo became friends after meeting at the Makaha International and surfing together at Rest Camp. As different as they were, the navy commander and the local park keeper saw each other as fellow surfers and family men first, ignoring the racial and cultural differences. Edward "Fred" Bakutis was half-Lithuanian and half-Polish, and his parents had met on a ship headed for America. Like Buffalo, Fred had lost his father when he was young and his stepfather had been abusive. "So times were pretty rough in his youth, kind of similar to what Buffalo went through," Bunky says of his father. Like an aspiring Horatio Alger, Fred did well in high school and went on to win a scholarship to the Naval Academy at Annapolis. After graduation, he was shipped out to the Pacific Theater and fought in the war as a navy pilot. During one mission, his Hellcat was shot down and he managed to bail out at the last minute. He survived for eight days in a rubber raft until an Australian sub picked him up. From there, his military career took off.

After his distinguished service during the war, Fred was made captain and stationed at Pearl Harbor. Living in Hawai'i, he fell in love with surfing and began shaping his own balsa boards at his home on the base. His son Bunky grew up on military bases in Hawai'i and around the country, but he was disappointed when his father was transferred to the Pentagon. Fred continued to rise through the ranks, becoming an admiral, but he hated the politics of Washington and the bureaucracy of the Pentagon. Longing to return to Hawai'i, he finally got his dream job when he was sent back to Pearl Harbor. With his high rank, Admiral Bakutis now found that people were always being obsequious and kissing up to him, so he found comfort in hanging out with old beach buddies like Buffalo, who weren't overly impressed that he was a high mucky-muck in the navy.

"One time he invited us for lunch at Barbers Point, so I was driving over there by the gate," Buffalo recalls. "These guys with two stars on their cars were waiting for us. 'Sir, are you Buffalo? Please follow me.' So we go over there, and we have lunch. We go over on the airfield they're not using to go dove-hunting. He was top brass," Buffalo says with a laugh, recalling his royal treatment that day. This was in direct contrast to his years as a low-level lifeguard in the army. But just as the generals admired the big Hawaiian for his ocean skills, Admiral Bakutis liked Buffalo because he didn't kowtow to him. "Both had their share of poverty," Bunky says. "So they had that common ground. No free rides, no braggadocio, no bullshit."

Wanting to escape the formalities of living on base, Fred would take his family to Makaha to surf and hang out on the beach with the Keaulanas. Buffalo and Momi spent a lot of time with the Bakutis family and watched Fred rise to the highest rank of the navy. When he became the commander of the Pacific Fleet, Fred invited Momi and Buffalo to the change-of-command ceremony at Pearl Harbor. Military bands were performing, and sailors in their crisp white uniforms escorted the Keaulanas to their seats in a sea of military officers and navy families. Amid all the pomp and ceremony, Admiral Bakutis happened to see Buffalo and Momi toward the back of the crowd and sent one of his men over to them. "He just happened to look and spot us way in the back," Momi says. "He had one military escort come over there and escort us right to the front where his family was." People in the crowd smiled and stared at the Hawaiian couple, wondering how they were related to the admiral.

According to his old friend Greg Noll, Buffalo used to treat Fred like a member of the family whenever he came to visit the park keeper's house. Once when they had "Da Admiral" over, "the phone rings, and Buff hands him this screaming Hawaiian baby with poop dripping out of his diapers," Greg says with a laugh. "It turns out the call was for the admiral, and they were asking if they could take some aircraft carrier out of Pearl Harbor. And the admiral's on the phone with this crying baby in his arms." At this point, the Keaulanas had four kids running around their cramped house and baby Jimmy in diapers. Taking advantage of the admiral's love of children, Buffalo would leave the kids with him in order to go for a quick surf session. "He had the admiral babysitting Brian while he was out surfing!" Momi says.

After his last tour of duty as commander of Pearl Harbor and Barbers Point, Fred Bakutis retired and bought a little house on Maile Beach, where he could surf every day and enjoy a laid-back lifestyle by the sea. He and his wife would throw parties and invite Buffalo and Momi to join some of their old navy friends. During one gathering, they met Admirals Highland and Wyman and their wives. All the couples would stand there chatting over cocktails, very polite and formal at first. But as the evening wore on and the alcohol flowed freely, everyone would loosen up and the men and women gradually separated into their own groups.

Although it must have been a little intimidating being with the wives of such high-ranking officers, Momi says they enjoyed coming to the Westside and being able to let their hair down. "We were laughing, and all of the wives said, 'You know, we're waiting for our husbands to get the hell out of the service so we can become normal people. We're always on parade. You have to watch what you're doing,' " Momi recalls. "So I said, 'Over here, nobody's looking over your shoulder—just be yourselves.' It was a place where they could just come and relax." And relax they did, says Bunky. "They would play music and sing and enjoy themselves until the midnight hour."

Just as Buffalo admired Admiral Bakutis, who was twenty years older, Bunky grew up rather in awe of the older Hawaiian waterman. As the son of a navy man, Bunky had always lived near the ocean and loved water sports, but he didn't like the military lifestyle or living on heavily guarded bases around the world. He had a restless spirit and loved to travel, though. After earning a master's in literature at Berkeley, Bunky had moved to Alaska, where he taught, wrote, and fished for salmon. He then returned to Hawai'i in '71 with his wife. After moving so many times, he was ready to settle down in Makaha. With the war in Vietnam still raging on, Bunky wanted to find a peaceful place where he could just surf, write, and work on his pottery. "I was living in a house my dad had bought earlier in his life. He must have bought the house in the fifties, just down on Poka'i Bay Street in Wai'anae. I did a lot of surfing for two years, so I just got to know a lot of people here." Buffalo took the younger surfer under his wing and looked out for him and his family. "He's my captain," Bunky adds. "He's like a father figure."

Along with being a mentor, Buffalo gradually became a good friend of Bunky's. "We got to know each other pretty well just by surfing together and hanging around the beach together, watching him fish, cook fish, and survive on the beach," Bunky says. Coming from a more privileged background, he was not only amazed by Buffalo's incredible fishing skills but also impressed with his generosity in feeding his friends on the beach. Just as he was about to enter the ocean with his speargun, flippers, and mask, he would tell his sons or the guys on the beach to start building a fire to cook the fish. The ocean was their supermarket, and Bunky would often have to serve as the bag boy.

Waiting at the surface with a net, he would watch Buffalo swim more than forty feet below and stay down for up to two minutes at a time. Sitting still at the bottom, the Hawaiian waterman would wait breathlessly until a school of fish would swim by him. He would then pull back the rubber slings on his spear so it was cocked and ready. Aiming for the biggest fish, he would then shoot his prey. The large fish would be wriggling at the end of his long, three-pronged spear as he swam to the surface. Buffalo would throw the fish at Bunky to put in the bag. After catching enough to feed their extended family on the beach, they would swim back to the shore. "Good things come from giving," Bunky says. "This is not only an old Hawaiian belief; it's a way of life for Buffalo. A way that all those down at Makaha Beach know: whenever Buffalo touched the water with his spear, get the fire burning."

Makaha was a small community, but it was growing fast. New people were moving in every day, including poor families who settled into the military's old Quonset huts in the valley and rich folks who built big houses on the beach. Tourists would stay at the Makaha Shores, which was built at the end of the beach, or at the Makaha Resort with its immaculate golf courses in the valley. Many of the wealthy new homeowners came from the mainland, looking for a remote Hawaiian getaway. The wealthiest newcomer to the area was a Texas oilman named Carlton Beal, who bought a small vacation house in Maile Point for his wife and five kids. A talented athlete and man of extremes, he could surf with the locals on the Westside during the weekdays and then play polo with rich haoles on the North Shore on the weekends.

An avid waterman, Carlton loved to dive and soon learned to surf. According to his youngest son, Kelly, Carlton would go out every morning at six at the Rest Camp at Poka'i Bay and there he would encounter another older gentleman in the early morning light. The other man turned out to be Admiral Bakutis. "There were two guys in the water, two old farts," Kelly says, "and they became lifelong friends and did all kinds of stuff together." Eager to explore the world, they took a trip to the South Pole once. Always up for trying something new, they pioneered a first prototype of water skis by nailing tennis shoes to barrel stays and pulling each other behind a motorboat.

The admiral then introduced Carlton to Buffalo and they started diving together. As a big collector of cowries and other exotic shells, Carlton would ask the local park keeper to show him the world beneath the waves. Kelly says Uncle Buff "knew the Islands, knew all the holes and where to dive," and helped Carlton develop a world-class collection of cowry shells. While he would go shell-hunting, Buffalo and Fred would be spearfishing. Because the three men loved to surf and dive, the ocean became the bond that sealed their friendship.

Although they were relatively poor, the Keaulanas had a way of drawing the rich and powerful into their inner circle. Like James Arness and Admiral Bakutis, Carlton was a self-made man who had created his own fortune. Originally from California, he had studied petroleum engineering at Stanford, did his graduate work at MIT, and eventually moved to Texas in the mid-fifties to tap into the oil and gas reserves out there. With America's economy booming after the war, his company took off, and so did his profits. As the head of BTA Oil Producers out of Midland, Texas, Carlton decided to enjoy his newfound wealth and live on one of Hawai'i's most pristine and remote beaches for part of the year.

In the mid-sixties, Carlton began building a huge new home right on the Point at Makaha Beach, where Greg Noll and his band of "merry pranksters" used to live in an old Quonset hut surrounded by *kiawe* trees. At first, the locals must have wondered who this rich man was, constructing such a big concrete house so close to the ocean. He even used dynamite to blow a huge swimming hole in the reef for his family and the community. According to Kelly, "There's actually a little plaque there in memory of my dad that says: 'This pond is dedicated to the mommas, babies, and lovers.'" Carlton christened his new home "Luana Kai," rest by the sea, and his four sons and one daughter were partly raised out here and still bring their families to the home throughout the year. The Keaulanas used to be frequent visitors to the house on the Point.

As a newcomer to the Islands, Carlton and his wife, Keleen, must have felt privileged to be welcomed into the local community by Buffalo and Momi, who were respected like Hawaiian royalty in the area. The oilman from Texas loved their generous spirit and the way their lives revolved around the ocean and all that it had to offer in terms of food and fun. The couple had a way of turning ordinary afternoons into exotic evenings simply by sharing themselves and their culture. They were still living in the park keeper's house, and the ocean was their kitchen and the beach their living room.

In preparation for their potluck dinners, Buffalo would go diving and an hour later would emerge from the water carrying fresh lobster, squid, and fish. Momi would bring delicious side dishes and help cook the catch on the big fire. After dinner, she would tell stories about Buff's wild adventures and engage everyone with her contagious laughter while he would just sit back and chuckle. Strumming his 'ukulele and singing Hawaiian songs, he would then entertain the circle of kids, parents, and friends. "You've got to take time to enjoy what you have," Momi adds. "And the most important thing in life is your family, and next come your friends."

Carlton knew the Keaulanas didn't have much money, but he felt like they could teach him something about true wealth. "Life's too short not to enjoy," Momi would tell him. "Each day we get up, we say, 'Thank you, God, for this beautiful day, for the gold in the sun, the blue skies, the diamonds in the sky with the stars.' You know, people are so wealthy, but they don't even know it." It may sound sentimental, but for haole families like the Beals trying to escape the growing materialism on the "mainland," the Keaulanas' authentic Hawaiian lifestyle touched them deeply. The Keaulanas' intimate connection to the land and the sea and their simple generosity helped the Beals understand why the Hawaiians referred to themselves as *keiki o ke kai,* children of the sea.

In fact, Buffalo had a childlike way about him, and he loved playing with kids and getting into all kinds of mischief. Once, when Kelly was about ten years old, Carlton insisted that he cut off his long, scraggly hair. But he kept resisting, and so Buffalo decided to make a game out of it. "Buff goes, 'Hey, what's the problem? Watch this,' " Kelly recalls. The big Hawaiian then took the electric clippers and cut a swath right down the center of his thick mane of hair! "See, Kelly, no problem, this is cool!" Buffalo told the boy. "Okay, do mine; do mine!" Kelly responded. "So we proceeded to cut all of our hair off. My mother then comes home, and she sees all the hair, she sees me, and she calls out the back door, 'Carlton, Carlton!' " Buff looked at his friend and teased him, saying, "Carlton, come here please." He laughed about what a scolding his friend was going to get from his wife. After hearing Keleen yell at him, Buffalo saw her chasing him out of the house with a broom a few minutes later.

As the park keeper and unofficial leader of Makaha, Buffalo Keaulana not only cleaned the area but also kept an eye out for all those who swam and surfed in the bay. His son Brian remembers riding on a horse along the beach while his father picked up trash and watched over the people in the water. Inevitably, some tourist would get caught in the rip currents and Buffalo would have to go save them. "He would clean the park, and then throughout the day, people would get ripped out into the ocean," Brian says. He remembers seeing his father swim out, grab the panicked people, and then bring them to shore. Sometimes the victims were tourists who wandered out too deep, and other times they were surfers who pushed themselves into waves too big. "He was actually saving more people than cleaning the park." The newly formed Lifeguard Department had no one stationed on the Westside at the time, so Buffalo had to serve as the unofficial guard.

One day during a big swell, Carlton was out surfing when he caught a large wave that almost killed him. He wiped out, and the big board struck him right between the legs. Buffalo happened to be paddling out at that moment and saw him go under. "That was an amazing rescue," Bunky says. "Carlton Beal was on a wave and fell, and the board hit him right in the 'chops' and just knocked him out. He was down on the bottom." Knowing the currents, Buffalo figured out where Carlton might be, paddled over to that spot, and dove down. He saw Carlton curled up in a fetal position on the ocean floor, unconscious. With the waves exploding above and the currents tugging below, Buffalo managed to dive down almost twenty feet and grab him. Buffalo pulled the older man to the surface and put him on his board, where Carlton began coughing and spitting up seawater. Without Buff there to rescue him, Bunky says, "he would have been a goner." Carlton wanted to repay Buffalo somehow for saving his life, but it would take a long time before he figured out how.

Carlton was just one of many people whom Buffalo saved, and many of the survivors wrote letters to the city officials, expressing their thanks to the big Hawaiian caretaker. "As a park keeper, he was saving people left and right," Honolulu lifeguard chief Jim Howe says. In honor of Buffalo's many rescues, Mayor Neal S. Blaisdell appointed him as the first lifeguard at Makaha in 1969 without making him go through the formal tests because he knew that the Hawaiian waterman had a deep innate wisdom about the ocean.

"He's not a book guy, but he was there," rescuing people and saving lives, says Howe. "He's a legend; he's the real deal." As a young lifeguard, Howe used to go out to Makaha and stay in the tower with Buffalo, sitting at his feet like a student just to soak in his wisdom and see him in action. "He may not have a lot of titles, but he sure knows about the ocean," Jim continues. "He's just absolutely a wealth of knowledge, and not only about the beaches and the ocean but about all the different people who have come and been a part of . . . all the ocean sports that are here on this Island."

Buffalo enjoyed sharing his insights about the ocean's wildlife and reefs with his friends, including oceanographer and big-wave surfer Ricky Grigg, who used to surf at Makaha. When the waves were flat, the Hawaiian lifeguard would go diving with the blond California surfer. Along with teaching him about *ko'a,* or fish houses, Buffalo showed Ricky where the best ones were hidden in the reefs. This was sacred information to Hawaiians. "Then, he told me something that I never forgot," Ricky says. "He said that the most important thing about the reef is the surf. Where you get tremendous surf rolling in, it tends to sculpture the bottom and flatten it."

Ricky went on to become a coral reef ecologist, earning a master's degree at the University of Hawai'i and a Ph.D. at the Scripps Institute in La Jolla, yet he never forgot those lessons that he learned from Buffalo. "He taught me more about coral reef ecology than I learned at the University of Hawai'i and Scripps together. I'm not kidding," Ricky says. "Buffalo was so much more to me than just a surfer. He was a man of great Hawaiian wisdom . . . He inherited a thousand years of what the Hawaiians learned, and he made me realize all of that when he taught me about the ocean."

As the unofficial tribal leader of Makaha, Buffalo would watch over all those who visited his little village by the beach. In 1969, Ernie Tomson and his son Shaun traveled all the way from South Africa to surf in Hawai'i as part of Shaun's bar mitzvah present. They were planning to stay on the North Shore but got lost and ended up driving to Makaha. The father and son were a little intimidated by the fierce watermen of the Westside, especially after witnessing a violent melee during their first day at the beach. A

Japanese surfer had run over a big Hawaiian on a plywood *paipo* board, cutting his leg. After wrapping a towel around his bleeding leg, the local grabbed the kid's surfboard and ran right toward where Ernie and Shaun were standing near some big rocks. The Hawaiian then smashed the board on the rocks into a hundred pieces of fiberglass and foam. "Wow, this is radical," Shaun recalls. "I better be careful down here."

Although they were a little intimidated by the locals, Ernie and Shaun were soon welcomed into the community by Buffalo, who made a kind impression on the fourteen-year-old boy. "He reminded me of a Zulu warrior," Shaun says. "I came from Natal, which was the home of the Zulu people. He was tall and regal and had this wonderful charisma and presence. He kind of took me under his wing. I felt very safe there."

The Tomsons were also taken in by the Sunn family, who invited Shaun over to their Quonset hut on the beach and showed the cute curly-haired kid from South Africa around the Westside. "That was the first time I experienced that whole mythical concept of aloha," Shaun says. "And that's one of the reasons why I kept coming back to Hawai'i, because of that special feeling I got as a young boy." Shaun would later become a world champion surfer in the mid-seventies, and he returned to Hawai'i each year as a young pro.

During his nine years as park keeper, Buffalo and his family had lived in the upstairs apartment of the bathhouse at Makaha. Their home was like a community center, where wayward surfers and Hawaiians could always come for a meal, conversation, and shelter. The kids had grown up at the beach, and the beach was their backyard. The world's best surfers had passed through their home, including regulars like Greg Noll, who used to sleep over after partying with Buffalo late into the night. Greg remembers passing out one night in the bottom bunk of the kids' room to the soothing sounds of the ocean, only to be wakened by a stream of warm fluid the next morning as little Rusty peed on him. At the time, Greg was one of the most daring big-wave surfers in the world, and it still tickles him today that that little *kolohe* (mischievous) kid who tinkled on him would later become a fearless big-wave rider.

Although the North Shore had replaced Makaha as the center of the surfing world and home to the biggest waves, the Westside still had its share of giant swells. Over the years, the Keaulanas had woken up to huge waves literally banging on their door. Buffalo had warned the city not to build the bathhouse so close to the beach, but they had ignored his warnings, and the building often paid the price. Brian remembers waking up one night to the sound of big waves crashing against the front of the house and breaking windows while the family was trapped upstairs. Worried they might all be washed away, Buffalo grabbed an ax and started smashing a hole in the floor, and they escaped through the back storage room below.

Every few years, the city would repair the two-story structure, but then another winter storm swell would do more damage. Even though the waves threatened to destroy their home, the Keaulanas were more in awe of the ocean's power than scared or resentful. When he was finally promoted to lifeguard, Buffalo and his family had to leave behind the little A-frame structure that had been their home on the beach. They moved up the road to Wai'anae, where they rented a little house. (Eventually, the waves destroyed the bathhouse, leaving only some battered bathrooms.)

Years later, the Keaulanas decided to share a Hawaiian homestead lot with Buffalo's mother and build a house on her property in Nanakuli. But they didn't have the money to build the house and the banks wouldn't give them a loan. Carlton heard about their predicament and offered to give them the money, but Momi declined. "My God, girl, how can I do something for you if you won't let me?" Carlton complained. Momi then asked if they could borrow it. Carlton agreed and also helped them by giving them some of the construction materials. The community rallied together to help them build the house. Many of the guys who had taken shelter in their home or been fed by the Keaulanas over the years came out of the woodwork to help. Like in a traditional barn raising, their extended family and friends worked together to lay the foundations and construct a spacious four-bedroom home for Buffalo and his family. "This is the house that love built," Momi says.

"For two years straight, I paid the bill every month right on time," she continues. In December of 1982, the Keaulanas received their annual Christmas card from the Beals, but this year Carlton included a little surprise. "I opened the card, and it says: 'Merry Christmas, Momi and Buff! We love you very much. Here's the deed to your house, paid in full.'" Momi started jumping up and down, screaming, crying, and laughing! "I couldn't believe the generosity of this man," she says, remembering that Christmas morning when they talked on the phone.

"I called him and said, 'You can't do that.'"

"No, it's done," Carlton said. "How do you pay someone for your life?"

"That's priceless."

"And so is Buff."

❧

In his first year as a lifeguard, Buffalo was working during one of the largest swells of the century. Large storms in Alaska's Aleutian Islands had created a series of swell trains that traveled across the Pacific Ocean, gathering steam and momentum as they rolled toward the Hawaiian Islands. On the morning of December 4, 1969, the waves rose rapidly as they started crashing into the outer reefs of O'ahu. Sirens began wailing on the North Shore, signaling it was time to evacuate as the waves started crashing into homes along the beach and washing out roads. Police and firemen cruised up and down the streets, trying to enforce the evacuation and rescue those whose homes were being inundated.

Meanwhile, Greg Noll and a couple of the best big-wave

riders were looking for a place to surf on the North Shore. But Waimea was too big and blown out, with thirty- to forty-foot waves closing out the Bay and rolling across the parking lot. Determined not to miss what was already being called the Swell of the Century, Noll drove around Ka'ena Point to Makaha, where the forty- to fifty-foot waves looked like they would devour the coastline. He had never seen such big waves, and some crazy desire compelled him to try and ride them.

Earlier that morning, James Arness's son, Rolf, had paddled out into the rising waves and tried to catch a few of the big outside sets, but they were too big. "I never made a wave," Rolf said later. "I would make the drop, but then I couldn't make it down the line." He was later joined by Lord James Blears's son, Jimmy, another young charger and future world champion. Only in their late teens, both boys were "goofy-footers" and had to paddle into the giant swells with their backs facing the wave. Buffalo paddled out with Fred Hemmings and more established big-wave riders like Randy Rarick, who were catching some large but still survivable swells beyond the Point. "It was a beautiful day," Buffalo recalls. "Then, the waves got bigger and bigger and bigger. By the time we came in at one o'clock, it was really big!"

When Greg Noll arrived, he saw only the most fierce surfers in the water, because everyone else had come in, afraid for their lives. In an interview with Drew Kampion years later, Greg said, "I ran to the Point to get a handle on what was going on, and Lord James Blears was out there with his camera, in tears. He said, 'Greg, do me a favor, try to talk Jimmy [Blears] out of the water; I'm afraid for his life.' Not what you want to hear when you're waxing up." Kneeling in the sand as he waxed his big board, Greg stared at the massive waves crashing down like thunder in the distance. He looked out at the tumultuous sea and wondered if this was the day he would die. Questions raced through his mind: Is it worth risking your life just to ride some monster wave? What are you trying to prove? Is it ego driving you or something deeper, some primitive desire to push yourself to the edge of the abyss? Waiting for a lull in the ten-foot shore break, Greg tried to tune out the voices of fear in his head and paddled out into the maelstrom. This was something he had to do.

After paddling hundreds of yards through the roaring surf, Greg took a few moments to rest in the channel. He watched mountains of water rise up and come crashing down in avalanches of white water. The beads of water on his board danced from the vibrations. Wondering if he could even make the steep drop, he saw a huge swell on the horizon and started paddling to catch it. The wave looked like a mythical creature of the deep, and it seemed to swallow the sky as it enveloped him. Greg took off, stood up, and started dropping down its massive face, but he couldn't ride fast enough. The wave devoured him in its huge, gaping maw and swallowed him whole. He spent the next minute flailing around in what felt like an eternal dark underworld as the rolling wave tossed him around in the churning water. When he finally surfaced and gasped for air, he was amazed to be alive. But he was far from the beach, and the rip current was quickly dragging him toward the jagged coral shore.

Buffalo was there on the beach when Greg took off on the wave that shook the surfing world. Estimated to be more than fifty feet high, it is still considered one of the largest waves any surfer has ever paddled into and survived. After watching him disappear beneath the waves, Buffalo finally saw his friend surface and get pummeled in the towering wall of white water. "I got my ass kicked on that wave, and there was a very strong current," Greg says. "I was struggling and struggling, and when I finally hit the point where I was thirty or forty yards off the beach, I looked up and Buffalo was in the lifeguard Jeep following me down the beach." Greg barely made it through the shore break to the last stretch of beach just yards before the jagged coral rocks, which would have been "the point of no return." Crawling to shore, Greg remembers collapsing on the beach and seeing his friend, waiting there for him. "Buff sticks a beer in my hand and looks down at me. I'm sitting there panting, and he goes, 'It's a good thing you wen make 'em, brah, 'cause there's no way I was comin' after you!' "

Though trying to make light of the situation, Buffalo knew how badly his friend was shaken up and how close he had come to death. But Buffalo didn't know how that massive wave would change Greg's life forever. After that fateful ride, he basically quit surfing, sold his booming surfboard business, and moved to Alaska to become a commercial fisherman. Like certain fish stories, people love to talk about Greg's epic ride at Makaha. That wave seems to grow even bigger each year, and it has become a legend in surfing lore. Even Greg jokes that he's gotten a lot of mileage and fame out of that mythic wave. But at the time, his need to push himself into bigger and bigger waves proved to be a dangerous drug.

"Surfing is like an addiction. You always need more size," Greg would say years later. "I think what finally happened was that I realized, that day at big Makaha, how the addiction was bordering on insanity. At some point, a guy has to ask himself, 'Are you going to slip over the goddamn edge or are you going to keep this thing in perspective?' " After Greg's brush with death, he finally managed to get the "monkey off of his back." But others were wrestling with a different kind of addiction.

During the late sixties and seventies, surfing was embraced by the counterculture movement as the ultimate way to commune with nature. For many, surfing was like a drug, and drugs became the fuel that propelled them to ride bigger waves and drop into a deeper consciousness. But once they crossed through those "doors of perception," some of those psychedelic surfers dropped out of reality and never quite recovered.

After almost drowning that epic day at Makaha, Rolf Aurness went on to surf another big swell at Waimea Bay. Eddie Aikau was the lifeguard on duty and tried to stop him, saying the waves were too dangerous. But Rolf was hell-bent on pushing the limits. He took off on one wave that was so massive that he free-fell fifteen feet down the vertical face before landing on his board, but miraculously he made the wave. "I actually felt like it was a near-death or out-of-body experience," he told journalist Drew Kampion years later. "But, like Greg, after that I said, enough is enough." After pushing himself too far physically and mentally, Rolf stopped surfing big waves and quit doing drugs.

In order to keep his kids off the street and out of trouble, Buffalo encouraged his boys and their friends to hang out on the beach and in the ocean, where he could watch over them. Brian's best friend, Melvin Pu'u, was one of those boys whom Uncle Buff practically took in as one of his *hanai* (adopted) sons. Mel's mom had died when he was five, and his sickly father passed away when he was fifteen, so he spent a lot of time at the Keaulanas' home and at the beach. "Buffalo was a father figure for most of us down there," Mel says. "Buff would grab me and Brian and make sure we weren't on the streets, because there's only so much trouble you can get into in the water!"

Too poor to own his own surfboard, Mel used to borrow Brian's or Uncle Buff's. One day when the waves were good, Mel came over to the Keaulanas and wanted to go surfing, but Brian had to finish his chores before going to the beach. He hated doing yard work, so like a Hawaiian Tom Sawyer, Brian managed to convince Mel to help him clean the yard. When Buffalo saw the two boys working so hard, he decided to come down and help, too. Brian then said he was going to take care of the backyard, but when Mel and Uncle Buff worked their way around to the back, Brian was nowhere to be found. They then went upstairs and saw him sitting down, watching television. Buffalo yelled, "Hey, you damn kid, what the hell you doin'?" Brian said something about just getting a glass of water and then ran back down to the yard with his father and Mel chasing after him!

At the beach, Brian, Mel, and the other kids used to sit under the lifeguard tower, reading comic books while Buffalo would keep watch over all the beach. "We grew up with the sight of

Buffalo saving a lot of people's lives," Mel says. "I can remember one classic situation where Brian and I were hanging out at the tower and there was this family that was being swept down the current line at Makaha Beach." Buffalo ran down the beach, grabbed the little boy, his sister, and their mother, and swam them to shore. The father had tried to help but was exhausted and being carried away. Buffalo saw the man flailing in the waves and yelled, "Stand up!" And to his amazement, the father was able to stand up on a hidden sandbar for a few moments to catch his breath before being swept away again in the fierce currents. Then Buffalo swam out and brought the father back to shore, where he and his traumatized family hugged and then thanked the big Hawaiian lifeguard profusely. "For me, that was one of the key turning points," Mel says, "that made me think, 'Oh, I want to be like him.'"

Buffalo rescued hundreds of people during his career. Yet like most lifeguards, he couldn't help but be haunted by those souls he couldn't save. His most traumatic experience occurred when he was called to rescue a man and his two kids who had fallen off the treacherous coastline near Ka'ena Point. They had been washed off a cliff by large waves and then were sucked into a jagged coral cave below. The Fire Department tried to rescue the man and his two children at first by throwing grappling hooks into the cave, which would fill up with water with every pounding wave.

"They think they're going to try and hook the guy," Bunky Bakutis recalls with horror. "Buffalo saw this and said, 'You guys gotta stop this—I'll go in.' This guy is set apart from other people just in his natural thinking and his ability to find a way." Police and firemen gathered on the cliff while Buffalo paddled his big rescue board near the mouth of the cave. He could hear the cries of the children and wanted to go in, but the rescue team was telling him it was too dangerous. Unwilling to sit there and do nothing, he paddled into the maw of the lava tube during a momentary lull in the waves and was able to grab the two kids and get out before the next set came crashing against the cliff in an explosion of white water.

After saving the two boys, Buffalo was told not to go back in for the father. "They said, 'No, you should come up with a better plan, because you might perish,'" Brian recalls. "My father said if he didn't go, there's no chance [of saving the man] because it's only getting bigger. And by then, it's too late, and you can't go in. At least now, he knows there's a chance he can go in." But as the light faded, the waves grew bigger and more deadly, and the Fire Department captain said it was too risky. Throughout the night, they could hear the man's cries for help from deep inside the cave. "As a small kid, I remember listening to the guy scream and his family screaming back," Brian says. "It was horrible. Then, in the morning, his body floated out. They threw a hook, gaffed him, and pulled his body out." The man's tragic loss had a profound effect on Brian, who would have to relive a similar incident as a lifeguard twenty years later.

Large and small injuries seem to be an unavoidable part of surfing and other water sports. Buffalo spent a lot of time teaching his children and the neighborhood kids about ocean safety and making sure they kept an eye out for other people. Several went on to become professional guards, including Brian, Mel Pu'u, and Rell Sunn. Having seen Buffalo perform so many rescues at the spur of the moment, this new generation learned that even the most ordinary day can suddenly turn deadly.

One day while surfing in 1972, Buffalo hit the backwash, fell, and broke several vertebrae in his neck. He was rolling around paralyzed in the surf, yelling for help in between breaths. When friends saw him floating helplessly in the shore break, they came running to his rescue. Everyone was shocked to see him carried up the beach, surrounded by a crowd of family and friends. He was then taken to the hospital in an ambulance. He was paralyzed for three weeks, and the doctors said he might not be able to walk or surf again. But Buffalo was determined to get back on his feet and into the ocean.

The community rallied to support the family, bringing them food, making donations, and visiting Buffalo in the hospital. His friend Peter Cole was also hospitalized at the same time after gouging his right eye on his surfboard fin. The two old friends spent some time recuperating together. After months of rehab, Buffalo was back in the water, surfing again. Every surfer has stories to tell about their worst injuries, though some are life-changing events. Jim Howe sustained a serious leg injury on the North Shore that left him temporarily crippled. "The doctors told me that I would never surf again," Jim says. But he was encouraged by Buffalo's dramatic recovery and vowed that he would follow his example. "That was definitely the inspiration to get back out there in the ocean!"

CHAPTER 6

The Birth of the Hokule'a

Hawai'i's pride, she sails with the wind
And proud are we to see her sail free.
—from Eddie Aikau's song "Hokule'a"

Buffalo was proud of his heritage, but many Hawaiians wrestled with a sense of anger because their culture had been suppressed for so long. After all, the missionaries had shunned cultural practices such as hula, surfing, and chanting as "immoral." When their descendants went into business and politics over the next two generations, they became rich and powerful. Missionary families such as the Thurstons and the Doles eventually took over the kingdom and later banned Hawaiian from being spoken. From then on, preachers, politicians, and teachers had basically espoused the same message toward Native Hawaiians and Native Americans: embrace Christianity, forget the past, and assimilate into mainstream American culture.

Buffalo was raised as a Christian, but he was not ashamed of his "pagan roots." Many locals resented learning only about "haole history" and very little about their own culture. They were basically being taught the same old story that their parents had been told: that the Hawaiian kingdom had been willingly given up by Queen Lili'uokalani to become a territory of the American government; that U.S. military bases and new hotels were signs of progress; and that tourism and commercial development were the first steps in the long march toward statehood and the fulfillment of the American Dream.

During the late 1960s and '70s, however, Hawaiian historians began writing about the oppression of their people and the overthrow of the Hawaiian kingdom. Inspired by these writers and the civil rights movement in the continental United States, local activists began talking about restitution for the lands that were taken away. The people grew angrier about the unfolding revelations about how their ancestors had been gradually disenfranchised: how the Great Mahele of 1848 had slowly but effectively deprived most Hawaiians of their land; how King Kalakaua had been forced to sign the "Bayonet Constitution," which basically barred Hawaiians from voting and holding office (if they didn't own a certain amount of land or earn a certain income); how a powerful group of plantation owners and businessmen had overthrown Queen Lili'uokalani by bringing in U.S. Marines; and how these powerful haole men had lobbied Congress to make Hawai'i an American territory.

Through books, newspaper articles, public talks, and demonstrations, the Hawaiian Renaissance revealed a new vision of

Hawaiian history and opened up the eyes of the people. "In the public and private schools, all of us learned in the books that there was this wonderfully smooth transition of power," Hawaiian lawyer Beadie Kanahele Dawson says. "I didn't really know the facts of history that surrounded the overthrow. The renaissance was a rediscovery of what had happened to us." After reading books by native historians like her uncle George Kanahele, she and others learned that traditional Hawaiians didn't believe that "owning" the land was possible or important.

"What was of importance was the 'ohana, the family. Hawaiians are basically a very inclusive people," Dawson says. "We never chased anyone from our shores—we welcomed everyone, and we still do. The tradition of hanai [a common form of informal adoption] is typical of the way Hawaiians welcome people, not just to the Islands, but into our homes, into our hearts, and into our families."

During the Hawaiian Renaissance, Buffalo and his family began to experience an awakening pride in their culture, which had been suppressed. In school, his sons and daughters were learning about Hawai'i's historical leaders: distinguished figures like King Kalakaua and Queen Lili'uokalani and their efforts to revive Hawaiian culture and resist foreign colonial powers. Known as the Merrie Monarch, Kalakaua had helped restore the hula and Hawaiian chants from near extinction by staging hula and music festivals. Both he and his sister Queen Lili'uokalani were talented musicians, composers, and writers who spoke several languages. Both leaders were and still are revered by their people.

Until the turn of the twentieth century, Hawaiians had had one of the highest literacy rates in the world (almost 90 percent), and native-language newspapers and journals flourished during this time. But after the territorial government banned the Hawaiian language from being spoken, the literacy rate rapidly declined. "The best way to destroy a culture is to take away their language," Brian says. Now Hawaiian teachers were trying to turn the tide and inspire their students to speak their native tongue and help resurrect their culture.

Starting in 1963, the annual Merrie Monarch Festival on the Big Island had celebrated the best hula performers in the Islands and become a source of pride for the people. The university began offering courses in Hawaiian language, history, and culture. But the greatest symbol of the Hawaiian Renaissance was a voyaging canoe called the *Hokule'a*. Created in 1975, this double-hulled, sixty-foot canoe was modeled after the traditional sailing canoes that brought the first Polynesian sailors to Hawai'i more than a thousand years before.

Ironically, it was a haole anthropologist from California named Dr. Ben Finney who came up with the idea of the *Hokule'a*. Ben was not only a respected professor and writer but an avid surfer and sailor as well. With his tall, lanky body, blond hair, and tan skin, he looked like he spent more time in the ocean than deep in the maze of the library. He was a rare breed of academic who led a kind of double life: among the local tribes of surfers and sailors, he was just called Ben; but in international scholarly circles, he was referred to as Dr. Finney. His treatises on Polynesian migration and "accidental" versus "intentional" voyaging had created waves of controversy in the academic world, but he had no idea how this canoe project would change his life and Hawaiian history.

Going against the prevailing ideas about Polynesian migration, Ben Finney asserted that their ancestors had been excellent navigators who had "intentionally" settled islands throughout the Pacific. But in a bestselling book and popular film called *Kon-Tiki*, Thor Heyerdahl had argued that the first Polynesian settlers must have sailed and drifted westward from South America and "accidentally" arrived on the scattered islands throughout the South Pacific. In other words, Heyerdahl believed that these so-called primitive people and their sailing rafts weren't good enough for "purposeful" voyaging over such long distances. To prove his point, the Norwegian ethnographer and adventurer actually built a log raft called *Kon-Tiki* and in 1947 he and four other companions sailed it for over one hundred days from Peru to the Tuamotu Islands. They also filmed the voyage, and the documentary won an Academy Award in 1951.

Many of the leading anthropologists of the day disagreed with Heyerdahl about the direction of the first Polynesians' migration, theorizing that they came eastward from Southeast Asia. But Ben says these Western scholars agreed with the Norwegian ethnographer that these indigenous explorers were "nautically and navigationally incompetent, which is a real intellectual insult." These theories went directly against the Hawaiian chants and legends that told of heroic Polynesian voyagers who had intentionally sailed all over the Pacific, using celestial navigation.

Based on his extensive anthropological research in Hawai'i and field studies in Tahiti, Ben Finney firmly believed the legendary stories about how the Polynesians had intentionally navigated their canoes all the way to the Hawaiian Islands. In fact, he believed they had settled a vast area called the Polynesian Triangle, which stretched from New Zealand in the south to Easter Island in the east and Hawai'i in the north. If this was true, the Polynesians would have been some of the greatest navigators in history, having formed what Captain James Cook once called "the most extensive nation on Earth."

In order to prove his theory, Ben came up with the idea of re-creating a replica of these ancient voyaging canoes and sailing it from Hawai'i to Tahiti. But unlike Thor Heyerdahl, Ben wanted to include the people he was writing about in the project, but he had no idea how passionate the Hawaiians would become about the canoe. What started out as a scientific experiment would soon evolve into a cultural revival, later erupting in a violent conflict.

Ben Finney had already built a smaller sailing canoe while teaching at the University of California, Santa Barbara, but now he was ready to build a larger, more authentic one for deep-sea navigating. Knowing he needed a Hawaiian partner, he sought out a man named Herb Kawainui Kane, who had just moved back to the Islands from Chicago. Herb had been a successful advertising designer, creating memorable characters such as the Jolly Green Giant. But he was unfulfilled as an artist and hungry to rediscover his roots. Back in Hawai'i, he immersed himself in every aspect of his culture, studying history, archaeology, anthropology, and the lost art of celestial navigation that his ancestors had once practiced.

Although they were bursting with ideas, Herb and Ben both knew they needed another organizer with more ocean experience, so they recruited a local waterman named Tommy Holmes. "We all got together and said, 'Let's do it; let's build a canoe,'" Ben recalls. "So we formed the Polynesian Voyaging Society in '73, and we raised the money. Herb started doing a conceptual design of the canoe." The trio threw themselves into the project and put hundreds of hours into researching the history of Polynesian voyaging and creating a replica of the ancient crafts. Initially, the three PVS founders worked well together, but their different backgrounds and diverging goals for the project would eventually tear them apart. "Ben was more interested in the scientific questions," Herb says. "Holmes was interested in the adventure of it. I saw cultural possibilities for the canoe to help stimulate a cultural revival."

No one embodied the spirit of the Hawaiian Renaissance more than Herb Kawainui Kane. Along with designing the canoe, he began writing articles about the *Hokule'a* for magazines such as *National Geographic*, which planned to do a documentary about their voyage to Tahiti. These magazines published pictures of his colorful artwork, which featured strong tattooed Polynesians sailing the first canoes toward Hawai'i's shores. In various articles, he referred to the *Hokule'a* as the "Spaceship of Your Ancestors," comparing these historic voyages across the Pacific to modern expeditions into space. Herb's paintings and articles inspired Hawaiians to look at their ancestors and their culture in a whole new light. He referred to his people as *kanaka maole,* the "native human beings" whose ancestors had originally settled the Hawaiian Islands.

"My feeling was that I didn't want to build another *Kon-Tiki,*" Ben says, referring to the fact that Heyerdahl's experiment didn't include any indigenous people. "It should be for the benefit of the people whose lives and past we were investigating. That was my idea, that was Herb's idea, that was Tommy's idea, even though we were the worst people to do it: two haoles and a Chicago Hawaiian. It's not politically appropriate." So they recruited Native Hawaiians to help build the canoe, but some of the workers began to feel like it belonged to them. Others wanted to take control of the whole project. "It was just such a hot moment in the changeover from the beaten-down mentality [of the Hawaiians] to the renaissance and revolt," Ben says. "This is such a hot-button issue, and we got caught in the middle of it."

The construction of the *Hokule'a* began in 1974 down at the docks at Snug Harbor in Honolulu. Scores of locals from all over the Islands showed up to help build, just hoping they might get the chance to sail on it one day. Everyone who read about the voyaging canoe in the papers wanted to be involved. In building a replica of an ancient voyaging canoe, the PVS leaders tried to remain true to the traditional design. In assembling the canoe, they didn't use a single nail—the hulls, crossbeams, deck, and two masts were all lashed together with miles and miles of rope.

Seeing footage of the canoe on the nightly news and hearing stories from friends who were working on it, Buffalo decided that he had to get involved with the project. As the *Hokule'a* began to take shape, he asked his captain if he could take some time off from lifeguarding so he could sail on the canoe. Although the Keaulanas were struggling to raise five kids on a limited income, Buffalo knew he had to do this and Momi supported him. Besides, the PVS leaders promised to pay the workers a per diem to help ease the financial burden.

During the course of her creation, many volunteers had become intimately involved with the building of the *Hokule'a*. Some worked until late at night and slept down at the dockyard, and a few even seemed to fall in love with the canoe. With her long, rounded hulls and the deep glow of her woodwork, she looked like a vision of Hawai'i's proud past, a vessel to carry their hopes and dreams. And men like Buffalo hungered to sail on her and experience the same sensation their ancestors must have felt during their voyages across the Pacific. Yet in the backs of their minds, they also wrestled with doubts about whether or not they would be able to sail her all the way to Tahiti. After all, their people had stopped voyaging more than eight hundred years ago. Buffalo had done a lot of near-shore sailing with friends like James Arness and Admiral Bakutis but hadn't done any deep-sea voyaging. In fact, no one had experience trying to cross the Pacific in a traditional Polynesian canoe without any modern equipment, not even a compass, quadrant, or sextant! The *Hokule'a*'s voyage to Tahiti would be the first of its kind in modern history, and this created a lot of uncertainty.

After years of planning and nine months in the making, the canoe was finally ready for her first launch at a sacred place called Kualoa on the eastern shore of O'ahu. On March 8, 1975, hundreds of people drove to this remote area and gathered on the beach to witness the birth of the *Hokule'a*. Dressed in traditional robes, the *kahu* recited a long Hawaiian chant that wove together new blessings for the canoe and ancient tales of Hawai'i's legendary voyagers. A Hawaiian man wearing a *malo* (loincloth) held a conch shell to his lips and blew into it like a horn, filling the humid air with its low, haunting wail. Bare-chested sailors wearing traditional *malo* began pushing the canoe down a ramp of logs on the beach. As bystanders watched in breathless anticipation, the flower-covered *Hokule'a* splashed into the bay and the crowd cheered. With her traditional Polynesian sails billowing in the wind, the canoe cut through the blue-green water as if she had sailed right out of Hawai'i's past.

The successful launch of the *Hokule'a* led to the first sea trials and training sails. Hawaiians of all ages turned out to sail on the canoe, including famous surfers such as Buffalo, who was forty-one at the time, and young canoe paddlers such as Nainoa Thompson, who was eighteen and had just graduated from Punahou School. "Here I am fresh out of high school, given this extraordinary opportunity to train with the crew in 1975," Nainoa says. "I'm in the midst of all these legends, and Buffalo is at the top of the list . . . He's a very quiet guy but completely in command." Buffalo had been selected to try out for the crew by his old surfing buddy Wally Froiseth, and Nainoa had been brought on by Herb Kane, who was acting as captain.

During the first sea trials, Nainoa remembers one time when they were sailing back into Kane'ohe Bay from Chinaman's Hat. Normally, they would come in through the deep channel to avoid the waves and shallower waters. But Buffalo was steering the canoe, and he headed for the surf. "I think everybody wanted to tell him, 'Don't do it,' but no one was going to tell him not to do it," Nainoa says with an awkward laugh. "He not only catches the wave, but he's perfectly lined up with the wave." The canoe weighed close to twenty tons, yet Buffalo managed to guide it right into the swell, which lifted up the stern and sent it racing toward shore. "He just surfed it right into Kane'ohe Bay," Nainoa says. "Nobody else could have done that because none of us had that connection, that ocean sense that separates everybody else from the true ocean people."

Along with helping to select the crew, Wally Froiseth was in charge of overseeing the training sails. Wally was not only an experienced sailor, surfer, and canoe builder, but was also well respected in the Hawaiian community. But he and others began to question whether Herb Kane had enough deepwater sailing experience to be captain of the canoe. In the meantime, Wally continued gathering together a crew of experienced watermen, including big-wave surfer and lifeguard Eddie Aikau, who was equally excited about sailing on the canoe. But Eddie also had misgivings about the planned voyage to Tahiti because he felt there was too much *huki-huki,* or pulling and jerking, in the tense tug-of-war between the PVS leaders and the Hawaiian crew members.

During their training, Buffalo and Eddie joined Wally on a practice sail from Oʻahu to Kauaʻi. The *Hokuleʻa* had sailed into Waiʻanae the day before, and hundreds of people turned out to see the canoe. In their eyes, the vessel was like a piece of living history, a work of art, and a time machine between the present and the past. Because the crew was still learning to navigate by the stars, they needed to sail at night, but they still had to use a compass and quadrant to chart their course.

Leaving around midnight, Buffalo and Wally were in charge of steering the canoe, using two long oarlike paddles by each hull (though they would later switch to a bigger center sweep, which was easier to steer with). "He was on the left side, and I was on the right side. The moon happened to be right in front of us, right on the course, so we would steer by the moon," Wally recalls, drifting back to that magical night. They were navigating by the moon, stars, and their own gut instinct, but the captain didn't trust their judgment. "Herb Kane couldn't understand, and he was so mad with us because he wanted us to go by the compass. But every time he checked the compass, we were right on course!" It was as if the moon's silvery light painted a shimmering path to their destination.

In contrast to their peaceful voyage to Kauaʻi, the return voyage proved to be disastrous. After they changed crew members, their luck suddenly changed as well. On the trip back, one of the hulls began taking in water during the night and the canoe later swamped under Herb Kane's watch. With the *Hokuleʻa* slowly sinking, Tommy Holmes decided to paddle back toward Kauaʻi for help. After being spotted by a passing ship, the crew then had to be rescued by the Coast Guard. Hours later, they found Tommy, exhausted and sprawled out on his surfboard, still miles from shore. The canoe was hauled back to shore in disgrace.

Ben Finney called for a formal investigation into the incident, and the conclusions split the PVS founders.

When the report came out, it stated that the *"Hokule'a* swamped due to lack of seamanship, an absence of knowledgeable command at sea and the omission of acceptable standards and procedures for all oceangoing vessels." Everyone shared in the blame: Herb Kane as captain, Tommy Holmes as officer on duty, and even Ben Finney as PVS president. After the accident, Herb gradually withdrew from the leadership of the voyaging society and returned to working on his paintings and fund-raising efforts for the canoe. Meanwhile, Ben and Tommy led the effort to rebuild the canoe and make sure that the interior compartments of the hulls were watertight. Unfortunately, most of the money that was supposed to go to the workers now had to be redirected toward the *Hokule'a*'s reconstruction. Hardly anyone was being paid at the time, and this understandably created rancor among the Hawaiians. After all, guys like Buffalo had families to support. But the PVS leaders said that if they couldn't do it, there were plenty of other guys who were waiting to get on board.

Before they could safely sail all the way to Tahiti, the Polynesian Voyaging Society needed a navigator who knew about "wayfinding," the ancient form of navigating using the stars, seabirds, and ocean swells as guides. But with the advent of modern instruments and ships, wayfinding had become a lost art that few practiced anymore. Because Ben and the PVS leaders wanted to sail to Tahiti using no modern or Western instruments of navigation, they had to find a traditional wayfinder to guide them on their twenty-five-hundred-mile voyage. Yet most of these natural navigators had died without passing on their unique knowledge to the younger generations.

After a long search, Ben was able to find a small Micronesian man named Mau Piailug from the island of Satawal who was one of the last traditional wayfinders left in the world. Like his ancestors, Mau had sailed all over Micronesia, charting his course by the stars each night. The constellations served as his sky map. In his research on Polynesian voyaging, Ben had met Mau years earlier and was greatly impressed with his skill in noninstrument navigation and his ability to work with people from other cultures. Mau was a master canoe builder, and he had helped oversee the repairs of the *Hokule'a* after it swamped off Kaua'i. But after retying the lashings on the canoe, Ben made him and the other crew members completely rework the ropes according to his theories of how the ancient Hawaiians had done it. This created a growing tension between the crew and PVS leaders. Mau was known for his calm and courage under extreme conditions, and it was said that he had survived two hurricanes at sea. But when he agreed to help navigate the *Hokule'a,* he was not prepared for the storm of conflicts and fierce emotions that would rise up during the long voyage to Tahiti.

Even Wally was surprised by the sudden onset of hostility on the part of Hawaiians who didn't know that he was married to a Hawaiian woman and deeply integrated into their culture. "I came on board when we were in Kawaihae," Wally recalls. "All these Hawaiians rushed at me like they were ready to throw me overboard. But Herb Kane told them, 'He's part of the group.' What I found out later is that this kahuna told Kimo Hugho to tell all the Hawaiians, 'Don't let no haoles on the canoe!' " Kimo was a tall Hawaiian sailor who resented the way they were being treated. After Herb's departure, the PVS directors had wanted Wally to be captain, but he turned them down. "I had to refuse it because, I said, 'This is a Hawaiian project, and you gotta have a Hawaiian captain,' " Wally recalls. They then asked Kimo to lead the crew because he was a respected and popular leader in the community.

Although Kimo Hugho was a firefighter, sailor, and surfer like himself, Wally says the two had different perspectives on the canoe and the crew. According to Wally, the tall, barrel-chested Hawaiian began to stir up resentment among the guys working on the canoe. Besides complaining about the long hours and lack of pay, Kimo promised many of the locals that they could sail on the first voyage to Tahiti. "He caused problems by telling everybody at every place he went that they could be on the crew," Wally says. "I was on the nominating committee for the crew, and we ended up with about eighty guys." But they could only select fifteen sailors for the voyage down and fifteen more for the voyage back. Saddened by the growing tension and competition to be on the crew, some sailors like Eddie Aikau decided to withdraw from the selection process and wait till the next voyage.

While working on the selection committee for the *Hokule'a,* Wally remembers Buffalo asking him to bring him aboard the upcoming voyage. "He wanted me to help him get on," Wally says. "He was so anxious to go. 'Wallace, get me on the canoe! Get me on the crew!' I put his name on a list, and I was on a committee to select the guys. Of course, even Tommy Holmes, when I told him about Buff, he says, 'Oh yeah, Buff's a good waterman.'" Many of the guys were talented watermen, but they hadn't done much deepwater sailing. "Buff was extremely comfortable on the ocean," Wally adds. "He turned out to be an excellent sailor."

When he was finally selected, he was both happy and anxious at the same time. "It was a heavy and great honor for our family," his son Brian recalls. "I remember there was a lot of blood, sweat, and tears getting ready for the voyage, a lot of preparation physically, mentally, and spiritually." After joining the crew, Buffalo decided to bring along his best friend, Boogie Kalama, a talented local musician, to sail with him on the canoe.

"Actually, Boogie wasn't on the crew, but being so close, Buff just told him, 'Come on,' so he came on, and they just went," Wally says. It was a power play on Buffalo's part, and he won. According to Boogie, "Buff told 'em, 'If Boogie no go, I ain't goin'.' He needed somebody he could talk to. None of the other guys could converse with him because they didn't understand him," Boogie says. "They didn't want me to go because I was the one that was saying there was a whole bunch of bullshit going on." Most of the controversy centered around money issues, because the workers who had helped rebuild the canoe still had not been paid. "A lot of people involved had families, and that's why they dropped out, because they just couldn't afford it," Boogie adds. But he and Buffalo decided to stay and sail on the *Hokule'a* at any cost.

A week before they were supposed to set sail, Captain Kimo Hugho staged an angry press conference near the canoe. Kimo told reporters that the sailors had worked without pay for months, were living in cramped containers and not being fed well. "He thought we weren't really being treated fairly, so he did a media blitz," a young Hawaiian sailor named Mel Kinney recalls. Like Nainoa Thompson, Mel was a proud young Hawaiian who was well liked by both the PVS leaders and the local crew members. Both Nainoa and Mel were chosen to sail on the return voyage from Tahiti. But during the press conference, both young men felt stuck in the middle of the tension between the two groups, with the PVS leaders on one side and the crew on the other.

"There's too many coaches trying to run a really good team," Kimo told reporters. "I told you in the beginning, you want the best watermen out here, and we got the best. But you got to take care of them and their families. I told you you created a monster— now take care of it. But most of all, take care of these guys." Kimo went on to say that the canoe and the crew were not prepared for the long and possibly fatal voyage. "We're not ready to go. There's dissention among the leaders, but there's unity among the crew . . . That's my feeling, but I feel I know what the Hawaiian people deserve. They've been taken for granted." In the National Geographic documentary *Voyage of the Hokule'a,* the filmmakers covering the event seemed to encourage the tension between the sailors and the PVS leaders.

That press conference was the last straw for the leaders of the Polynesian Voyaging Society who felt that Kimo was undermining them and not being a good team player. "So they decided to replace him with David Kapahulehua on the day of the launch!" Mel says. "Of course, that caused a lot of tension." David was a quiet Hawaiian man with years of experience as a sailor, but he came onto the scene late and had trouble asserting authority over the crew. Standing on the shore of Honolua Bay on Maui, surrounded by cameras, the stunned sailors wrestled with anger and tears as Kimo was asked to step down so David could take his place. For the sake of the canoe and its crew, Kimo's father asked his son to shake hands with the new captain as a sign of forgiveness. Both Hawaiians were reduced to tears as they shook hands and hugged. "That was a tense moment for everyone," Mel adds. "It was very intense."

Mau, the Micronesian wayfinder from Satawal, addressed the crowd and the crew gathered on the shore just before they set sail. The dark-skinned man spoke in his native tongue, and everyone listened as his son translated. "Now, we are going on the ocean. There everything we do is different from what we do on land. On the ocean, we don't eat the same or sleep the same or work the same. We do what the captain says—he is our mother and father. Our problems, our quarrels, we leave on land. We must change all our ways so we can survive." Then, the *Hokule'a* set sail, with friends and family waving from the shore. Unfortunately, most of the crew didn't take Mau's advice, and the anger and quarrels they stowed deep inside would eventually erupt on the high seas.

"That's how the boat left, and you can't leave that way," Mel adds. "All that tension was carried down." As a Native Hawaiian crew member, he felt the same frustration with the PVS leaders; but as a student at the University of Hawai'i, he had also come to respect Finney and the other leaders for their vision and mentorship. As Mel and Nainoa watched them sail away, the two young sailors hoped that all the tension would be released during the long journey down to Tahiti. Instead, it only escalated with each day.

What happened over the next thirty-four days of their voyage is a subject of intense debate, and many of the crew members have conflicting versions of what went down. "There were sixteen different guys on that boat," says Brian Keaulana, "and you could write sixteen different stories, depending on firsthand experience." But toward the end of the journey, two main factions emerged between the Hawaiian crew members and the haole leaders. For Buffalo and the crew, the voyage was part of a larger cultural revival. But for Ben Finney and the PVS guys, this was also an important scientific experiment. Although Captain David Kapahulehua was Hawaiian, he was a friend of Ben Finney, so the other crew members just assumed he was on the side of the PVS leaders.

The voyage got off to a rough start when the PVS leaders chose to navigate a course above the Hawaiian Islands heading into the wind, instead of sailing through the more tranquil Kealakaihiki Channel. Kealakahiki translates as the "way to Tahiti," and many Hawaiians were frustrated that they didn't follow the traditional route. Although they had an escort sailboat following them a mile or two behind, Mau and the other navigator, David Lewis, had no access to Western equipment or modern technology. No radar, no maps, not even a compass. Only the vast, desertlike ocean with its endless dunelike swells. But with Mau's intimate understanding of the night sky and the help of veteran navigators such as Lewis, they managed to map out their course based on where certain stars rose and set on the horizon each night. In this way, they hoped the heavens would guide them all the way to Tahiti, the ancestral homeland of Hawai'i's people. It should have been a trip that united them, but the uncertainty of not knowing if they were on the right course or terribly lost began to take its toll on the sailors.

To reduce the anxiety of being so far from land, drifting in the middle of the world's largest ocean, Buffalo wanted some of the creature comforts of home, like coffee and hot food. But Ben had ordered that they follow a strict diet of dried taro, bananas, and only foodstuffs that the ancient Hawaiians would have eaten. This meant that most of the food was bland and cold and much of it had spoiled. The sailors began to grumble. Being a practical man, Buffalo decided the crew needed coffee because it was so cold at night and hard to stay awake, so he lit up the small stove he had brought on board and began making coffee. "He passed the coffee around to everybody," Boogie recalls. "All the scientists said, 'No, we don't want it.' He came up to Mau, and Mau drank and said, 'Oh, good, this is what we need.' After that, every day, we made coffee."

Some crew members had smuggled *pakalolo* and a radio on board so they could smoke, relax, and listen to Hawaiian music during the long, lonely nights at sea. Ben and the captain had strictly forbidden these things and argued that they might compromise the integrity of the voyage and the scientific experiment. Sailing a mile or two behind, the escort boat was sending back daily reports of the *Hokule'a*'s position, which was sometimes reported on the radio. Because they were able to tune into radio stations broadcasting from Hawai'i during certain parts of the voyage, Ben argued that they might hear the nightly reports about their progress across the Pacific and maybe tell Mau whether he was on course or not. But Buffalo and six other crew members just ignored his orders and stared defiantly at him like he was a killjoy. They started congregating in the little grass *hale* at the front of the deck, where the acrid scent of smoke mingled with the muted sounds of the radio and Boogie's guitar.

Several weeks into the voyage, the canoe began to seem sluggish in the water and heavy in front. Buffalo suspected that water was leaking into the bow compartment of one of the hulls. He shared his thoughts with the leaders, but Ben kept insisting that the hulls were watertight. Knowing he was right and sick of being talked down to, Buffalo took matters in his own hands. He took a hammer and a chisel and started slamming away at the divider in the hull! "The captain and the scientists were all asking me, 'What's Buff doing?' " Boogie recalls. After Buff broke through the first bulkhead, a little water trickled out. But when he slammed through the second divider, Boogie says, "almost one hundred gallons of water came pouring out from inside the hull." The hull rose up, and the canoe began sailing much faster. "See, I knew there was water inside there!" Buffalo said triumphantly.

Ben saw that Buffalo had been right, but the damage had been done, literally and figuratively. "The bow compartment, which was guaranteed to be watertight by the guys who did the work, wasn't watertight, and Buff took the lead on that," he grudgingly admits. Still simmering about the way Ben talked down to them, the Hawaiian sailors could be heard muttering jokes like, "The only good haole is a dead haole."

Tensions mounted daily between the PVS leaders and the crew around the issue of navigation, especially when they reached the doldrums at the equator. They drifted endlessly for days under the fierce gaze of the sun. Ben Finney and Dave Lewis started questioning Mau's directions, saying the canoe was off course, while Buffalo and the crew stuck by the small Micronesian man. According to Boogie Kalama, Mau would tell the locals, "I know what they're saying, but you cannot do nothing. The wind blow that way, we gotta go with the wind." When it changed direction, Mau was able to get them back on course, but a rift had developed between the two navigators, further dividing the crew.

Being a troublemaker and sensing that this rift would make a good story for their documentary, the photographer on board encouraged animosity on both sides. According to Ben, "One of the National Geographic photographers was a dopehead from a ski resort in Aspen. He was a young man who didn't have any sense. He was sniffing stuff off mirrors and running around nude." Ben continues, "It was lucky he didn't get killed. They said I was lucky not to get killed, but he was in more danger than I was."

After more than a month at sea, the crew began to see certain seabirds that suggested they were approaching their destination. When they finally came in sight of the Tahitian islands, Dale Bell, the National Geographic producer, came out in a motorboat with bottles of champagne and started tossing them to the crew members. The Hawaiian contingent took their bottles to the bow and started chugging down the cool, crisp champagne. On the surface, it seemed like a nice way to toast the success of their long, arduous journey. But deep down, Ben suspects that Bell had planned to get the crew drunk. This way, they would release all the tension that had been boiling inside them and he could capture it on film. Sure enough, after the bottles were emptied, the Hawaiian crew members emerged from their hut in the front of the canoe and walked toward the haole crew members. The Hawaiians looked angry and ready for a fight.

Surrounding Ben, the captain, and Dave Lewis against the starboard rail, some of the Hawaiians started yelling at the leaders for not paying them enough money and for talking down to them during the voyage. Like a small mutiny, they listed their grievances and started pushing them around. According to Boogie Kalama, Dave Lewis then called Buffalo a "stupid *kanak*," and that's what sparked the explosion. Buffalo lost his temper and slugged Lewis and the captain. Then Buffalo jumped on Ben Finney and hit him in the face. As crew members rushed to pull them apart, Mau stepped in and said, "Buff, stop!" The brawl ended as quickly as it started.

Afterward, Buffalo came up and offered Ben his hand in the form of a wordless apology. Suffering from an infected sore on his foot, Buff had been in a lot of pain and had just snapped. It was clear he felt bad about what had happened, but the other crew members were still seething. "Everyone else was looking daggers," Ben says. "It's sort of hard to eat humble pie, but you have to do that and turn the other cheek."

Before setting sail, Mau had told the crew to leave their

problems on land and work together as a family, but they had
not heeded his warning. According to crew member John Kruse,
the fight and dissention during the voyage had infuriated the
small Micronesian wayfinder. "On the trip, Mau said your problems on the canoe when you do deep-sea voyaging, those little
problems that everyone takes for granted and that we can always walk away from on land, those little problems become big
problems at sea," John says. "So you have to think as one big
family, and if you make it you're going to make it as a family;
and if you die or get lost at sea, you're gonna die as one family.
Some guys get stir-crazy when they can't see the land. The ocean
can be unforgiving." After sailing across the Pacific together, the
crew had made it as a family of sorts, but it was a bitter and divided one.

Despite the conflicts on the canoe, the voyage was basically a
resounding success. On the bright and clear morning of June 4,
1976, the *Hokule'a* sailed into Papeete Harbor. After thirty-four
days at sea, the canoe had completed its epic twenty-five-
hundred-mile voyage to Tahiti, using only the stars as guides.
In anticipation of their arrival, the governor of French Polynesia
had declared the day to be a public holiday. More than eighteen
thousand Tahitians, a big portion of the Island's population,
waited by the shore to welcome the *Hokule'a* and their Hawaiian "cousins" home. The police had erected barricades to hold
back the crowds. But when they saw the double-hulled canoe
sailing through the blue-green waters of their harbor, the people burst through the barricades and began wading in the water
to touch her.

Boogie Kalama would always remember the day, partly because it was his birthday but mostly because of the huge crowds
who were ecstatic to see a traditional Polynesian voyaging canoe sail into their waters. "They came from everywhere because
this was like their ancestors coming home." Hundreds of canoes
and boats from other islands sailed out to greet her tired crew.
Mobs of locals tried to climb aboard, almost capsizing her with

their enthusiasm. "They saw this as an extension of their past, and we hadn't done this in eight hundred–plus years," John Kruse says. "All of a sudden, they see this thing on the horizon, and it was like 'Whoa, man, this is history!'"

In the midst of all the celebrations, Mau Piailug slipped away from the canoe and left a message saying he wasn't coming back. Before reaching Tahiti, Mau had told Ben that he wanted to go home and wasn't going to sail back to Hawai'i with the new crew. Ben tried to convince the wise old wayfinder to stay, but Mau had made up his mind to leave. The tension on the canoe had taken a heavy toll on everyone involved, especially its founder. When they landed in Papeete, Ben's family was there to greet him, and they were stunned by what they saw. Although he tried to look happy about the voyage's success, they could see beneath his smile that he had lost considerable weight and had a black eye and bruises on his face.

Shortly after the arrival of the *Hokule'a,* Wally Froiseth flew down to Tahiti to take part in the celebrations and congratulate the crew. At the airport, Ben rushed up and told him all about the conflict with the Hawaiians and his fight with Buffalo. Wally could tell that Ben was still shaken up by the conflict and tried to reassure him that everything was going to be okay. Seeing Buffalo in the distance, Wally started to go up and greet him, but Ben tried to stop him. "I started to go talk to Buff, and he said, 'Oh no, no, don't go; don't go.' I said, 'Come on; don't worry.' He said, 'No, no, don't you dare; he's a wild man.' I turned around and said, 'Don't worry.' So me and Buff we meet like old friends, no problem."

Ben and Wally had radically different views of Buffalo and saw two sides of the same man. Ben, on the one hand, could only see the man who had challenged his authority and seemed angry at haoles. For instance, Ben had arranged for the crew to stay for free at the local YMCA, while he and Tommy decided to pay for their own rooms at a nice hotel nearby. So Ben couldn't understand why Buffalo, Boogie, and the other Hawaiian crew members had angrily barged into the same hotel, insisting that the PVS leaders pay for their rooms. "We were not going to stay at the YMCA while those guys stayed in the hotel," Boogie says. "We came in the same canoe. So we ended up at the hotel because we forced our way into the hotel."

Wally, on the other hand, could only see the lighter side of Buffalo and how happy he was that the Tahitians were treating him and the other crew members like cultural heroes. The locals gave the Hawaiians all kinds of gifts and welcomed them into their homes like long-lost cousins. Running into Buffalo at the hotel, Wally said he was excited by the reception and proud to be Hawaiian. "At that time, he began to feel more of his own heritage. It was really a wonderful thing to see. He was stoked, and he couldn't talk about it enough."

Like a double-edged sword, the Hawaiian Renaissance was a powerful weapon in the hands of the Hawaiian crew. For the first time in a long while, they felt a renewed pride in their cultural heritage after sailing on the *Hokule'a*. Yet they also rediscovered a pent-up rage that had been dormant for the last century. The Tahitians could relate to the Hawaiians' anger about the way their traditional culture had been suppressed. After the arrival of the first white men in their tall ships, the Tahitian people had endured centuries of colonial rule. Having lived in Tahiti and learned the language and culture as part of his research, Ben Finney knew the pain these people felt was similar to what the Hawaiians were experiencing.

"France did the same trip on the Tahitians as we've done on the Hawaiians—made them feel bad about themselves, made them *kaumaha*," Ben says. "*Kaumaha* literally means 'heavy' and also 'psychologically heavy, depressed, angry, frustrated'. . . . You know your lands have been taken away, and you're left with the dregs and you're looked down upon." Intellectually, Ben could understand their collective frustration as a people, yet emotionally, he had a hard time relating to the effects of their enduring pain. He still resented his treatment by the Hawaiian crew members. After all, Ben had helped conceive of the *Hokule'a* and had built it in part for the Hawaiian people. But he couldn't understand that Buffalo and the others still resented him for acting at times like he controlled the canoe and knew what was best for his people.

In order to heal the wounds of that original voyage, Wally tried to explain to Ben the cultural differences between haoles and Hawaiians. Although Wally never graduated from college, he grew up in Hawai'i and in some ways understood her people better than the brilliant professor with a Ph.D. in cultural anthropology. "That's the reason I wanted him to try and understand these guys' thinking," Wally says. "You can't think that the way you think is the way they think—you've got to think in their terms and how they feel.

"After this whole thing was over, years later, Buff gave a lu'au," Wally continues. He invited all the crew members who had ever sailed on the *Hokule'a* and many people on the Westside to honor Mau Piailug, who had come back to help with the subsequent voyages. Ben Finney said that he didn't want to go because of all the anger and resentment between him and Buffalo. "No worry, you know, he doesn't hold any grudges," Wally tried to reassure Ben. "Just come with me and everything's going to be okay, no problems."

Driving down the coast to Makaha and staring at the ocean, both men had time to recall the long journey of the *Hokule'a*, from its inception and construction to its first sea trials and the tumultuous voyage to Tahiti. When they arrived at the lu'au, Buffalo walked right toward them. He welcomed them and gave each man a hug, as if they were old friends. But during the ceremony, the new president of the Polynesian Voyaging Society paid tribute to the younger crew members who had just finished a recent journey to Tahiti. But he neglected to honor Mau and the first crew, and this upset Buffalo and the other sailors.

According to Boogie Kalama, Buff stood up and said, "You know this party was made to honor our navigator and the crew members of the first journey and their families, and that's why all my people did this. Now, you shame us by doing something like this and not mentioning all the people from the first journey." Ben Finney felt like he was back on the canoe and being attacked again. After the outburst, the PVS leaders and crew members talked about it, apologies were made, and the dispute was resolved. The crowd resumed drinking and having a good time, but Ben could still feel the sting of the lifeguard's angry words.

"You know, Finney didn't understand it," Wally says. "Like when I grew up here, you go to a lu'au and you'd fight with somebody, and the next day, everybody would be great friends. You don't hold anything back, there's no hatred involved, just emotions at the time, and that's it. That's the way Hawaiians are," Wally adds. "Maybe I understand the thinking of the Hawaiian people because I've been here a long time." Both he and Ben had lived in Hawai'i for years and had surfed, fished, and sailed with locals like Buffalo. But only Wally had truly embraced the local ways. Marrying a Hawaiian woman and becoming the father of a proud Hawaiian family, he was fully accepted into their culture. Buffalo would remain lifelong friends with Wally, but he and Ben never really reconciled.

Despite their differences, all of the PVS leaders and crew members set the course for the *Hokule'a*'s future voyages around the world. In 1980, Nainoa Thompson had become the first Hawaiian wayfinder in modern times to navigate a voyaging canoe back to Tahiti. Since then, the *Hokule'a* has sailed more than one hundred thousand miles across the Pacific, from Hawai'i to New Zealand in the south, Easter Island in the east, and Japan in the west. In 2010, Nainoa hopes to navigate the double-hulled canoe in an epic voyage to circumnavigate the globe. Over the years, the *Hokule'a* has encountered many more storms, controversies, and the tragic loss of one of its sailors, but she has never stopped voyaging.

CHAPTER 7

⊗

Hawaiian Royalty

If just for a day our king and queen
Would visit all these islands and see everything
How would they feel about the changes of our land?
—"Hawaii '78," The Makaha Sons

When Buffalo returned from his voyage to Tahiti in 1976, he was a changed man. Sailing on the *Hokule'a* had taken him on a long journey back to his ancestral roots and restored a long-lost sense of pride in his cultural heritage. In spite of all the *pilikia* (trouble) aboard the canoe, the voyage had transformed his image of himself and others' perception of him as a Native Hawaiian leader. Sitting in his orange lifeguard tower back in Makaha, Buffalo would stare at the blue-green water and relive the highs and lows of the journey. He searched for ways that he could share his love and knowledge of the ocean with his own people and help them rediscover their culture.

Looking around the community, Buffalo could see restless young locals who were drifting toward unemployment, drugs, and crime. Others were moving away to find jobs in the city. After the demise of the Makaha International, the area had experienced a downturn. Now the North Shore was the new hot spot for surfers, tourists, and contests, and even his own kids were eager to get into the action. As an aspiring pro surfer and mentor to the hottest kids from Makaha, Rell Sunn took Brian under her wing and introduced him to the North Shore. "She was like my older sister," Brian says. "Rell would pick me up and take me to Haleʻiwa and Chun's Reef and expose me to a lot of places on the North Shore." She had gone from babysitting him at Makaha to surfing big waves with him at Sunset Beach. He was excited to experience the size and power of its waves, but he was surprised by the different culture out there.

"The Westside is real different compared to the North Shore," Brian says, adding that the people over there are segregated into bodyboarders, bodysurfers, and surfers. "A piece of equipment makes that person different. Whereas here [in Makaha], we all bodysurf, we all bodyboard, we all canoe-surf, we all windsurf. We're more waterpeople over here. If it's flat, we go diving and fishing. If the wind is up, we go sailing." Yet as an aspiring young surfer who wanted to go pro, Brian realized that the North Shore was the place to be. This "seven-mile miracle" of pristine coastline hosted the biggest waves, best contests, and most photographers. After ABC's *Wide World of Sports* began covering the Duke Classic in the late sixties, competitive surfing on the North Shore had taken off with the addition of the Pipeline Masters and the Smirnoff Pro in the seventies.

Surfer-turned-promoter Fred Hemmings ran the contests and did commentary for the TV networks, which broadcast the events all across America. With his square jaw and clean-cut demeanor, "Dead-ahead Fred" became the face of professional surfing and was determined to develop a pro tour. He had been there for the first broadcasts of the Makaha International in the mid-sixties and then began doing commentary for the Duke Classic in the early seventies, but he realized they needed more of an organized international contest circuit. In 1976, he and pro surfer Randy Rarick developed the governing body of the world tour known as the International Professional Surfers (IPS). A few years later, Fred and Randy would create the Triple Crown, which would become the final climax of the world tour. These three final contests took place on the North Shore each November and December, ending with the Pipeline Masters, which is still the most exciting and longest-running surf contest in the world.

With the rise of professional surfing, the Hawaiian "sport of kings" was slowly being transformed by corporate interests and promoters who saw its growing commercial appeal. Fred arranged for big companies such as Ocean Pacific, Hang Ten, and Smirnoff to sponsor contests because they wanted to associate their products with tan surfers and the laid-back beach lifestyle in Hawai'i and California. Some "soul surfers" protested against its rising commercialism and referred to the top pros as "sell-outs." One surfer wrote that professional surfing was like "fornicating with mother sea," while the pros argued that they were being screwed by the corporations and contest promoters who were making all the money.

For competitive young surfers like Brian Keaulana, these contests were the height of glamour and glory. To enter and become part of the tour, Brian had to compete in the pro trials at Sunset Beach. As a teenager, he had already won amateur contests and picked up sponsors like Town & Country Surf Shops, but he was now going up against the world's best surfers. Although Brian may have been a better all-around waterman, he had a hard time breaking into the big leagues. Yet in the eyes of the locals on the Westside, he had become a hometown hero.

While still a student at Wai'anae High School, Brian also began working as a junior lifeguard at Makaha with his father and Rell Sunn, who had become the first female guard in Hawai'i. Buffalo took pride in the fact that his son seemed to be following in his footsteps, yet he could also see that Brian was being lured away by the glamour of becoming a pro surfer. As he and other young surfers began migrating to the North Shore, Buffalo became discouraged by the younger generation's focus on cutthroat competition and media attention. Recalling his own glory days as a competitor, he wanted to find a way to revive the friendly spirit of the Makaha International contests.

Reflecting on Buffalo's career as a surfer, Ricky Grigg says, "He was surfing at a point when history took the spotlight off Makaha and turned it toward the North Shore. For that reason, his career was sort of broken by a shift of emphasis away from Makaha over to the North Shore, and he didn't go with it. He was a loyal guy stationed in Makaha. That was his place, his home, his heart. He didn't care about being noticed or famous or big-time. He wasn't trying to be a famous surfer." Although Buffalo had been featured in a few surf flicks in the sixties, most of the newer films focused on younger, radical surfers from Australia and South Africa who were carving names for themselves on the North Shore scene.

This new crop of Aussie surfers charged onto the North Shore scene in the mid-seventies, acting like they owned the place. Featured in the film *The Golden Breed*, the Aussie invasion was headlined by Wayne "Rabbit" Bartholomew, Ian Cairns, and Peter Townend, or PT, who won the first world championship title in 1976. Their radical new style of surfing simulated a roller-coaster ride as they raced up and down the face of the wave, but their boisterous behavior, cocky attitudes, and self-promotion did not amuse the locals. And none of them was more outrageous than Rabbit Bartholomew.

Nicknamed Rabbit for his speed and manic behavior, the pale Aussie loved the showmanship of professional sports and wanted to emulate Muhammad Ali's banter in the boxing ring and John McEnroe's insolence on the tennis court. But Rabbit's brash behavior clashed with the local culture's emphasis on *ha'aha'a,* humility, and the Hawaiians took deep offense at the brash, trash-talking surfer from Down Under. After Rabbit published an article called "Bustin' Down the Door" in *Surfer* magazine, he and the other ex-pats suddenly became the focus of intense Hawaiian rage. At the height of the hostilities, Rabbit was beaten by an angry group of locals who threatened to kill him if he didn't leave town.

Meanwhile, many young local surfers adopted the media-grabbing, aggressive attitude of the Aussies and the contest scene became even more commercial and competitive. Arguments in the water erupted into fights on the beach or in bars. The owners of companies such as Lightning Bolt were told they couldn't sponsor "outsiders" like Rabbit and the other Australians. Of course, there was a history of animosity between the Hawaiians and Aussies that dated back to conflicts at the Makaha International and more recent scuffles between Buffalo and Nat Young, the brash surfer from Sydney who won the 1966 World Surfing Championships. During one of the Duke Contests at Sunset Beach, where Buffalo was working on water patrol, Nat had accused him of not looking out for the Aussies in the big waves. As a lifeguard who took safety seriously, Buffalo confronted Nat after the contest. Buffalo made it clear that he would save Nat in the water, but on the land he'd better watch out.

"The North Shore is not what surfing is really about," Ricky Grigg says. "It's hairy; it's heavy; it's spectacular. But the heart and soul of surfing is still over there at Makaha." According to Ricky, the Westside retained the original spirit of Hawaiian surfing because it never became inundated with big money or media hype. "As the North Shore became sort of tired out, in the sense of being overdone by the media, Makaha started to re-emerge as a place where the Hawaiianness of the sport still survived. It was due to people like Rell Sunn and Buff that that was happening. Their personalities were so soft and yet so strong at the same time that it sort of built a new image of Makaha as having always been the place where real Hawaiian surfing was done." And no event would embody the playful and authentic spirit of the place like the annual Buffalo Big Board Classic.

"It's all about fun and aloha," Brian says. "That's what makes my dad's contest so different." Buffalo and his friend Adam Holbrook wanted to put on a fun local event for the community. While the North Shore contests featured aggressive young pros ripping their shortboards across the waves, the Classic invited guys of all ages and sizes to compete on all kinds of equipment, including traditional longboards (generally over nine feet in length), body boards, and outrigger canoes.

Like the Makaha International, it was a fun amateur contest, with events for older watermen (over forty) and younger surfers (under forty). Years later, there was even a 250-pound division for bigger guys like Buffalo. To make sure the competitors were over the weight limit, the local organizers would tie 250 pounds' worth of Primo beer on one end of a seesaw and make the competitors walk the plank to see if they could lift the cases of beer on the other end. In one event, they had to perform a series of silly tricks on their longboards. Guys would do headstands on their boards, sit with their legs crossed like the Buddha, and then lie on their backs with their arms and legs in the air like a dead cockroach.

Buffalo hoped to get people off the streets and into the ocean, where they couldn't get into trouble with drugs or crime. "Dad really saw the community not having any sense of values and just running amok," Brian adds. "What he did was told all the beach boys, 'Look, we're going to have one golden weekend, and everybody who comes to this festival and contest needs to be treated like kings and queens. There's no ripping off people.' All the guys that are crooks he made them all cops. He made them

T-shirts and put down 'Maka'i Ke Kai,' which means 'police-
men of the ocean'. . . . Dad really laid the law down. I think that
was the turning point for a lot of the guys because it became
such a perfect weekend."

Even the criminals in the community pledged their support
to help Buffalo maintain order and cut back on crime. If anybody gave him or Momi any trouble or acted out of line, they
might have to face these tough guys. "They was people you
should be afraid of," Buffalo says. "These are the people who
helped make our surf meet a success. In the country over here,
even the parents have a hard time controlling their kids. But I
had control because if you wanted to be bad, I'll show you some
bad guys." Just the threat of having to answer to one of these
toughs scared a lot of local delinquents straight and helped to
keep order. Meanwhile, the corporate sponsors liked the fact
that they could come down to Makaha and feel safe. "We know
both sides of the street," Momi says with a laugh. "We walk in
the middle."

A local radio DJ named Frank B. Shaner used to help out at
the Classic and emcee during the contest. Frank remembers
how Buffalo ran a tight show down there. "He was a big bruddah," Frank says of the stocky Hawaiian lifeguard who was just
over six feet and 250 pounds and whose wild hair and mustache
were tinted blond by the sun. "I remember one time at his contest, this tourist lady came up to him and said, 'You know, somebody busted into my car, and I lost my camera and everything.'
And Buffalo would make an announcement: 'Okay, anybody
find this lady's camera, bring 'em up, no questions asked.' I'm
thinking, 'Oh, man, this is a long shot, right?' About an hour
later, she got her stuff back. Amazing." That's the kind of respect that Buffalo commanded in Makaha.

Buffalo recruited his buddies Bunky Bakutis and Boogie
Kalama to help him run the contest. "Buff's whole intent was to
make two weeks out of the year where the rule was 'Thou shall
not steal.' And getting all those guys who were ripping people

off to stop it and do something real," Bunky says. "That was the impetus: 'Hey, let's do something that makes us proud of who we are.' That's what he learned on the *Hokule'a*." The first Buffalo Big Board Classic started in 1977, a year after his return from the voyage to Tahiti. Bunky was a reporter at the time, and his stories about the Classic headlined *The Honolulu Advertiser*. Instead of covering the overly serious contests on the North Shore, he wrote about how this was a whole new kind of event. "We started with pretty radical ideas like there would be no winners," Bunky says. "Everybody got a trophy." They also integrated Hawaiian culture into the event and began it with a big parade and a Hawaiian court.

As part of the opening ceremony for the Buffalo Big Board Classic, the Keaulanas organized a traditional Hawaiian court procession that would gather early in the morning as the sun was rising and march to the beach. "It was great because we got the *Hokule'a* down there and we had a royal court, like how you have the king and queen," Boogie says. Buffalo was the king, and a feisty *kupuna* (elder) named Frenchy DeSoto was the queen.

Frenchy was a respected Hawaiian activist, community organizer, and matriarch of one of Makaha's most prominent families. She had started off working as a janitor at the State Capitol at 'Iolani Palace, but she became frustrated with the politicians who weren't doing anything for the Hawaiian people. Deciding to run for office in the newly formed Office of Hawaiian Affairs, Frenchy won a seat and began a long career representing her people in state government.

Along with surfing, she and her family liked racing stock cars and motorcycles, and her mechanic husband won many races in the Islands. But her son John was the most gifted athlete of the family. He played college football, won tandem surfing titles, and later became famous as a national motocross champion. Known as the "Flyin' Hawaiian," John DeSoto would perform at big dirt-bike shows around the country. He would jump his motorcycle high into the air and do incredible aerial tricks, which the crowds just loved. Following in his mother's tracks, John later rode his high-flying popularity into political office as a city councilman.

Though John DeSoto would become an influential politician in Honolulu, Buffalo was still the King of Makaha. Dressed in robes like traditional tribal chiefs, Uncle Buff and Auntie Frenchy were carried on platforms to the beach by Hawaiians wearing the gourd helmets of ancient warriors. His sons, Brian, Rusty, and Jimmy, wore Hawaiian *malo* and proudly carried the *kahili* (royal standards with ornate feather tops) in front of the procession. As in the traditional Makahiki ceremonies of old, the robed kahuna would inaugurate the contest by blowing into their conch shells and performing a welcoming chant. After the solemn procession and festive hula performances, Buffalo would paddle out and catch the first wave, and then the fun and games would begin.

Buffalo not only presided over the Classic, but he also competed in the contest. Inspired by the hula performances, he would say that his style of surfing was influenced by the traditional dances. "Riding a big board properly is much like dancing the hula. You've got to move around on the board, get the feel of the surf, and then flow with the waves," Buff says. He focused on the traditional style of longboarding he had grown up with because it was more fun. "Big boards, those ten feet and longer, are for us older surfers," he would say. "We need the extra length so we can hang out our big *'opu* [stomachs]. Leave the small board hotdogging to the kids."

Buffalo wanted to avoid the overly competitive and commercial atmosphere of the North Shore pro contests, which the big corporations had taken over. "Where's the fun and friendship? Is winning so much more important than enjoying good waves with a few friends? I don't think so. Look around you here. Look at the smiles and happy talk. When we surf, it's for fun and good sportsmanship. You don't see too much of that nowadays. Surfing events nowadays are like a business."

Building on the sense of pride he felt after sailing on the

Hokuleʻa, Buffalo decided to organize a local *hui* (club) of young Hawaiians so he could teach them how to be better sailors, surfers, and all-around watermen. "Then came the formation of the Makaha Beach Boys, which was a group of guys down here with Buffalo as their head," Bunky says. "Buffalo's idea was to build a double-hulled canoe [like the *Hokuleʻa*]. He had just come back from Tahiti, and that was a total inspiration. There was a kind of empowerment for him." So they purchased Hobie Cats and windsurfing equipment to train the local guys. Part of the inspiration for organizing the Makaha Beach Boys and teaching them how to sail came from the excitement over the Polynesian Voyaging Society's second journey to Tahiti in 1978.

During the Second Annual Buffalo Big Board Classic, Eddie Aikau and his family came down to Makaha, sharing the good news that he had been selected to sail on the next voyage of the *Hokuleʻa* in '78. Already known as one of the best big-wave surfers and lifeguards in Hawaiʻi, Eddie was looking for a new adventure that would test his skills as a waterman and bring him closer to his heritage. He had won the Duke contest a few months before at Sunset Beach and had recently been chosen as one of sixteen sailors to sail back down to Tahiti.

Days before the second launch of the *Hokuleʻa,* Eddie drove down to Makaha to talk to Buffalo and Boogie about the imminent voyage. "I just had to come out and see you before we sail," he kept telling them, as if seeking their advice. They could sense he was nervous and seemed to be having second thoughts about sailing to Tahiti. After all, the crew hadn't had much time to train properly in deep-sea conditions. They talked about how the Polynesian Voyaging Society had decided not to have an escort boat follow the canoe to avoid any speculation that the boat might be helping guide the *Hokuleʻa.*

At that time, Buffalo was studying for his own captain's license so he could train younger sailors. But he sensed that Eddie seemed to be having premonitions that something bad was going to happen during the voyage, so Buffalo told him he didn't have to go. But when he realized that Eddie was determined to sail on the *Hokule'a,* Buffalo reassured him, saying, "No worry. I give you all of my aloha." Then, the three men embraced solemnly in the darkness, and Buffalo and Boogie watched as Eddie drove off into the night.

On the windy afternoon of March 16, 1978, the *Hokule'a* set sail from Magic Island with sixteen crew members headed for Tahiti. The sun was already setting and the seas were rising as the vessel departed without an escort boat. Thousands attended the ceremonial send-off and lined the shore to watch the double-hulled voyaging canoe sail across the choppy harbor and gradually disappear around Diamond Head. Although the gale-force winds sped them along, the crew didn't realize that one of the hatches in the leeward hull was slightly open and began slowly taking on water in the darkness.

About five hours later, the crew discovered the flooded hull and tried bailing out the water, but it was too late. A rogue wave hit the canoe, which was already listing, and it capsized in the Moloka'i Channel. The crew clung to the overturned hulls throughout the night. They had no way of contacting help because the radio had drowned and the emergency beacons had drifted off in the howling darkness. That night, Eddie Aikau volunteered to paddle his surfboard to the Island of Lana'i, which was about twelve to fifteen miles away. But the captain refused his request, saying it was too dangerous. By the next morning, two seasick sailors were suffering from dehydration and hypothermia and one was going into shock. So when Eddie asked again to go for help, this time the captain relented. Around 10:30 A.M. on March 17, Eddie paddled off on his rescue board toward the distant Island of Lana'i and gradually faded out of sight.

Miraculously, the rest of the crew was later rescued after their last flare was spotted that night by a passing airplane. Coast Guard helicopters hauled them out of the churning seas and carried the exhausted sailors back to Honolulu, yet there was still no sign of Eddie. In spite of a weeklong search and rescue operation,

Eddie Aikau was never seen again. The state of Hawai'i was hit hard by the loss of their native son who had saved hundreds of lives at Waimea Bay as a lifeguard. Buffalo and all the crew members who knew Eddie and had sailed with him were particularly devastated. Hundreds of friends and admirers turned out for his memorial service at Waimea. A Fire Department rescue helicopter hovered over the Bay, dropping thousands of flowers over the water. In order to pay tribute to their friend the next year, Buffalo decided to dedicate the Big Board Classic to Eddie's memory.

On the gray morning of the opening ceremony, the mournful sound of the *pu* could be heard echoing off the cliff walls as Native Hawaiian heralds blew into their conch shells. Wearing traditional gourd helmets and holding staffs, Hawaiian warriors led the procession to the beach, followed by the white-robed kahuna, who chanted his homage to Eddie Aikau. More bare-chested men carried the platform with Buffalo, the king, and his entourage, and on the next platform was Frenchy DeSoto, the queen and mother figure of the community. Except for the chant honoring Eddie, no one spoke or made a sound, and almost every eye glistened as they stared toward the sea, remembering their fallen brother.

After staring at Buffalo on top of his platform, Fred Hemmings later wrote this description of the man: "*Ka Mo'i*. The king. Buffalo K. Keaulana. A face of a thousand years. A face drained by the rigors of modern life. A face made rugged by the burden of leadership, a proud face, a face of a warrior king, a determined face. Yet a face with eyes of compassion. A face that reflects the glory and dignity of his people." During the tribute, hula dancers performed in honor of Eddie, the fallen *keiki o ka nalu* (child of the waves). Meanwhile, the Aikau family stood stoically on the beach, lost in their memories. After the ceremony ended, Buffalo and his attendants paddled out into the lineup with a *ho'okupu*, or offering to the god of the sea. Then they caught a wave and rode it back to shore as the crowd cheered. The contest and con-

Bonga Perkins
Photograph by Stuart H. Coleman

Craig Davidson in Rell's old lifeguard
tower, Makaha Station 47 Bravo
Photograph by Stuart H. Coleman

Rell Sunn and her daughter,
Jan *Photograph by Pam Ka'aihue*

Rusty riding his longboard at Haleiwa in 1993 toward his first world championship *Photograph by Jeff Divine*

Brian Keaulana, the author, and Mel Puʻu clowning around
Photograph by Minako Kent

Brian Keaulana, Dave Parmenter, and Terry Ahue canoe surfing
Photograph by Minako Kent

Brian Keaulana and Kathy Terada tandem surfing at Buffalo Big Board Classic in Makaha
Photograph by Minako Kent

Brian Keaulana surfing at Makaha, a cover shot for *Surfer* magazine in 1980 *Photograph by Jeff Divine*

1965 World Championships in Peru: Wayne Schaefer, Estelle and
Joel DeRosnay, George Downing, Fred Hemmings, Buffalo, Wally
Froiseth, and Paul Strauch *Fred Hemmings Collection*

Buffalo Keaulana and Ants Guerrero canoe surfing *Photograph by
Minako Kent*

Israel Kamakawiwoʻole playing his ʻukulele *Photograph by Betty Stickney, Courtesy of Mountain Apple Company*

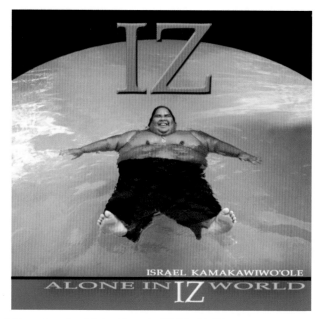

Israel Kamakawiwoʻole's *Alone in IZ World* CD cover *Courtesy of Mountain Apple Company*

Rell Sunn and her Menehunes in Biarritz, France *Tony and Jan Sunn-Carreira Collection*

Rell Sunn dancing hula at the Buffalo Big Board Contest *Photograph by Jeff Divine*

Rell Sunn hanging five on the nose of her board *Photograph by Jim Russi*

Rusty Keaulana cutting back *Photograph by Jeff Divine*

Wally Froiseth *Photograph by Stuart H. Coleman*

Ben Finney *Photograph by Stuart H. Coleman*

cert could now begin, though Eddie's memory would hover over the events like a band of clouds that occasionally blocked out the sun.

After struggling for months to complete the course for his captain's license, Buffalo was ready to give up. But Captain Bob Alverson at the Maritime Academy kept telling Buffalo he could do it and wouldn't let him stop trying. Motivated by the instructor's belief in him, Buffalo stuck with it, passed all the tests, and earned his maritime license. Later that year, the governors of Hawai'i and Alaska arranged for Buffalo and Captain Alverson to fly to Fairbanks to work with the local Aleutian people. They hoped the Hawaiian lifeguard could motivate the Native Alaskans to study their own culture the way Buffalo had embraced his through the *Hokule'a* and his Big Board Classic.

"He went to show the Aleutian Indians that somebody with hardly any education had earned his maritime captain's license," Momi says. When Buffalo asked the Indian Affairs representative why the locals weren't reviving their traditional culture, he said a lot of the kids were obsessed with snowmobiles and drugs and not really interested in the older people and their traditions. But the Aleutians were impressed by the heartfelt words of the soft-spoken Hawaiian lifeguard, especially the ones who wanted to rediscover their own culture. After working with the Native Alaskans, Buffalo came home more determined than ever to make sure the kids in his own community learned about their vanishing cultural heritage. That's when he and the Keaulanas threw their support behind Rell Sunn, who had recently inaugurated her own event to teach kids about surfing, water sports, and sportsmanship.

⚬

Around the time that Buffalo's Big Board Classic became an annual event in Makaha, Rell Sunn created her own surf contest for the local kids. A few years earlier, Rell had decided to host a small event as a birthday party for her daughter, Jan. Dividing the kids into heats, Rell and others judged their rides and then gave out her old surfing trophies to all the competitors. The handful of Jan's friends loved it so much that Rell decided to put on another event the next year, but this time she would try to find corporate sponsors to donate prizes. "My mom liked it because it became the community family thing," her daughter, Jan Sunn-Carreira, says. "The moms potlucked, some parents judged, but if their kids surfed, they couldn't judge. Then, it got so crazy that sponsors had to be called in." Rell started with local sponsors like the Watanabe Gas Station and the Wai'anae Store, but as the event grew, she brought in bigger corporate sponsors like the surf company Quiksilver.

Rell decided to call her event the Menehune Contest and hold it on the North Shore at Hale'iwa Beach, and the event quickly became a huge hit. Brian was too old for the twelve-and-under contest, but his younger brother Rusty won his division, and the victory changed his life. Holding his trophy and seeing the smiles of his friends and family, Rusty had a vision of becoming a surf champion one day. Fourteen years later, he would win his first world longboarding championship at that same beach.

For the first year or two of the Menehune Contest, Rell had to scrape together prizes and give the winners her old trophies. But with each year, more and more kids showed up for the competition as the surfer dads cheered and coached from the beach. Surf companies and corporate sponsors began donating bigger and better prizes and looking out for the next generation of surf stars. As the contest grew, Rell decided to move it from the North Shore back to Makaha and hold it during the long Thanksgiving weekend so they could have three days to run the event.

As one of the pioneers of women's professional surfing, Rell saw early on the potential growth of the sport and how it could transform young lives, just as it had her own. She would eventually compete all over the globe and become the sport's biggest advocate, but she always longed to return to her childhood home on the Westside.

Born in 1950, Roella Kapolioka'ehukai Sunn grew up in a Quonset hut in Makaha, where her beach-boy father taught her how to surf at age four. Her name was like a prophecy, symbolizing her passions in life. "Most Hawaiian grandparents name you before you're born," Rell told *Surfer* magazine. "They have a dream or something that tells them what the name will be." Her middle name means "heart of the sea," and indeed her heart would always belong to the sea. Her godmother gave her the nickname Rella Propella because she was always buzzing around so fast. "Actually, I was born Roella, a combination of my parents' names: Roen and Elbert. But I hated it, and no one used it, so I changed it to Rell."

Her dad was half-Chinese and her mom was half-Hawaiian, and together they had one son and four daughters, who grew up to be some of the most talented and beautiful surfers on the Island. Rell's brother, Eric, was more of a fisherman, like his father, but her sisters, Val, Anella, and Martha, all competed in the Makaha International in the late sixties. Martha, also known as Kula, won the event three times.

Following in her sister's wake, Rell won the Hawai'i Junior Championships at sixteen and traveled with a team chaperoned by Duke Kahanamoku himself to the World Championships in San Diego in 1966. She put her surfing career on hold in her late teens when she abruptly moved to Oklahoma with her boyfriend, Lazarus, a soldier in the army. They got married, had a baby girl, and moved to another military base in Germany for a year. During that time, the marriage unraveled and Rell became homesick for Hawai'i. After separating from her husband the next year, she returned to Makaha, where she resumed her surfing career. It was tough being a single mom and trying to compete in the few, disorganized pro contests for women, but Rell managed to place third in the Lancers Cup at Sunset in '75. She was ranked sixth on the newly formed World Tour in 1977 when she started her Menehune Contest.

After her divorce, Rell was living in Makaha and struggling to support herself and her young daughter. Seeing how Buffalo and the other lifeguards seemed to enjoy working at the beach, Rell decided to become a lifeguard herself. But there were no female guards at that point, and there seemed to be a silent underlying prejudice against hiring women in what was considered a male club. "If men could do it, she didn't understand why she couldn't do it," her daughter, Jan, says. "She dove better than half the men, she surfed better than half the men, so she was like 'What the hell?!' " Though the lifeguard tests were physically challenging, she beat most of the male competitors in the swimming, running, and paddling races.

After proving that she could compete with the men, Rell joined the ranks of the lifeguard service on the Westside and cut a path for other women to follow. Pua Mokuʻau became the second female lifeguard in Makaha, and they grew to be best friends. The two women worked, surfed, and danced hula together in the same *halau*. As lifeguards, these slim, dark angels from the Westside rescued many pale tourists from the ocean's strong currents. When the waves were big, they risked their lives to save victims from drowning in the surf and often had to resuscitate them back to life. Only in their mid-twenties, Rell and Pua were loved and respected as leaders in the community.

Rell's most dramatic rescue happened when she was working at Pokaʻi Bay, just up the road from Makaha. It was a peaceful summer day at the Bay, with hardly any wind or waves on the water. There was a large family down the beach having a picnic under a tree, and they weren't paying attention to their kids. Suddenly Rell looked up and saw something floating in the water and realized it was a baby. "I was on the beach, and saw her running and yelling," Jan recalls. "The baby was blue. She flipped it over and was doing mouth-to-mouth [resuscitation]. . . . I remember the baby barfed up the water, and it was okay. She warmed it up and called the ambulance." She was shaken up and had so much adrenaline that she spent the rest of the day jogging up and down the beach.

While pursuing her other career as a professional surfer in the mid-seventies, Rell had to take unpaid leave from her life-guarding job and recruit sponsors to help pay for her to travel to the distant contests. She also had to hide the fact that she had a child because "how are you going to get a sponsor as a single parent?" Jan asks. "Yet she was going for her dream, making a name for herself. She was broke because at the time women's pro surfing wasn't even on the map."

During one trip to South Africa, they traveled more than twelve thousand miles to compete in the Gunston 500 outside of East London. After their exhausting and expensive trip, Gunston officials told them they hadn't planned for a women's event and had no prize money. The officials eventually scraped together some money, but it was ridiculously small. Rell and the other female surfers had to spend more money to get there than they could possibly win, so it was a lose-lose situation. "The purse was like six hundred dollars when it costs like sixteen hundred dollars to get to Africa to even surf in the event," Jan adds. "It was a sick pipe dream if you think about it."

Rell was constantly arguing with Fred Hemmings about the lack of money for women's surfing, but he would say they had to go out and get sponsors themselves. To augment her income, she started doing commentary with Fred for different events filmed by ABC's *Wide World of Sports*. While covering the Tandem Surfing Championships at Makaha one year, the director asked Rell and Fred to go catch a wave together, do a tandem pose, ride right up to the beach, and then run up to the camera and welcome everyone to the event! The director had never surfed and clearly had no clue how difficult his request would be to fulfill, but they both agreed to give it a try.

The pair paddled out in front of the cameras and huge crowds and caught a wave and Rell grabbed Fred's hands and jumped up on his shoulders. Although Fred thought that he was in charge, he later said, "She told me what to do in very explicit terms for the entire wave. We rode up the beach on the back of the wave, stepped off the board and sauntered up to the camera and microphone. I still marvel that we did it just as the naïve TV director had outlined," Fred writes in his book *The Soul of Surfing Is Hawaiian*. "She made it happen by the sheer force of her will."

Rell pushed Fred to treat the professional female surfers the same way he would the male pros. Pushing back, he decided to see if they could handle surfing with the men in the big waves at Sunset Beach, where they were filming the Smirnoff Pro. Rell used to tease Fred for telling the TV producers, "You know, there's big surf at Sunset, and we'll send 'em out in the same-sized surf as the men, fifteen to twenty feet, and one of them might die—who knows, maybe the whole heat might die!"

Pressured to go out in big, stormy surf that year, Rell and a strong cadre of other women charged into the massive waves and held their own. Some of them experienced nasty wipeouts, which the TV producers caught on film. "That's what they wanted—carnage!" Rell added with a laugh. She and the others gradually convinced Fred and other promoters to invest more money in women's professional surfing, but it was still not much of a living. The women could make more money in the bikini contests than in the surfing competitions. In spite of their poor treatment, Rell and her sisterhood of traveling surfers continued fighting for their rights, supporting each other, and laughing through the hard times.

It was a hard life, but Rell and her good friend Jericho Poppler enjoyed the adventure of the World Tour. "That was easily the prime of women's pro surfing," Sam George told *Surfer* magazine. "Aside from their great ability, Rell and Jericho were the most glamorous girls who have ever done the tour, by far. They were a talented, dynamite combination. I first met Rell in Australia for a Bells Beach contest in 1977, and she was doing a radio interview to stir up some interest. Rell goes, 'We want all you Aussie surfers to come down here, 'cause we'll be rootin' for all the locals.' Well, she had no idea what 'root' means down there (imagine a four-letter word for sex). People went berserk, just turned out in droves. Two beautiful girls, rooting for the guys at Bells [laughter]. But the thing about Rell, without even trying, she had sex appeal. She was just plain sexy. And she knows that's lacking on the women's tour today."

When sponsors wanted to photograph world champion Margo Oberg at Makaha for a surf ad, the locals wouldn't let her catch many waves. But when Rell stepped in and said Margo was a friend of hers, all the guys cleared out of the way for the shoot. Seeing how the locals revered her, Margo later wrote that Rell was the "Queen of Makaha," and the title stuck. Rell was not only a beloved leader for the Westside community, but she cast a magic spell on people everywhere she went around the world. "She was the most perfect beach woman I ever met in my life," says surf photographer Warren Bolster. "I had a huge crush on her. So many guys did. She had beauty, elegance, extreme coordination, and a very sophisticated surfing style. I can still see her on *Wide World of Sports*, running up the beach with a flower in her hair, doing the great commentary."

Although Rell managed to make a living through her surfing and lifeguarding, she was wary of letting her daughter pursue such financially unstable professions. While struggling to make ends meet, Rell spared no expenses for her daughter's education. Along with taking piano lessons and hula, Jan also attended Kamehameha School, her mother's alma mater and the only private school for Native Hawaiians. Although Jan didn't want to become a boarding student at Kamehameha, her mother insisted she live at the school and get the best possible education. During this time, Rell herself went back to college and earned a degree in cultural anthropology at the University of Hawai'i, while also working as a lifeguard, taking hula and judo lessons, and competing on the pro circuit.

"Rella Propella" was always on the go, and there were not many guys who could keep up with her frenetic lifestyle. Her natural Polynesian beauty and grace attracted many men, but her first love was surfing and from then on her heart always belonged to the sea. "I was four years old, and I knew I was in love," she told surf journalist Bruce Jenkins. After receiving her first surfboard, Rell slept with it in bed. "I'd touch the rails and fondle it. That's just the way it's always been. Can you imagine being four and knowing what love is?"

It seemed that any man who vied for her deepest affections would have to be a waterman. After shooting many pictures of her for *Surfer* magazine, photographer Jeff Divine fell in love with the elegant surfer girl. They dated and traveled together on surf jaunts for a few years, and his portraits of her appeared in magazines around the world. Though his home was in Southern California, he basically lived with her in Makaha. Even when he was away on assignment, she was never alone because guests would always stop by every time they were in town.

Whenever Rabbit Bartholomew ventured over to the Westside, he made sure to visit Rell's place first. Rabbit had developed a crush on Rell, who was a few years older. "There was no use falling in love with her because she was a princess," Rabbit says. "I was just some grubby little beach urchin." Even though he went on to become the world champion in 1978, he had been humbled by his near-death encounters with the angry locals on the North Shore the year before. Rabbit was equally intimidated by the fierce reputation of the surf warriors on the Westside, but he knew that he would be okay because he was a friend of Rell's.

"I'd drive over to Makaha and pull straight into Rell Sunn's, and then it was the full welcome. Once I did that, I felt really comfortable over there, because it is a pretty intimidating place," Rabbit says. "It was like a different world once I pulled up to her house and went in and got that beautiful aloha. We'd sit around, have a cup of coffee, and talk story, and then she'd say, 'Get out there!' I felt like I was going surfing at my home break.

You had that feeling like, 'Wow, Rell just blessed me!' I went out there buzzing."

Rabbit's praise for Rell might sound over the top, but she had that kind of effect on people. She was so full of life and warmth that her eyes seemed to sparkle like sunlight on the water. Locals referred to her as the Queen of Makaha because she seemed to have a regal air about her. "She was royalty in the true sense of the word," Rabbit says. "From the very first time I saw her, I always looked at her as royalty, way before I had any knowledge of Hawaiian royalty. She was a princess, and then she became a queen." Even though Frenchy DeSoto was honored with that title each year at Buffalo's Big Board Classic, the feisty *kupuna* says, "Rell was the Queen of Makaha, not me. I was the *ali'i* of Makaha for that one week." Watching Rell dance hula at the Classic or cheering on the kids at the Menehune Contest, Frenchy could see that "she was proud of her heritage, proud of who she was."

Along with the contest, Rell would host an annual Easter egg hunt for the local *keiki,* painting hundreds of eggs and then hiding them in the reef. In this way, she made sure the children had fun and also taught them a little about the reef and coastal ecology. She was passionate about preserving the environment and always had the kids clean up the beach after every event. Rell and Jericho later became involved with the newly formed Surfrider Foundation, a grassroots environmental organization that was dedicated to protecting the ocean and beaches. Inspired by her love of surfing, nature, and Hawaiian culture, kids were always coming by her house. Locals loved hanging out at "Rell's Motel" because she made them feel so comfortable. If Rusty or any of the local kids needed help in school or some advice, they would come to her place. "Rell was the best," Rusty says, remembering how she looked after him and helped with his burgeoning career as a young pro surfer. "She was my hero, my idol, my everything. I won her first contest actually, and I still got the trophy."

Sunny Garcia was another of her "kids" who won her Mene-hune Contest at Haleʻiwa in 1979 and went on to become a world champion. "Rell would always lend me boards when I surfed Makaha and let me stay at her house," Sunny says. "I was like the illegitimate child. I used to stay there whenever I could. I came from a poor family, and my own mom couldn't afford boards. So I used to borrow a lot of stuff. Fortunately for me, I had an aunt like Rell that had a lot of boards and would let me use them all the time."

Sunny was a troublemaker, getting into fights at school and often cutting classes to go surfing. "As a young kid, I got told all the time I was a punk. I had to be straightened out quite a bit," Sunny adds. "Rell would always sit me down and tell me that I should be nice to people and treat them the way I wanted to be treated, like a mom would do, but without the beating. Rell was a very gentle person. She could talk, and you could get it. Rell was so liked and well respected that it didn't matter whether she could fight or not; you just didn't disrespect someone like that."

Along with being a mother, a lifeguard, and a community activist, Rell was one tough wahine who had a black belt in judo. She could put someone in their place if they got out of line, yet she hardly ever used force. The kids and her community sponsors loved her so much that they didn't want to disappoint her. She was also very *akamai* (clever) about how to get sponsorships for herself and her protégés like Brian.

After surfing in the Menehune Contests as kids, Sunny, Rusty, and another local teenager named Johnny Boy Gomes began competing in pro-am contests all over the Island and later across the world. Following in Brian's wake, they began picking up corporate sponsors along the way. At the time, Brian was working as a lifeguard with Rell and his father. Brian was also competing on the local circuit and doing modeling for department stores on the side. Each year, all the Keaulanas and their extended family would help set up and compete in the Buffalo Big Board Classic and the Menehune Contest because they were fun events that brought the community together.

As Rusty, Johnny Boy, and Sunny won more contests, they collected more sponsors and saw more of their pictures in the surf magazines. Inflated with their newfound fame, they began acting cocky and earned a reputation as aggressive competitors in the water and hotheaded locals on the beach. These ambitious young pros didn't like anyone getting in their way, and they would later get embroiled in scuffles on the pro tour. But they all became like humble Boy Scouts around Buffalo and Rell because they loved and respected them so much. As Sunny once put it, "Uncle Buff is the King of Makaha, and Auntie Rell is the Queen."

CHAPTER 8

Wild Life

In wildness is the preservation of the world.
—Henry David Thoreau

As part of the Buffalo Big Board Classic, the Keaulanas and their extended network of friends decided to host Hawaiian music concerts on the beach. They wanted to showcase some of the state's best local musicians and raise money for the voyaging canoe they hoped to build. Buffalo originally sought out Don Ho in Waikiki to help support the event and left with a one-thousand-dollar check to pay for the first concert. Carlton Beal helped finance the event for the next two years, donating the money to pay for the musicians, the stages, and the sound system. The stage would be lined up against the far western fence, and Hawaiian groups would come down to play for the thousands of people dancing on the beach.

During the concerts, Hawaiian and Tahitian groups would play onstage and hula dancers from different *halau* would perform on the beach. Meanwhile, the surfers were competing in the waves—the music, dancing, and surfing all seemed to flow together! "I tell you, there was nothing like it," Bunky Bakutis says. "You could go out there, and you'd hear all the music, and you had to have fun. It was the funnest thing in the world. It brought you back to Waikiki when you could hear the Beachcombers playing on the side. It brings out that really beautiful feeling when music was part of surfing."

A talented slack-key guitar player himself, Boogie Kalama was asked to be in charge of the entertainment each year. He invited the biggest names of the Hawaiian Renaissance to perform, including Cecilio & Kapono, Olamana, the Brothers Cazimero, and of course the Makaha Sons of Ni'ihau. Fast becoming one of Hawai'i's most popular new bands, the Makaha Sons consisted of Israel Kamakawiwo'ole, his brother, Skippy, and a group of local boys who met down at the beach in the seventies. Together, they helped revive traditional Hawaiian music with their soulful lyrics and harmonious voices. But it was Israel, better known as Iz, who would leave the biggest legacy. In Hawaiian, Kamakawiwo'ole roughly translates as the "fearless eye or face," and in time he would live up to that name.

If Buffalo was the new king of Makaha and Rell its queen, Israel became its new crown prince. Born into a local family of musicians who were known for their Hawaiian values and religious devotion, the pudgy toddler grew into a mischievous, wild-eyed teenager. Iz was a paradox: he dropped out of school, yet he loved learning about Hawaiian culture; he experimented with drugs, yet he enjoyed the natural high of playing music on the beach with his family and friends; and he was massively obese, yet he felt light and free while swimming in the ocean. During his short, tumultuous life, Iz developed a reputation as a wild man with a violent temper and an enormous appetite for food, alcohol, and partying. Yet years later, he would renounce violence and drugs and embrace his cultural and spiritual roots.

Israel Kaʻanoʻi Kamakawiwoʻole came into this world in 1959, the year Hawaiʻi became the fiftieth state. Throughout his life, he would wrestle with the tension of being both Hawaiian and American. He loved his native culture and grew up steeped in its traditions and music. But in school his haole teachers hardly said anything positive about his people or their history, so he resented them and talked back in class. His parents were both Hawaiian, and his mother's family came from the isolated island of Niʻihau, southwest of Kauaʻi. Israel's grandfather was a Protestant minister, and he took the boy on a pilgrimage to their ancestral home in Niʻihau one summer. The trip was like a religious experience for the young boy. The mischievous child was astonished to see that only Native Hawaiians were allowed to live on this remote and rustic island, where horses were the main form of transportation and Hawaiian was the only language spoken. Hearing the musical and spiritual language of his ancestors spoken would later influence his own music. Israel felt like he had taken a trip back to Hawaiʻi's mythical past.

In Rick Carroll's book *IZ: Voice of the People*, Israel's uncle Moe Keale says that his father hoped the trip would leave an enduring legacy for his grandson. "He wanted Israel to know the past so he could face the future." Growing up in Honolulu, Iz began to sense his people were treated as second-class citizens in their own land. But he was doted on like a little prince in his home, and his parents and grandparents let the boy get away with occasional temper tantrums and defiant acts because he was such a cute, pudgy rascal. By contrast, Skippy was more disciplined and trained hard to become a talented musician and football player.

Israel's family lived in a relatively poor neighborhood of Kaimuki, near their grandparents' home in Palolo Valley, but they inherited a rich heritage of music. He and his three siblings, Skippy, Lydia, and Leinani, grew up singing with their family and friends at church, backyard parties, and lu'au. As the youngest boy, Iz was spoiled and enjoyed clowning around on his 'ukulele and being in the spotlight. Their father, Henry, originally worked at Pearl Harbor doing construction, but he later helped their mother, Evangeline, manage the Steamboat Lounge in Waikiki, where some of the best musicians of the day would perform. As kids, Iz and Skippy would often be invited to sing onstage with legendary performers such as Gabby Pahinui and Eddie Kamae. When the Steamboat Lounge closed and Iz's parents lost their jobs, the Kamakawiwo'ole family moved from Honolulu to the remote little town of Makaha, where the land was cheap and the living was easy.

Although Skippy liked living in the country, Iz hated leaving his friends and the bright lights and excitement of the city. But as with his visits to Ni'ihau as a child, he eventually grew to love the laid-back Hawaiian lifestyle in Makaha. His family would camp on the beach down the coast at Makua in the summers and grew close to other local families like the Keaulanas. While trying to catch waves on his wooden *paipo* board one day at a spot called Yokohamas, Iz met Uncle Buff. The friendly lifeguard gave Iz some pointers about where to surf and kept an eye out for the hefty teenager. In spite of their size, their friend Jacqueline "Skylark" Rossetti says, Iz and his siblings "would swim like dolphins and play in the ocean. That was a kind of freedom for Israel. He was half his body weight in the water. He could move, he could swim, and that's where he felt the most comfortable."

Brian Keaulana was a few years younger and remembers first seeing Israel at Wai'anae High School, where he already had a reputation as a rebel. Instead of going to classes, he and his friend and cousin Mel Amina would take instruments out of the band room and sneak into the bathroom to practice. When word got around about these impromptu sessions, other students began to show up. Soon Israel and Mel were hosting their own private concerts in the boys' room for their male and female classmates. Smoking in the boys' room was a relatively minor problem, but having concerts there landed Iz in a heap of trouble. He began hanging out at the beach, jamming with other musicians, teaching each other new chords and songs. After getting into trouble with the administration one too many times, Iz later dropped out of high school to pursue his music career.

Brian remembers how he and Israel used to joke around and play pranks on each other. "He was the Hawaiian comedian, witty as hell. You cannot outwit Israel. He got one fast brain, fast mouth, and don't stand too close to him because his hands were pretty fast, too!" Once while Iz was sleeping, Brian and Mel put poi in his hand and tickled his face. Unconsciously scratching his itchy nose and eyes, the sleeping giant smeared his face with the poi, which dried like glue. "Then, we played a nasty trick," Brian recalls with a laugh. "We grabbed one piece of toilet paper, burned it, blew the smoke in his face, and yelled, 'Fire, fire!' He tried to get up, run, and open his eyes, but he kept bumping into the walls and stuff. He wanted to kill us guys . . . I think we were apologizing for one week before we got in arm's length."

Brian's favorite memories take him back to the times when he would just hang out at the beach with Israel and Skippy after school. He and others would listen to them play music and sing all afternoon and into the night. Brian also loved eating with the Kamakawiwoʻoles because there was always plenty of good home-cooked food.

Israel's uncle Moe Keale was also a popular musician who used to sing with the Kamakawiwoʻole family. Though he was a big man himself, standing at six feet and weighing almost 345 pounds, Moe soon realized that their diet was killing the family. "Everyone back then ate the same thing: plenty rice, plenty starch, plenty fat," Moe says. "No one ever said it was bad for me." Like his uncle, Skippy managed to control his weight when he played football, but once he quit, the pounds stayed on like extra padding. Mel changed his diet completely, but his nephews stuck to their daily feasts and ate two to three courses at every meal. Or they went out for the standard plate lunch fare of rice, macaroni salad, potato salad, fried chicken, and a Spam *musubi*. But their favorite was the *loco moco* plate, a beef patty on a bed of rice, topped with a fried egg and drowning in gravy.

The situation only worsened when they starting eating at fast-food restaurants like McDonald's, which came to the Islands in the sixties and offered the cheapest food around. It soon became clear that "Israel had an eating disorder," Moe says. "So did Skippy; they all did." By the time they formed their band, both brothers weighed over 350 pounds each, yet the blend of their guitar and 'ukulele sounded as light as the wind.

Out in Makaha, Iz started performing with his brother, Skippy, and a young musician named Jerome Koko. Iz had met Jerome down at the beach one day when they both cut school, and they started jamming on their 'ukulele. They soon hooked up with two skinny local boys named Louis "Moon" Kauakahi and Sam Gray and formed a band called the Makaha Sons of Ni'ihau. The band was more like one big family, because Moon married Iz and Skippy's sister Lydia and they were later joined by their cousin Mel Amina and Jerry's brother John.

The Makaha Sons became the hardest-working group on the Island, playing at lu'au, parties, and proms, sometimes doing three different gigs a day. With his commitment to God, Hawaiian culture, and music, Skippy was the heart and soul of the group. But it was Israel's angelic voice and devilish personality that brought the fans to each event. "Bruddah Iz was a good guy," Boogie Kalama says. "He was *kolohe* (mischievous) but musically great. Every time we had events, he would be the first to step forward and say, 'Oh yeah, we'll help Uncle Buff.' The Makaha Sons were the first on the list, and the others would fall behind."

The Makaha Sons had deep roots in their culture and had been inspired by older groups like Eddie Kamae's Sons of Hawaii, who had breathed new life into old Hawaiian music. They were also influenced by younger bands like the Sunday Manoa, which began incorporating political messages about the plight of the Hawaiian people into their songs. The group had a reputation for singing about serious issues like cultural oppression and desecration of the land in songs like "Hawaii '78." But they were also known for fun, lighthearted hits like "Pakalolo," Israel's tribute to marijuana, the Islands' most popular cash crop, whose burning scent lingered in the air during their rehearsals and performances. Like the legendary Bob Marley, whose reggae sounds were popular in the Islands, Iz was known as a wild man who liked to party.

When Israel, Skippy, and the other band members lumbered onto the stage, the crowds on the beach would whistle and yell their support. Wearing "slippers" (rubber flip-flops) and mismatched T-shirts, the Makaha Sons sang in Hawaiian, which had been banned for much of the century but was just starting to make a comeback. As the leader of the band, Skippy guided the group toward singing traditional Hawaiian songs like Liko Martin's "Nanakuli Blues." Later renamed "Waimanalo Blues," the song described how the once-pristine Islands were now being overrun by hotels, tourists, and new developments. But as the band performed sweet melodies like Moon's song "Kaleohano," a vision of old Hawai'i would emerge there onstage. As Rell and her hula sisters danced to their music, the audience would watch as their hands and bodies told moving stories about their ancestors and the harmony of the land, sky, and sea.

Skippy's wife, Donna, was a hula teacher, and she helped train Brian and the local beach boys to dance so they could perform while the Makaha Sons were playing. "She taught all of us ancient hula basics and everything," Brian says, recalling how the Makaha Beach Boys would practice until they could barely walk. "We used to call her the 'pain lady' because we used to dance basics for two hours straight." Afterward, they would go to the beach, sit, and just look at the waves because they couldn't move. "It was real tight. That time was a real turning point," Brian says, referring to how closely the community had come together to revive Hawaiian values and traditional practices such as the hula. People were impressed that some of the best surfers on the Island could dance so well.

Rock-and-roll bands would also perform at the Buffalo Classic, and the drunken crowds would dance on the beach. The Westside knew how to throw wild parties, and in between bands they would hold bikini contests. The men in the crowd would go crazy watching these beautiful young women glide across the stage in their skimpy bathing suits.

When Rell and other women complained that they wanted equal entertainment for the female audience members, Buffalo decided to add a men's Speedo contest. Bodybuilding was the rage on the Westside, and the local guys worked out in preparation for this annual event. Brian, Mel, and other surfers would strut their stuff onstage, wearing only small Speedos, body oil, and big smiles on their faces. As they flexed their muscles, the fans and female judges would scream and yell their approval.

As the Buffalo Classic grew in size each year, corporate sponsors and surf companies would donate brand-new surfboards and prizes for the winners. In a poor community like Makaha, this was like winning the lottery. "As we got bigger and bigger, we got more stuff, and the more stuff we had, the more stuff we gave away," Momi recalls. "Some people said, 'You guys are crazy, because you give all this stuff away—what do you keep for yourself?' I said, 'If I could put all those smiles in the bank, I would be a wealthy lady!' We had fun, and that was the whole point of the meet. When it stops being fun, that's when we're going to stop."

Although the Keaulanas offered no cash awards for the surf

contest, the competition for cool prizes and bragging rights was intense. Friendly rivalries between local families like the DeSotos, the Rappozas, the Pu'us, and the Keaulanas became so fierce at times that they had to bring in outside judges. Bernie Baker was a well-known surf photographer on the North Shore who was brought in each year to help judge the contest, and he and the others' decisions sometimes generated controversial results and reactions. "In the heat of battle and competition, there is no place anywhere where the fur will fly as severely as it does in Makaha," Bernie says with a laugh. But Momi Keaulana was like his City of Refuge, and he always knew she would protect him and the other judges. "I knew that nobody would start anything within eyesight of Auntie Momi. She'd have their ears and their nose in her grasp way too quickly. . . . I can't imagine how many people she's had to straighten out in her life to keep peace in the valley."

Unfortunately, with the concerts getting rowdier each year, putting on the event became less fun, especially when the TV networks started approaching the Keaulanas about televising the events. "We had ABC, NBC, and CBS approach us, and they wanted to run our surf meet," Momi says, recalling how the corporate executives tried to buy out their contest.

"We'll pay you this," they told her, offering large sums of money, "and then we'll call the shots."

"Excuse me," Momi said. "I don't think so."

"Lady, are you against making money?"

"Yes, I am," she said. "We have a pie over here—how can I split that pie into a thousand pieces? It can't be done. We have all these people giving their aloha and help, and all of a sudden, we're going to play greedy? We do what we do, and we enjoy doing what we do, and if you don't like it, we don't give a damn!" Momi told them. "That's how we feel." After turning away the greedy corporate sharks, the Keaulanas began to re-evaluate the format of the Buffalo Big Board Classic. The event grew larger each year, and more outside troublemakers were coming down to Makaha just to party and raise hell. As the crowds and traffic got out of control, the cops started arresting people. TV sponsors kept offering the Keaulanas money to buy the rights to the Classic, but they didn't want these corporate outsiders coming in and trying to run the show. Still, there was a lot of money involved in running the event, and other local groups began to clamor for a share of the proceeds of the two-week event.

"As the sniping increased, we decided we would just disband the whole thing," Bunky says. "What we were all about was enjoying what we're doing—we didn't want a war with somebody else while we're doing it. So we stopped the concert because at the same time the crowd was getting huge. As you get bigger, more and more people start to come down that don't really respect the ocean and what this place is all about." Buffalo and his extended family of locals were sad about canceling the concerts, but the events had just become too much of a hassle. Besides, groups like the Makaha Sons who played almost for free could make more money by doing shows in town.

Instead, the Keaulanas decided to return the focus to the ocean and water sports. "We started thinking about what we could do, what kind of events we could create that would encourage cameraderie. Brian came up with the idea of team surfing where there are two guys on a wave . . . So that started this sense of community." Other events included tandem surfing and mixed-doubles bodyboarding. Yet even without the big concert, people came from all over to attend the Buffalo Big Board Classic because it was a fun weekend of surf, water sports, and sun.

Just for the sheer fun of it, Brian would do stunts where he would take a beach chair, umbrella, and surf magazine out on his board, catch a wave, and then sit down and act like he was reading the mag. Once he took out a ladder on his board and climbed up it while surfing to shore. Shots like these began appearing in surf magazines, and readers loved the crazy antics of the Makaha watermen and their stories of the wild life out there.

Just as Buff's Classic kept changing year after year, Rell would add new events to her Menehune Contest as well. Because the crew at Makaha used to have fun with their pets in the surf, she decided to host a Wet Pet Contest one year during the Menehune event. It all began when Rell used to bring her dog Shane to the beach and take him surfing. The *poi* (mixed-breed) dog would sit poised at the front of her board, riding all the way to shore, and if she wiped out, he would jump back on for another ride. The crowds on the beach just loved seeing Shane surf, and the dog seemed to love it, too.

Frenchy's son Bruce DeSoto grew up with Rell in Makaha, and one day she asked him, "Why don't you surf with your dog?" Bruce always had a crush on her and their dogs got along well, so he decided to give it a try. "My dog liked it because he was right alongside Rell's dog," Bruce says. "They looked at each other, you know, like 'Hey, this is all right!'" Seeing how much fun they were having, Brian decided to bring out Chop-Chop, a friend's pet pig, and another guy brought out his pet duck. The local *keiki* enjoyed watching the Wet Pet Contest.

"The kids were watching and laughing," Bruce says with a big smile. Local TV stations often feature cute animals in the news, so a couple of reporters came out to cover the story. But one newspaper writer later contacted the SPCA, and their representative called Brian to complain about taking the animals out of their element. In Bruce Jenkins's article "Buffalo's Soldiers," he described their following conversation on the phone.

"You cannot take a pig out of his environment," the SPCA representative told Brian sternly.

"The pig wanted to surf," said Brian. "He jumped on the board, walked up to the nose, and did a spinner [a 360-degree turn]."

"But pigs can't swim," the animal rights activist said.

"Funny you should say that," Brian responded. "The pig beat the duck in the swimming contest."

"Well, they have hooves, though. They can slip on fiberglass."

"We thought about that. We put on a rubber mat [on the board]."

"But the pigs have no pigmentation. They get burned in the sun."

"Yeah, we put colored zinc all over him. Worked great."

"Brian," the man finally said in an exasperated voice, "could you just help me out and not take that pig in the ocean?"

Not wanting to upset the animal rights groups, Brian refrained from taking out Chop-Chop or their pet donkey into the surf. Although the first annual Wet Pet Contest became their last, Rell and Bruce continued to take their dogs surfing, and they became regulars in the lineup. Rell had thirteen dogs in her life, and they all surfed. The last and most famous one was Shane, who would sit on her porch just waiting for the next surf session. "Dogs go out once, and from that point on, they know they're different," she told *Surfer* magazine. "Shane surfs, he canoes, he rides on the front of my board. He comes back here, kind of crosses his legs on the porch, looks at the other dogs, and he's like, 'Yeah . . . riff-raff.' All animals are that way. From the time they get on that board, they know they're special." After Brian took Chop-Chop out there, Rell says that the pig "acted differently from that day on. Went back to the farm and had an attitude."

As part of their menagerie, Buffalo and Bunky also had pet donkeys that had been given to them by a rancher in Makua. The Keaulanas named their donkey Jenny, and she was a wild one who wouldn't let anyone ride her. Buffalo would goad his friends into trying, and she would just kick up her hind legs and send them flying to the ground. "But that jackass used to run away from our kennel, and she would run down the road, and all the kids would chase her," Buffalo says. Sometimes he would have to lure her back into the kennel with beer, which they liked to drink together.

"I would hold up the beer, and I would pour some out, and she would come running. Heeee-haaww!" Buffalo would have to hold the beer to the side so he wouldn't get run over by Jenny. "And then you pour it into her mouth, and you betta have another one ready. And then I walk her inside." Unfortunately, the Keaulanas had to give Jenny back to the rancher eventually because they were afraid she was going to bite or kick one of the neighborhood kids. But Jenny had trouble adjusting to life back at the ranch. "Because it got that human smell," Buffalo says, the other donkeys would "stay away from her or bite her. It was a hard life for that animal at the ranch, so my friend gave it to another Chinese guy who used it in his banana fields so it could run around. Finally, they killed it and made jerk meat out of her. They make good jerky."

As a hunter and fisherman, Buffalo felt at home in the natural world of predators and prey, even when he came close to being eaten himself. As a girl, Rell used to follow Uncle Buff around like a puppy and watch his every move when he would dive and spearfish. In awe of his natural abilities, she remembers watching once when he paddled out on his board to go spearfishing. After spearing a few fish, Buffalo saw a shark cruising right toward him and the bloody catch in his bag. So he jumped on his board and began paddling toward the shore. "When the shark made a pass at him, he would immediately look in the bag and throw fish away from him," Rell later told *Surfer*. "Now this big crowd's gathering on the beach, tourists and everything, and he's throwing stuff and the shark just keeps coming back to him as a source. All the while, he's paddling toward the beach, and when he got up there, the shark was cruising around on the inside. So he took his shorts off, threw them to the shark and just walked bare-butt down the beach. It was like 'Here, take this, too.' Neatest thing I ever saw in my life."

Although Uncle Buff used to call Rell his "little China Doll," she had grown up to be a fearless woman and an accomplished diver under his tutelage. During one dive near Kaena Point, she paddled out on her board and speared a number of fish and octopus. But her biggest catch that day was when she shot a forty-five-pound *ulua* through the head with her spear and had to dive down thirty-five feet to retrieve it. She looked like a mermaid with her fins and long hair flowing behind her as she descended into the depths. Rell found the *ulua* stuck inside a cave and wrestled it up to the surface holding the spear. After almost blacking out from lack of oxygen, she brought the huge fish to the surface and then hauled it onto her board, which was heavy with the fish and octopus she had caught earlier. When she heard some local fishermen yelling from the shore, she proudly lifted up her catch to show them the huge *ulua,* but they were pointing toward a large dorsal fin coming up behind her.

"I turned my head seaward just in time to see a fourteen-foot tiger shark sliding under the surface barely fifty feet away, knifing toward my board, my sixty-five pounds of octopus and fish, my *ulua,* and my legs, not necessarily in that order," she later wrote in an article about the episode. Torn about what to do, she sacrificed her prize *ulua* and got onto her board and paddled toward shore as the tiger ripped through the fish.

"My lungs, my arms, and the fishermen were screaming as I paddled away from the snapping, churning orgy," Rell said in her story, which she called "The Woman Who Shot Ulua Vance." Growing up in a time when the best divers and surfers were men, she loved being able to hold her own in the ocean. "Out there, under the deceptively placid surface, was a world blind to gender," she wrote. "Though I was taught by men, I was formed by and subjected to the rigid laws of a seemingly lawless realm that treated me and every grazing *ulua* or marauding shark with the same utter equanimity."

Bruce DeSoto became another protégé of Buffalo's and used to go diving with him and learned a great deal by watching him spearfish. Once, as a kid, Bruce followed Buffalo into the ocean one night to hunt for lobsters at a place called Yokohamas, just down the coast from Makaha toward Kaena Point. Diving down, he would shine his flashlight into the dark coral caves below while looking for spiny creatures. While searching, he would suddenly see Buffalo's big hand reaching by his head to pick a lobster hidden on the cave wall right next to him. Uncle Buff had what the locals call squid eye and was able to find lobsters, squid, and other sea creatures that most others couldn't see. Cooking their catch later on an open fire, Bruce heard all kinds of fishing tales on the beach, but the most amazing one was about Buffalo's encounter with a big tiger shark.

Once while diving at Yokohamas with his friends Homer Barrett and "Teddy Bear" Davis, Buffalo speared a big three- to four-pound squid. While watching Buff from above, Homer saw a gray shadow in the distance that looked like a small shark. But the closer it came, the bigger it got. "Buff was coming up with the squid and turning like a corkscrew as he came up," Bruce says, so he could see what was around him. "First he saw Homer pointing, and then he turned and saw the shark. Buff released the squid as the shark approached." Right before the fifteen-foot tiger hit the squid, the creature opened up like a fan and wrapped its tentacles around the shark's nose. They watched the shark go into a frenzy trying to get the squid off, dragging it across the bottom and against the coral. Finally, the agitated shark managed to eat the squid and was now looking right at Buffalo and his two buddies. "*Ope,* time for go!" Buff shouted.

The three guys started paddling in on their boards, with Bear in the middle and Buffalo and Homer on either side. The shark circled them and then came right down the middle with its fin scraping their boards, lunging at Buffalo with its jaws wide open. At that instant, the big lifeguard slammed his fist down on the shark's nose, its most vulnerable spot. "The buggah shakes his head like 'What?!'" Bruce says. The shark then swung around and knocked Buff off of his board with his powerful tail. "Buff falls off his board, climbs back on, and says, 'Let's get outta here! Give the guy another squid!'" He then threw one of their catch to the shark and looked over his shoulder to see the large tiger devour it as they scrambled to shore.

Greg Noll's favorite story about going diving with Buffalo

was when they were in his motorboat one day near Yokohamas. After sharing shark stories, they put on their gear and were about to dive in the water, but Buff held back. "Go ahead, haole; you go first!" he said. After diving in, Greg looked at his Hawaiian friend sitting in the boat, wondering why he hadn't gone in the water yet. Buffalo then looked at him and said, "Anybody stay home?" Meaning, any sharks down there?

Even though they laughed about the danger, the threat of being mauled by a shark was very real. On November 2, 1992, a bodyboarder named Aaron Romento was surfing about thirty yards off of Ke'au Beach Park on the Wai'anae Coast when a ten- to twelve-foot tiger shark suddenly attacked him and bit his leg. Aaron managed to break free, and friends brought him to the beach and called the lifeguards. Pua Mokuau was the first to respond, and she immediately wrapped towels around his legs and tied a tourniquet to stop the bleeding. But as she held the young man in her arms, he bled to death on the beach.

❧❧

Along with life-and-death encounters with wildlife in the ocean, conflicts in the community started to arise between the locals and the soldiers from nearby bases who would come down to party or surf. The tension between these groups stretched back to the time when the first American marines helped overthrow Queen Lili'uokalani and worsened when the military seized control over huge tracts of land during World War II for military bases. In fact, the U.S. military was one of the largest landowners in the state, but what enraged Hawaiians more than anything else was how they used portions of the land for bombing practices. After the bombing of Pearl Harbor, the government began bombing the island of Kaho'olawe, off of Maui, and Makua Valley, down from Makaha, using the land for target practice and war games. George Helm had lost his life trying to save Kaho'olawe from the bombing in 1977, and others were angry that these sacred lands were never returned to the Hawaiian people.

The tension between Native Hawaiians and the military was always simmering beneath the surface, and sometimes just an angry look from a local surfer or a cocky word from a soldier could bring it to a boil. It didn't help that many of the servicemen came down to the beach acting like cowboys while the locals acted like they owned the place and decided who was allowed in the water. "Growing up, I was pretty aggressive," Mel Puʻu says, "and luckily a lot of times Brian was there to calm me down. We always watched each other's backs. We grew up in a rough neighborhood, so you had to learn how to defend yourself and take care of your family." Occasionally, even a hardworking, peaceful lifeguard like Brian could be lured into a fight when he felt someone was disrespecting him, his family, or his friends.

"Brian was a really shy kid who never did drugs, never bothered anybody, but he got into some big scrapes," Mel says. "One night we were out with Brian's sister Jodie. She and her boyfriend got into this hassle with a bunch of military guys, and by the time I got there, Brian was already in full swing. He's flying all over the place, kickin' guys, like a bunch of 'em. I jumped into the pile and I noticed these three big guys were trying to corner him. I picked up one guy and slammed him into a Jack in the Box sign . . . and Brian took care of the other two."

Arguments out in the water could often lead to brawls on the beach. Sitting in his lifeguard tower at Makaha, Mel saw a local guy and a soldier arguing as a group of drunken white servicemen gathered around. Mel remembers them looking like "a big pile of sugar" next to the dark local. After another soldier came from behind and whacked the Hawaiian surfer with the lid of a metal cooler, all hell broke loose. "There was this one guy who was really black in the middle of all of these white guys, and they were jumping on him. All of a sudden, you could see all these black ants come running and overwhelm the pile of sugar," Mel recalls, as he and a big pack of Hawaiians pounced on the soldiers. It turned into a huge brawl. Soon after, the ambulances came and hauled away the wounded servicemen.

"The military actually went in and developed a community relations program to try to get the people to communicate with the military and vice versa, because there was a lot of things like that going on," Mel says, shaking his large bald head. As a lifeguard, he tries to maintain peace on the beach. But as a descendant of Hawaiian warriors, he is willing to fight for control of the land. "We live here; this is our backyard. And then you have someone coming in your house, saying, 'Hey, try move.' Not going to happen. We've been here from the very beginning, and we're going to be here till the end. That's why Wai'anae and Makaha got a big reputation."

Even before the arrival of Westerners, Makaha was known for its fierce fighters and thieves. But after the overthrow of the monarchy, many more Hawaiians were pushed into the corners of the Island. Waimanalo on the Eastside and Wai'anae on the Westside were considered the least valuable areas back then, and Hawaiians were forced to eke out a living on this homestead land through farming and fishing. Like Little Bighorn, Makaha was the last stand, and Hawaiians had to fight back to keep their lands. "In order to live here, you had to be a warrior," Mel says. "This is where you would get the best fighters."

In spite of his reputation as a tough fighter, Mel considers himself a laid-back person who is happiest when he is in the ocean surfing or playing his guitar on the beach. Though he is a talented musician who still performs at lu'au and special events, he knew that he had to get a job as a lifeguard to support himself and his family. He says it was tough for local guys like Israel and Skippy to make a living on their music. "When it comes down to hardships, people do what they need to do to get by. As an entertainer back in those days, you don't make that much money. I'm a musician also, and no one appreciates the talent. I learned a lot from Israel; I learned a lot from all the musicians that came down here. I learned to play by watching."

As a kid, Mel used to fetch beers for guys like Uncle Boogie

Kalama, who taught him how to play slack-key guitar and songs like "Maui Brown Eyes." Playing with Israel and Skippy on the beach, Mel was amazed by how talented they were. But even with their success in putting out a new album every year for four years and performing at big venues, the Makaha Sons were still struggling to pay the bills and make ends meet. Except for the Kamakawiwoʻole brothers, all the band members had day jobs and couldn't survive on just their music gigs.

Whenever Israel and Skippy wanted to escape from the pressures of the modern world, they would return to their family home and go camping at Makua. Here there were no bills, debts, tourists, or record companies, just the natural elements. They could swim in the ocean under the hot sun and relax in the cool of the *kiawe* trees by the beach and then gather with friends and play music under the stars. Living on the land not only refueled their bodies and minds, but it inspired their music. After all, *Makua* means "parent," and this was the mythical land where the first Hawaiians were brought into being. Parts of the valley were so pristine and undeveloped that they used these sites for many historical scenes in *Hawaii,* the 1966 blockbuster movie based on James Michener's best-selling novel. Sacred worship sites and burial grounds could be found throughout the valley.

Yet as sacred as Makua Valley was to the native people, the U.S. military continued to use the area for live-fire target practice long after the war. Government officials had tried to evict the Kamakawiwoʻoles and the many other Hawaiian families who had set up camps on the beach, but they kept coming back, insisting that this was their land first. Makua became a rallying cry for many activists like Frenchy DeSoto, who was now chairwoman of the Office of Hawaiian Affairs. The nearby surf break was called Free Hawaiʻi in protest of the military's occupation of the land.

"Makua Beach is like standing in the middle of the Pacific

Ocean and having the United States on one hand and Hawai'i on the other," Skippy once told a local reporter. He had come down to interview the Kamakawiwoʻole brothers about their rising popularity and political consciousness. Being younger and less serious, Israel just listened and let his older brother do most of the talking. "Where else can you go in the world and have a nice sunny day of picnicking with your family and directly behind you in the valley they bombing and having maneuvers? While you enjoying part of your land, at the same time you watching part of your land destroyed. That's what hurts so much.

"One day we were there and had a lot of small children, including Auntie Frenchy's little grandchild," Skippy added. "And she's on the sand and we were in the water and watching her. They started to bomb and that girl went crazy. She so frightened and she ran up to her grandfather and she grabbed him and just hid her face in his chest because she was so afraid. You know, brah, we all had tears in our eyes because that's what we must leave for our children today," Skippy said, with both anger and sadness in his voice. "She is so innocent, as innocent as the beach itself."

With the continued bombing of Makua and Kahoʻolawe, Skippy and Israel would take their feelings of frustration and depression and channel them into their music. They started playing regularly at a place called Hank's Place in their old neighborhood of Kaimuki, where they developed a devoted following. Four nights a week, they would perform a diverse array of Hawaiian songs and Israel would entertain the crowd and call out local politicians in the audience to return the land to the people.

Toward the end of the evening, they would become more serious and sing "Hawaii '78." The song was written by their friend Mickey Ione about the imagined return of Hawai'i's last king and queen and their reaction to what had become of their kingdom. The solemn lyrics and haunting melody moved the rowdy crowds to tears and silence, and the song later became the anthem of the emerging sovereignty movement:

If just for a day our king and queen
Would visit all these islands and saw everything
How would they feel about the changes of our land?
Could you just imagine if they were around
And saw highways on their sacred grounds
How would they feel about this modern city life?
Tears would come from each other's eyes
As they would stop to realize
That our people are in great, great danger now.

For the refrain, they sang the immortal words of King Kamehameha III: *"Ua mau ke ea o ka 'aina i ka pono,"* which translates as, "The life of the land is perpetuated in righteousness." These words later became the state motto and a rallying cry for Native Hawaiians. As the final part of the refrain, the Sons then sang these heartrending words: "Cry for the gods, cry for the people / Cry for the land that was taken away / And then yet you'll find Hawai'i." Whether Hawaiian, Asian, haole, or anything in between, people in the Islands were moved by these lyrics. The words struck a chord deep inside locals and tourists alike about the loss of Hawaiian land and their culture.

CHAPTER 9

Over the Edge

I not scared myself for dying 'cause I believe all this is just temporary.
This is just one shell, because we Hawaiians, we live in both worlds.
—Israel Kamakawiwoʻole

When Keoni Watson was growing up in Makaha, he was one of the only blond-haired haole kids in his school. He looked like Casper the Friendly Ghost next to his dark classmates. Originally from Kansas, his parents, Mike and Sarah, had moved to Makaha after serving in the Peace Corps in the sixties. They had worked as teachers in Iran for two years and decided to check out Hawai'i on their return to the United States. In spite of its fierce reputation, they chose the Westside of O'ahu, because the local schools were recruiting new teachers. With the Vietnam War still raging, the Watsons had been looking for this kind of remote outpost. "This was as far away from my draft board as I could get at that time," Mike laughs.

One of the Watsons' friends from the Peace Corps lived in Honolulu, and they invited him to come out to their new place for a visit. But he said that it was too dangerous out on the Westside. "He wouldn't even come out here, and we'd gone through the whole damn world together!" Occasionally the Watsons and their two kids would drive down the coast just past Makua, where the road ends, to sit on the beach. Looking out over the endless blue of the Pacific, the couple must have felt like they were living at the edge of the world. Like Dorothy in *The Wizard of Oz,* they had wandered far from their native home in Kansas, but they liked living in the land of rainbows.

Though Makaha seemed like a rough area at first, the Watsons gradually grew to love it. After meeting the Keaulanas and the local families, they began to feel more at home. "We knew nobody here, and they just welcomed us in, especially Buffalo and Rell and those people at the beach." Still, it was tough for haole kids like Keoni and his friend Mark Cunningham, who were trying to blend into the local scene. "As a kid, I remember I didn't go to school on the last day of the seventh grade because that was 'Kill Haole Day,' and that was in the lily-white suburbs of Niu Valley," Mark says. "I can only imagine what being a haole in Wai'anae High School was like . . . Sometimes, it was just a look [what the locals call stink eye] or the slightest eye contact that could provoke an ass-kicking." But Keoni's father says that his bright-eyed son survived just by smiling at everyone and assuming they were friends.

Even though he had a Hawaiian name and spoke pidgin, Keoni felt like a kook at times because of his almost white hair and limited surfing skills. But once Rell took him under her wing and he became friends with Brian, Rusty, and Jimmy Keaulana, he was adopted into the local tribe as their blond-haired mascot. It was hard for them to imagine that years later he would go on to become one of the top surfers in Hawai'i.

Keoni's first surfboard was a beat-up old board that his father found in a Dumpster. To make matters worse, Keoni was naturally goofy-footed and always went left at Makaha, which is a right-hand break. The shy blond-haired kid would catch waves and ride them straight toward the shallow coral reefs. "Rusty grabbed me one day as I was coming up the beach, and he goes, 'Hey, brah, you're going to hurt yourself. Brah, you go left, and Makaha is one right. You gotta go backside.' So he was kind of teaching me," Keoni says.

Naturally goofy-footed himself, Rusty had learned to surf backside and then switch stance on his board like his father so that he was facing the wave as it broke to the right. He helped teach Keoni to go backside, showed him new tricks, and urged him to get a better surfboard. One day after history class, Rusty approached Keoni's father, Mr. Watson, and said, "Ho, you gotta upgrade that kid's board." Rusty had always been a rascal in class, but Mike appreciated his looking out for Keoni. Together, they found a used board, which had an airbrushed psychedelic design on the bottom that Keoni said looked like the measles. But it was better than his old board from the Dumpster, and it helped improve his surfing.

As a young boy, Keoni looked up to the Keaulanas and was blown away by their surfing abilities. "Rusty and Jimmy were the hot guys, and Brian was like the badass," Keoni says. "He had a cover shot on that Makaha issue of *Surfer,* hitting the backwash. It's all glassy, and he's totally in the air. That issue is awesome because it's all about Makaha."

The cover shot and article marked a turning point for the community, bringing the new generation of hot surfers out of obscurity and into the spotlight. Still living on the Westside with Rell, Jeff Divine began publishing more of his photos of the Keaulana boys, while she wrote a couple of articles about the Westside gang in *Surfer*. Jeff was later asked to be the photo editor at *Surfer* in San Clemente, California, and he agonized over whether to take the position. He didn't want to move away or be apart from Rell, yet they both knew this was a dream job he couldn't refuse. After the couple parted ways, his photos of her, Brian, and the Makaha gang continued to appear in the magazine like postcards from Jeff's time there.

Brian had been stoked to see his picture on the cover of *Surfer*, but he was humble about the publicity he received. This may have been partly because he realized that his younger brother Rusty was slowly becoming his equal, if not a better surfer. "Brian would be the first to admit that Rusty had the most talent in the family," Keoni says. Part of Rusty's talent came from his restless energy to try anything and a relentless desire to compete. Whereas Brian was trying to be the best he could be, Rusty seemed so competitive that he needed to be better and have more sponsors than his brother or anyone else. Along with being able to switch stance, Rusty could do tricks like a 360-degree turn on a longboard that most surfers couldn't do even on a shortboard.

Rusty was also known for his love of joking around and playing pranks on people. Although he wasn't a great student, he did have a clever sense of humor. When the film *Apocalypse Now* came out, Mike Watson says Rusty went around class asking everyone if they had seen the new movie *Opaka Lips Now*. Then the practical joker would cross his eyes and purse his lips together like a fish. Because his parents were health-food nuts, Keoni wasn't allowed to have candy, so he was constantly bumming sweets from the other kids at the beach. One day, Rusty asked if he wanted to try this new kind of candy called ex-lax, and the naïve haole kid just gobbled up the chocolate laxative!

"I go home that night and just lost my guts," Keoni laughs. When he explained to his parents what happened, his dad decided to talk to Rusty. The next day at school, Mr. Watson told him, "I heard you gave my kid ex-lax." Rusty mumbled, "Uh, yeah, I think so—maybe it was my cousin." Mr. Watson laughed and said, "Good, teach that kid a lesson." Rusty admitted that Brian had pulled the same trick on him a few days before.

In spite of Rusty's pranks, he helped Keoni become a better surfer and encouraged him to start competing. Rell Sunn also took a liking to the little towheaded kid and wanted him to enter her Menehune Contest. But Keoni didn't think he was good enough. "I had always heard about Rell's contest, but I was really shy about it," he told surf journalist Bruce Jenkins. "But Rell got on my case, and she wouldn't let up. She would come by every day and tell my mom, 'We gotta get Keoni in the contest. It's the best event—nobody loses; everybody wins; everyone gets a prize. It's a great day.'" Keoni was still self-conscious about his old board and his abilities, but Rell kept working with him on his backside form and teaching him about different wave conditions.

"I was still scared about the contest, but one day I come home and there's an unreal, beautiful thruster in the house," Keoni said. "Used, but in really good shape. Rell had brought it by for me. Now I had no excuses. I had to go surf that contest. I can't remember if it was that year or the next, but I wound up winning the surfing and bodyboarding divisions. I walked down the beach with five dollars and came home looking like I'd robbed a store. I had a brand-new surfboard, brand-new bodyboard, a pair of fins, two trophies, and two bags full of wax, stickers, all kinds of stuff. And I knew right then. This is me. This is what I want to do." Rell encouraged Keoni to enter more amateur contests and shared her secrets for winning. In 1982, she was at the top of her game and ranked second in the women's World Tour, so she knew her stuff. Even when she was away, Rell still kept in touch with Keoni. "I'd get postcards from all over the world where she was on tour.

"She taught me all kinds of things about strategy," Keoni told *Surfer*'s Bruce Jenkins. "She's the sweetest person, but you should hear the stuff she taught me to do in heats! I mean heavy, no-prisoners stuff. And it worked. I listened to everything she told me. It was always me, Ross Williams, and Jason Magallenes in the top three around Hawai'i when we were growing up. And even then, she still took care of me. Every night she'd have at least three things going on—parties, dinners, speaking engagements—and she'd always talk my mom into letting me go along. If I was late for something or didn't do my homework, she'd tell my mom, 'Sarah, the waves were so good, the inside section was just going off,' and my mom couldn't even get a word in. She knew Rell was teaching me all the right things."

Rell also helped Keoni get his first corporate sponsors, introducing him to some of the top surfers and executives in the growing surf industry. "She had style," Keoni says. "There would be some industry thing, and she'd say, 'Hey, come with me. It will be good for you to come and meet these guys. But we're going to surf beforehand.'" After driving into town and surfing at Ala Moana Bowls before the big banquet, they would change into their party clothes in the parking lot. "She'd be doing her eyelashes on the way there, driving the VW Bug. And then she'd get there and just look beautiful. All the other girls had been primping for hours, and Rell would just walk in and she was the knockout." Rell would then charm the bigwigs and introduce them to her blond prodigy.

With his winning smile and fun-loving personality, Keoni made friends with the biggest names in the industry. He would follow up and write them letters, and they would send him shirts and clothing. His father says Keoni soon accumulated several sponsorships, which he kept in folders in a little briefcase. "So he comes in, the surfer with his briefcase, and points out his portfolio [of sponsors]." Unlike Jeff Spicoli, the stoned surfer played by Sean Penn in the movie *Fast Times at Ridgemont High*, Keoni was a sharp kid who knew what he wanted.

The sponsors loved him because he was polite, professional, and eager to build a career in surfing. "We never bought the kid anything other than underwear," his father laughs. "We never had to buy him any clothes or boards because Rell got him sponsorships." She also motivated him to join the National Scholastic Surfing Association (NSSA), where he competed in California against the best young surfers in the country and became friends with future world champs like Kelly Slater.

Just as Keoni was rising up through the amateur circuit, Rell was climbing the ranks of women's pro surfing in 1982. She was poised to become a champion when her life suddenly changed. While competing in Huntington Beach, Rell was drying off on the beach after a heat when she felt a strange lump in her breast. Touching her chest, she could feel her heart racing and hoped it was just a cyst. Rell could be fearless in the face of towering waves, but this little lump scared her more than any wipeout she had ever experienced. She eventually went to the hospital, and the doctors put her through several tests. Rell was too young for something like cancer, and as a single mother without health insurance, she couldn't afford to get sick.

"It was very traumatic," she said later. "After the examination, I sat there while six different doctors came in and out of the lab, all looking at me and nobody saying a word. I already knew before they told me." Yet she was devastated to learn about the malignant tumor and angry that the doctors had treated her so coldly, without offering any support. Rell was only thirty-two and couldn't believe this was happening to her. "I'm the kind of person it can't happen to. I was running ten miles a day, surfing every day. I was never sick." She flew home and shared the news with her family, the Keaulanas, and other close friends, who seemed more upset than Rell. But she was determined to fight the cancer and had no doubt that she would win.

Gradually, news of Rell's cancer spread through the "coconut wireless network," but she didn't have the heart to tell Keoni. Rell would come over to talk with his mom, and he would find them both crying in the kitchen. "She kept telling me everything was fine, but I knew something was wrong," Keoni told

Surfer. "Finally, one night we were at this party down the street from my house. I was hurting so bad inside, I couldn't stand not knowing anymore. I guess she looked at me and knew it was time. So she said, 'Why don't you go home, go to sleep, and later I'll come wake you up and we'll talk surf talk.' I went home and didn't sleep at all; I was just waiting there. Sure enough, she came over and told me what was going on. I just cried for days. And, of course, for Rell it was about *me* having a problem now. She was consoling *me*."

Keoni's mother later developed breast cancer, and Rell began a support group to help her and other women going through the same painful process. "She helped my mom out a lot," Keoni says. "My mom had the same thing but not as bad. She had surgery too, so it was good because she was right there for my mom and talked her through the whole thing. She was really supportive and told her what to do. They caught it early."

Keoni began spending more and more time with Rell. "I remember going to her house, and she'd be like, 'Did your mom take the wheat grass?' It was amazing how she was still there for so many people, regardless of what she was going through. . . . She was always like, 'Oh, everything's good,' but you know she was hurting. But you would never see it. That was what Auntie Rell taught me—make everybody feel like they're the most important person at that moment." With her daughter boarding at Kamehameha School, Rell took comfort in Keoni's upbeat and youthful presence. He was like a son to her. "Rell was his surrogate mother," Mike says. "Keoni would spend his whole summer in her lifeguard stand."

After having her lymph nodes removed and going through radiation treatments, Rell threw herself back into surfing and tried to put the whole cancer behind her. To make some extra money to pay for her hospital bills, she began doing surf reports for a local radio station. That's where she met the radio personality Frank B. Shaner, who wanted to know more about the beautiful young surfer from Makaha. "Surfing was her thing, and I just sort of picked it up and went along for the whole ride," Frank recalls after meeting her at the station one day. On one of their first dates, they went surfing in Makaha and he was blown away by how good she was. "I watched her surf and said, 'Hey, wait a minute, you are fantastic! Where did you learn to surf like that?'" Only later did he realize that this local wahine and part-time DJ was also a pioneer pro surfer. Rell looked so healthy that he had no idea about her cancer.

When Rell first invited Frank to surf at Makaha, he was a little intimidated about interacting with all the big local brothers who were very protective of Rell. Although he had native roots and was a popular DJ and comedian, he was still a "town guy," born and raised in Honolulu. "I have Hawaiian blood. My mom is Hawaiian-Chinese-Portuguese. My dad is German, Irish, Dutch, Scotch and water!" Knowing laughter is the best weapon to disarm people, Frank used his sharp wit and self-mockery to entertain the locals. He often joked about the fact that he was balding by saying his Hawaiian name was Nohea, which means "handsome" in Hawaiian but also sounds like "no hair." Although he made inroads into the community, Frank knew he was a long way from town and his humor could only take him so far on the wild Westside.

"There was an element out there that was pretty rough, no doubt about it. There were some pretty bad characters out there," Frank says. "Some boys would hurt you just to hurt you. It's good to know who you know and be humble. . . . It's about respect and knowing what the hell is going on, who's who and what's what." He jokes that even the dogs had hostile attitudes and could be incredibly aggressive. "One dog attacked my car, boom!" he says. "I had a big dent in my door. I looked in the rearview mirror, and the frickin' dog gave me the paw, the dirty bastard!" But after dating Rell awhile and getting to know the Keaulanas, Frank was gradually given a warm welcome in Makaha. "Once you make friends out there and once you show you're sincere about their whole life out there, then you can be brought in and be a brother real fast." He and Rell eventually decided to make it their home.

"We got married on the beach at Makaha," Frank remembers. "She looked so beautiful. She was dressed in white and had flowers in her hair." It was an informal wedding with a large group of friends and fellow surfers, DJs, and musicians. One of the Islands' top performers, Henry "the Wild Hawaiian" Kapono, served as a groomsman, and his wife, Pam Ka'aihue, was one of the bridesmaids. Henry had been one of the first Hawaiian musicians to achieve international success with his band Cecelio & Kapono, and the duo traveled all over Asia and America.

During the reception at the Makaha Resort, Henry played along with the Makaha Sons. The Keaulanas and all the big local families were there to help them celebrate. After an evening of eating, drinking, and dancing, everyone stumbled out into the darkness and went home. Frank had moved into Rell's place at Makaha and was looking forward to spending some quiet time with his new wife. But they were inundated with a steady stream of visitors, and he soon learned why people called her small cottage Rell's Motel—because her door was always open. "People would just walk in the house, go in the icebox, and say, 'Hey, Auntie, what you got?' "

Brother Iz visited them on occasion and would park outside in his truck. Because it was so difficult for him to move around, Rell and Frank would often come outside and talk story with him as he strummed his 'ukulele. She would share some of her freshly caught *poke* (raw fish), which she had just cut up and seasoned, and they would eat, drink beer, and look at the ocean. Iz would tell stories about his wild evenings performing at Hank's in town and partying almost till dawn. He never wore a watch or seemed to worry about anything other than playing his music and having a good time. "Israel was just a frickin' free spirit, man," Frank says. "He was always just a child, and he had this attitude about him that was just beautiful. When he would play his 'ukulele and sing, you'd look at him and hear that delicate sound coming out of this mountain of a man."

Although the Makaha Sons were quickly becoming one of the bigger groups in Hawai'i, Israel and Skippy were having financial and health problems. Most of the members had day jobs, but for the Kamakawiwo'ole brothers playing music was not just a career; it was their life. No matter what was bothering them, they would always try to put on a good show and find comfort in their guitar and 'ukulele and the sound of Hawaiian music. "What you see on stage is four guys just having a blast," Skippy once told a reporter. Yet Skippy went on to say that what fans didn't see was how "really depressed we are." While performing, they seemed happy and full of life, yet behind the scenes both brothers were struggling with obesity, depression, and a growing frustration about the condition of their people.

Raised in a devoutly religious home, the Kamakawiwo'ole brothers were frustrated about the injustices they witnessed every day while commuting to town to perform. Driving through the Westside, they couldn't help but witness the poverty of its people and the homeless groups camped on the beaches across from massive military bases and luxury condominiums. They could feel every pothole in the road and could smell the stench drifting down from the landfill and the smoke from the oil refinery. They could see the Hawaiian flags flying upside down in front of many homes, and they understood the symbolic gesture. After all, the Hawaiian kingdom had been overthrown and their culture turned upside down.

The Westside had become a dumping ground for the Island's refuse and industrial wastes, and all these things left a bitter taste in their mouths. Sometimes that bitterness was directed at haoles, and Iz was known to provoke fights with guys he felt were disrespecting him, his band, or his culture. Yet once they had a few beers and started playing their instruments onstage, the music tended to melt away any lingering resentment. Occasionally, they would play popular songs from the past like the

Byrds' hit "Turn! Turn! Turn!" whose timeless lyrics could be traced back to the prophet Ecclesiastes, who seemed to sum up the spirit of the times: "To everything there is a season, and a time to every purpose under the heaven: A time to be born, and a time to die . . . A time to weep and a time to laugh."

One night while driving home from a performance on Maui, the guys in the van spotted a car stuck in the middle of the road with a flat tire. It was raining, and a couple of tourists were trying to change the tire. But the jack had buckled and was stuck underneath the car. The Makaha Sons and their intimidating crew of big Hawaiians got out of the van and walked up to the driver, who looked scared to death. Skippy asked what the problem was, but the haole guy just stared at them helplessly as if they were going to eat him. In an interview with music critic Jerry Hopkins, Skippy recalls what happened next:

> We say, "What's the matter, brah? You need help?" He just looks at us. So we all went over and picked up his car and said, "Okay, brah, change the tire." We stood there holdin' up the car until he got the tire changed and we put it down [Skippy recalled in his poi-thick pidgin]. The whole time, his girl is inside the van, staring at us. She cannot believe what she see. Finally, the guy was *pau* (finished) and we gave him an album and said, "Here, brah, this is us. Always remember the Makaha Sons of Ni'ihau."

The band also had a soft spot for community causes, and they would volunteer to play for free at baby lu'au and local fundraisers for hula *halau* and canoe clubs. They sometimes did several gigs in one day, but playing so much for so little money began to take its toll on the band. Though generally kind and generous, Israel was known to erupt like Kilauea Volcano on occasion and his molten anger would pour out in a stream of epithets against haoles.

One day in 1981 while driving their van through Waikiki, Israel, Skippy, and Donna saw a white guy pushing a baby carriage right in front of them, as if challenging them to stop. They swerved and screeched to a stop to miss the stroller and the tourist, who yelled at them. Already infuriated that the man would endanger his child this way, Israel exploded when he heard the tourist's comments and jumped out of the van to confront him. Israel and the tourist got into an argument. Before Skippy could stop him, Israel punched the man in the face and broke his jaw. The cops arrived soon after, arrested Iz, and took him to jail. He was later convicted of assault and battery and sent to prison, but his time there would be short-lived.

While imprisoned at the Oʻahu Community Correction Center, Israel was last in line to receive his meds when he found himself surrounded by four Samoans, who suddenly jumped him. Though big and heavy, Iz was fast, and he struck a couple of them down. A big fight broke out between the Samoans and the Hawaiians, who started climbing the fence to help the popular singer. The fight turned into a riot, and it took guards a while to break up the rival gangs and rescue Iz. Fearful of another riot, the warden transferred Iz to a local hospital where he was treated for his wounds and the extreme cellulitus in his legs.

Lying in bed, he tried to recuperate and figure out how his life had turned into such a mess. It was only when he hit bottom that he realized what he had been longing for all along: love and companionship. Staring at the ceiling, all he could think about was his childhood sweetheart Marlene. While the world seemed to be spinning out of control, Iz would close his eyes and see her face. Just recalling the first time they met and their ongoing conversation over the years would bring him a sense of peace.

Shortly after moving out to Makaha as a teenager, Israel had run into the pretty young Hawaiian girl named Marlene Kuʻupua Ah Lo. Both of their families were camping on the beach when the teenagers struck up a conversation. "We met in high school," Marlene recalls. "I was fourteen, and he was sixteen. He was going to Waiʻanae High." She was a pretty hula dancer who had grown up in ʻAiea near Pearl Harbor. After swapping family histories, they later realized that they had played at the same playground as kids. Although they lived on different sides of the Island, the hefty 'ukulele player became infatuated with the slim hula dancer. After they exchanged phone numbers, Israel went home and wrote her number with a red Magic Marker on the kitchen wall. "Back then, he used to tell me he was going to marry me. He would even tell my mom, and I would tell them that he was a sick puppy, because that wasn't even in my thoughts back then."

Because Marlene lived in town and Iz was way out on the Westside, they didn't see each other much. But he always kept in touch over the years. "He used to always call me, and I was like a big sister to him. He would tell me about his girlfriends, friends, and family," Marlene says. She adds that he didn't actively seek trouble, but it always seemed to find him. In fact, she says his sister Lydia used to call her, asking, " 'Can you talk to him? He's not listening; he's not behaving.' So we would just talk, and he would listen." She always had a calming effect on him.

When the Makaha Sons started performing in town, Israel would invite Marlene and her sister to come to their performances at bars like Hank's Place. "We used to go and watch them play, and they would call us up to dance [the hula]," Marlene says. A talented dancer, she later joined a hula group that spent two years performing in Japan and across the United States. It was during that time that Israel began to spin out of control. When she finally returned to Honolulu, Marlene heard that he had been calling and asking for her. She was stunned to hear about the riot at the prison and his illness.

Wanting to help, Marlene went to see Israel at the hospital. "So I ended up going to visit him," she says, "and that's when everything started up again." Walking into the room, she couldn't believe how big he had become. But there was still boyish playfulness in his eyes that she couldn't resist. Israel couldn't believe how beautiful she was just standing there, looking like the answer to his prayers. During another visit while they were busy catching up, a haole man appeared in the doorway. Israel realized it was the tourist whose jaw he had broken. It turned out that the man was a pastor and he had come to reconcile with the big Hawaiian. It was a stiff and awkward conversation, but at least they made peace.

Although the state couldn't drop the assault charges at that point, they didn't send Iz back to prison. Instead, Marlene says, "he had to do community service and pay a fine." During this low point in his life, he had rediscovered love, and it had given him something to live for. It seemed like he was getting his act together. Iz would eventually go back to prison years later, but this time it was to perform for the prisoners, most of whom were Hawaiian. During one benefit concert, a prison bell rang and Israel immediately shouted, "Recess!" The inmates cracked up laughing. But deep down, his heart ached for those brothers like himself who were locked up in their own cells of anger, resentment, addiction, and obesity.

Not long after reuniting with Marlene, Israel proposed to her; and to his surprise, she accepted. During his performances, he would boast about his fiancée and invite her to dance hula while the Makaha Sons sang. He was in love and wanted the world to know. The Keaulanas would drive in from the Westside to watch them perform, and Frank and Rell would drop by after working at the radio station. And that's how Marlene got to know Israel's extended 'ohana from Makaha. Israel would always acknowledge his friends in the audience and "talk story" about playing pranks with Brian and Rusty as kids and learning to surf from Buffalo. "It was just like one big family," Marlene says. "There's so much love. . . . Uncle Buff was like his father, and Auntie Momi was like his mother."

The Makaha Sons' record sales continued to climb up the local charts. They won critical reviews from music critics like Jerry Hopkins, who had written for *Rolling Stone* and penned biographies of Elvis and Jim Morrison. In the liner notes of one of the Makaha Sons' albums, Hopkins wrote: "The Makaha Sons do again what they always do so well—mix the old with the new, wearing their rich Hawaiian heritage like a feather cloak, yet never denying modern ears and tastes."

In spite of the band's rising popularity and his own engagement to Marlene, Iz was restless and always looking for some new sensation. Before and after gigs, he would smoke a little weed, get the munchies, and then eat incredible amounts of fast food. He also began experimenting with drugs and partying all night, all in the vain hope that some elusive high might satisfy his cravings. Skippy could only watch in frustration as his younger brother drank too much and pissed away his talents.

Marlene was equally upset about Israel's antics, but he had a way of charming her into forgiveness. He would apologize, sing her a song or share a funny story, and then they would make up. As Iz and Marlene grew closer together, he and Skippy gradually grew apart. They both had serious health problems that were causing problems with the band. "Israel and Skippy would get sick all the time, so there were no commitments," Marlene says. "Gigs were paid up front, and they couldn't commit. Moon would have to play or gather [other] band people to play. So Moon just said, 'Let's take a break.'"

Louis "Moon" Kauakahi grew up in Makaha and had been with the band from the beginning, but he was frustrated with the Kamakawiwo'ole brothers. The valedictorian of his class at Nanakuli High, he went on to become a serious student of Hawaiian music, language, and culture. As a soldier in the army reserves, he was punctual and responsible and resented Skippy's health problems and Israel's partying, so Moon decided they should take some time off. It was a tense time because he was married to their sister Lydia and the family was being pulled apart. During their extended break, the brothers began going stir-crazy. Marlene says they both needed to go back to work. "For the two boys, there was only their music."

When they resumed performing, Skippy organized a weekend "powwow" at Makua for a group of Native Americans and his Hawaiian friends so they could share their cultures. Having worked with the Aleutian Natives in Alaska, Buff and Momi helped organize the event, and they were amazed by the outpouring of indigenous stories and music. With their experience organizing the Buffalo Big Board Classic concerts for years, the Keaulanas also helped the Indians and Hawaiians set up a new annual festival called Our Celebration of Hawai'i.

The all-day outdoor show was held at the 'Ohikilolo Ranch in Makua with many Hawaiian bands and hula dancers. Building on the former glory of the Buffalo Classic concert, the celebration was now the biggest event on the Westside. Thousands gathered in the valley to hear the Makaha Sons and bands like the Brothers Cazimero. Onstage, Israel and Skippy acted like nothing was wrong and put on a great show. The crowds kept asking for one more song, yelling, *"Hana hou! Hana hou!"* Behind the stage, close friends and family could see the tension between the two brothers, but no one realized that this would be the last time they would ever play together.

While Skippy brooded over issues like Hawaiian rights and sovereignty, Iz was more concerned about drinking and having a good time, even if it meant missing gigs or inconveniencing the other band members. Skippy tried to set him straight, but he knew that his spoiled younger brother would just continue doing whatever he wanted. The tension between the two brothers rose until they finally stopped speaking to each other. Even though he was engaged to Marlene, Iz continued partying around town. Meanwhile, Skippy stayed at home strumming his guitar, retreating into a cocoon of sadness and resentment. Envious of his younger brother's immense talents and angry that he misused them, Skippy could feel his pulse race; at times like his heart was literally breaking.

The tension finally escalated when Skippy asked the band members to meet for a rehearsal for an upcoming show. Israel said that they didn't need to rehearse because they had been playing together for years. As the older brother and leader of the group, Skippy insisted that not practicing was unprofessional and lazy. So he gave Israel an ultimatum and said that he needed to call by Friday at midnight to let Skippy know if he was coming to the rehearsal. If he didn't call, Skippy would take it as a sign that Iz wanted to quit and they should break up the band.

At a time when the family should have been coming together for Israel's wedding, they were being torn apart. As the deadline approached, the distance between the two brothers widened. "Skippy was up and down all that night," his wife, Donna, said in an unpublished interview with Jerry Hopkins. "He'd lie on that couch and then get up and pace and then lie down on the floor. Midnight came and Israel never called." Afterward, Skippy confessed to his wife, "My heart is broke."

The impasse between the two brothers grew to such a point that Skippy missed the most important day of Iz's life. On September 18, 1982, Marlene and Israel were married at a local church in Kalihi, and Skippy never showed up for the ceremony. Marlene and Israel had the reception at 'Ohikilolo Ranch in Makua Valley, where the family had spent so many summers lounging and singing together on the beach. Although they had only invited five hundred guests, almost a thousand showed up. But Skippy was not there. "We got married, and he never came to the wedding," Marlene says with a sad look in her eyes. Israel got sick at the reception, partly from partying too hard the night before but also because his brother wasn't there, so he and Marlene left early. Skippy's absence had cast a shadow over their big day, but this was nothing compared to the darkness he would cast over their lives three weeks later.

On October 1, Henry "Skippy" Kamakawiwo'ole's heart finally broke. He died of a massive heart attack at the age of twenty-eight. "We never got to see him or talk to him. So that hit Israel really hard because that was his oldest brother," Marlene says. "He was like the man of the family."

During his memorial service at a mortuary in Honolulu, hundreds of friends and fans came to pay tribute to Skippy. Hawaiian music filled the room as performers from all over the Islands played their guitars and 'ukulele and sang their final farewells. His family was gathered around the huge casket, which was surrounded by horseshoe-shaped stands of flowers. Friends whispered their condolences to his wife and sisters as they filed past the coffin and took one last look at the gentle giant of Makaha.

During his eulogy, Jerry Hopkins spoke about Skippy's deep spiritual devotion, his love of family and friends, and his deep concern for the land. "This past summer, Skippy organized a campout on Makua Beach, inviting a group of American Indians to join him and his friends," Jerry said in a trembling voice, "to exchange legends, music, dance, sports, and crafts. He learned there were others who cared about the land, the planet, and what was happening to it. It was appropriate, I think, that we could hear the rockets exploding in nearby Makua Valley. Skippy's message that week, voiced over and over and over again, was that it was his generation that was charged with the preservation of the 'aina. If there is one word to describe Skippy, it is 'aloha.'"

After the service, a long caravan of cars drove out to the Westside. Gathering at his favorite beach, friends watched as the family spread his ashes in the ocean at Makua. Israel and the Makaha Sons sang some of Skippy's favorite songs. They were flooded with memories of the countless times that they had all sat and played music together on this beach, singing all day and into the night. All of their old friends were there with them, including Rell and the Keaulana clan. Uncle Buff and Brian remembered watching Iz and his brother swim and ride their wooden *paipo* boards in the blue waves and marveling at how agile these giants were in the water. While the band played,

Skippy's wife, Donna, performed a hula in his honor, and then she dove into the water where his ashes had been scattered.

Devastated by his brother's loss, Israel felt like he had fallen over the edge of a steep cliff and was drowning in despair for months after the funeral. He tried to get the band members back together, but their leader was gone. After playing several gigs without Skippy, the band took a year off to rehearse and try to find their new sound. Eventually, Louis "Moon" Kauakahi would emerge as the new leader, setting up the gigs and making sure they rehearsed. But it was Israel who continued to be the voice and personality of the band, and he would be the one to carry on his brother's spirit.

Skippy's loss was tempered somewhat when Israel met the second love of his life. Within a year of Skippy's death, Marlene gave birth to a baby girl named Ceslieanne "Wehe" Kamakawiwoʻole. Wehe would become incredibly close to her father, and as a child she would climb over this mountain of a man. Although there would be many ups and downs in his relationship with Marlene, their love of Wehe always brought them closer together. Just as Iz took care of her as a little girl, she would later help her mom take care of him when he became seriously ill. Having suffered through his brother's death, he began to see his family and friends and even life itself in a new light. Israel came to believe there was only a thin veil separating this world from the next, and at times he felt like he was living on both sides.

CHAPTER 10

◑◐

What It Means to
Be a Lifeguard

*When beholding the tranquil beauty and brilliancy of the ocean's skin,
one forgets the tiger heart that pants beneath it.*

—Herman Melville

When Mark Cunningham became a lifeguard in 1976, his first assignment was at Poka'i Bay on the Westside. The hit movie *Jaws* had come out in 1975, and many people were still afraid to go in the water. But Mark was more worried about the locals on the Westside. "I was living in the lily-white suburbs of Niu Valley, and they made the rookie hop through the hoops and drive as far as he could." As a "skinny haole kid" from town, Mark was well aware of the fact that older guards referred to the Waiʻanae Coast as the "Wild, Wild West," where there was "only one road in and one road out."

After meeting Buffalo and the Keaulanas, Mark says his opinion of the Westside changed. "He and the rest of the family have been nothing but warm and welcoming and nice to me. I was part of the lifeguarding ʻohana." Mark later moved out to what he calls the Californicated North Shore, where he was a lifeguard for almost thirty years, but he never forgot the kindness of the Keaulanas. As a world champion bodysurfer, he often returned to Makaha to compete in the Buffalo Big Board Classic. After three decades of service, Mark knows what it means to be a lifeguard, and he has seen their image change dramatically.

"Early on, a lifeguard's reputation was sort of saddled with the Waikiki beach boy kind of stereotype," Mark says. "A lot of people thought of lifeguards as just there to hit on the girls or go surfing . . . But that stereotype was there for a good reason. We used to have a damn good time at the beach, whether we were in uniform or not. I imagine the same thing was happening out on the Westside. It's like the further you get from Honolulu, the more flexible, shall we say, the rules and protocol become. I know we were having a real good time on the North Shore back in those days, and I assume the same thing was going on out on the Westside. . . . We got away with a lot of shenanigans, but, thank God, no one ever got hurt or died due to us not paying attention. Everything's just evolved and grown and become more efficient."

Mark says that a lot of the changes were due to the leadership of Brian Keaulana, who wanted to see lifeguards become more professional and respected. "It's just been a real effort over the years with a lot of people trying to change that image,"

Mark says, referring to the stereotypes about lifeguards. "We are first responders; we're in public safety; please think of us as you do police, firemen, and paramedics."

With all the social and health problems on the Wai'anae Coast, Brian could see that the local first responders were spending most of their time just putting out domestic fires and reacting to drug-related crimes. But he believed it was better for lifeguards to work with the community and become more proactive in preventing crises. He had watched his father break up many fights and then try to teach the local kids a lesson. "Dad tells them, 'You gotta remember one thing—God is watching you guys. Tell God to forgive you—look up and ask God forgive you and forgive each other. Now shake hands—shake hands before I make you guys kiss.' " Like Buffalo and Rell, Brian wanted lifeguards to become more like mentors for young people in their community. Their job was to watch over them in the water *and* on the land. But it was a tremendous challenge trying to save many teenagers and young adults from the treacherous undercurrents of drugs and crime that were taking over parts of the Westside.

"My whole life, there were always drugs around; there were always thievery and violence," Brian says. "I could've ended up like a lot of my friends: some of them are in jail, some of them died, and some of them lost their minds because of drugs. As kids, you take chances, not realizing that you have a choice. I think the next generation needs to understand good and bad choices." Growing up in Makaha, Keoni Watson says, "I managed to stay clear of all the kind of stuff that can sidetrack you. . . . On the Westside, if there's no surf and nothing to do, it's trouble. But I was lucky because I had guidance from Rell and Brian."

If Brian was working at the beach and kids like Sunny Garcia cut class to go surfing, he would make them sit under the lifeguard tower until school was out. Brian didn't want the younger kids cutting school or doing drugs. "I thought it was so cool that he didn't drink and didn't smoke," Keoni says about Brian. "I wanted to be a badass like him. We'd go to an awards banquet and the swipe would be going around, and Brian would just say, 'No, thanks.' He would just do his own thing." Although he was mature for his age and serious about his career as a lifeguard and surfer, Brian still had a youthful innocence about him. In fact, Keoni says Brian would often sit up in his lifeguard tower, reading comic books about Superman, Spider-Man, and the Silver Surfer. "Here's this badass, legendary surfer, and the guy's reading comic books up in the lifeguard tower—it was hilarious!"

As straitlaced as Brian was, some of his friends were much more mischievous. They used to hang out with guys who were drinking too much, doing drugs, and getting into crime. There had always been a lot of pot and booze, but then cocaine and crack became more available. Part of the problem stemmed from the U.S. government's so-called War on Drugs, which ended up doing more harm than good.

In the eighties, the feds initiated Operation Green Harvest in Hawai'i to eradicate the growing and distributing of marijuana, one of the least addictive and least harmful drugs around. Although the campaign was eventually successful in reducing the amount of *pakalolo* available in the Islands, the vacuum was filled with crack and ICE, two of the most addictive and destructive drugs ever invented. According to Brian's uncle, Ants Guerrero, these drugs devastated the community. "You used to buy a bag of pot for ten dollars but no way nowadays," Ants says. "But they sell ten dollars of that ICE, and you take that a couple of times, and bingo, you're the Boogeyman. You're up all night, and you're instantly hooked."

While many reckless teenagers were experimenting with beer and pot, the ones who tried ICE or crack often became hard-core addicts. But Keoni says he decided to stay far away. "I just never wanted to get involved with anything creepy because I knew it would break my parents' hearts and it would break Rell's heart. I never wanted to fall out of their good graces because I had so much to gain by learning and hanging with them."

Along with mentoring many younger kids in Makaha, Brian and Rell would spend endless hours in their lifeguard towers just watching the kids frolic in the small surf. But the waves and rip currents in Makaha could change rapidly, turning deadly at times. So the local guards had to be vigilant, waiting for something to happen and trying to anticipate accidents. Like his comic book heroes Superman and the Silver Surfer, Brian was always ready to spring into action to save someone's life; but he also knew that he was risking his own life in the process. Before the use of Jet Skis, Brian says, "the rescues before were real dramatic, life-and-death kind of stuff." Once, as a rookie lifeguard, he had to make one of the most daring rescue attempts of his life. The waves were huge, and the guards had been pulling people out of the surf all morning.

Then, way out in the distance, Brian saw a tourist sprawled out on a rental surfboard and paddling toward the big outside sets. More conservative guards would have waited until he got into trouble, but Brian was more proactive. "That's ninety percent of being a lifeguard, being preventive," Buffalo's old friend and fellow lifeguard Kimo Hollinger says. "But then you gotta be able to put your life on the line when you gotta do your job."

Brian grabbed his big, orange rescue board and went after the tourist. Paddling out, Brian saw a monstrous wave rise up and crash down on the man, who was now floundering in the white water. Brian managed to grab the man and put him on the front of his board and start paddling outside of the impact zone. But seeing a huge wave rising up on the horizon like a tiger ready to attack them, Brian turned toward the shore and told the man, "Look, our chance of survival depends on how hard you can hang on." They went flying over the falls of the enormous wave, bouncing in front of a roaring wall of water.

Miraculously, they managed to stay on the board together as

Brian steered them to a small patch of beach sandwiched between jagged rocks. "The guy bent down, grabbed my legs, and
just started thanking the Lord," Brian says. After catching his
breath, the bronzed lifeguard asked the man if he had ever surfed.
The tourist said, "No, I never did." Incredulous, Brian asked,
"What made you paddle out? You know how dangerous this wave
is?" The man said he had just flown to Hawai'i and, looking out
the plane window, he thought, "The surf looked billowy." Brian
had never heard of the word "billowy," but he put it in his report.
Then he went home that night and looked up the word in the dictionary. He couldn't believe that the man thought those giant
waves were soft and cloudlike. "It's amazing," Brian says. "It was
life threatening." Over the years, he encountered many people
who were equally naïve about the power of the ocean. "Anyone
can comprehend the beauty of the ocean," Brian says, "but it takes
a certain kind of person to understand the beast." Recognizing his
dedication and ability, his superiors promoted him to lieutenant.

As Brian rose through the ranks of the lifeguard service, he
also continued to surf competitively. Sponsored by Town & Country, Hawaiian Style, and other companies, he was known for his
ability to surf anything from two to twenty-five feet, using all
kinds of equipment from shortboards to longboards, from outrigger canoes to bodyboards. When they introduced tandem surfing
to the Buffalo Big Board Classic, Brian decided to add that to his
repertoire. Having seen a pretty hapa woman named Kathy Terada perform with former champion John DeSoto, Brian asked if
she would work with him. Ten years older than Brian, Kathy was
a nurse-practitioner who worked at the Wai'anae Comprehensive
Health Center. She knew Rell Sunn and Pua Moku'au from her
hula class and started hanging out with them at the beach. Kathy
got to know the Keaulanas, who welcomed her and her husband
into their extended family. "When we used to have the Makaha
Concerts in Makua Valley, Rell used to dance hula with Kathy
and Pua," Brian says, "and Israel would play music with the
Makaha Sons of Ni'ihau." It was like one big 'ohana.

Talented athletes, Brian and Kathy began training and practicing their moves on the beach. Then they would go out surfing and he would lift her into a series of poses like the Star, where he would hold her above his head with one hand on her back while she formed a graceful arc. Their mind-boggling acrobatics helped them win many tandem events at the Buffalo Classic, and Brian would often take home trophies from the other events as well. But the contest was set up in such a way that if you accepted the first-place prize, you couldn't compete in the event the next year. So Brian would usually give away prizes like brand-new surfboards to good friends or younger, less fortunate kids. During these ceremonies, Kathy used to watch the local girls just staring at the tall, handsome Hawaiian.

Though young and available, Brian was shy around women and so dedicated to surfing that he was practically married to the sea. But Kathy, Rell, and Pua began thinking that he needed to find a good woman. Nobleen Cabanilla was one of the cute local girls who used to come down to the Buffalo Classic to watch the concerts. She was a friend and fellow hula dancer with "Brian's angels," which is how Momi referred to Rell, Kathy, and Pua, the three women who looked after him. They decided to set Nobleen and Brian up on a blind date without telling either of them.

"Do you want to come with us to a C and K concert at the Shell?" the three women asked Nobleen, who said she'd love to go. "Okay, our friend's going to pick you up," they explained. "We'll meet you there." They then asked Brian to pick up their friend Nobleen and take her to the Waikiki Shell, the outdoor amphitheater where Cecilio & Kapono were performing. When Brian went to get her, Nobleen says he arrived in "an old red Pinto that had all *kine* stickers and was falling apart." Apparently, the stickers were the only things holding the car together, because when she went to open the door, it fell off! He managed to get the door back on, and they had a chance to talk and get to know each other on the long drive to the Shell. At the concert, they all sat on the grass under the stars and listened to popular C&K songs like "Friends" and "Good Times Together."

After that first date, Brian and Nobleen started dating. The shy surfer and talkative dancer made a handsome couple, yet they had different interests. Brian was more committed to surfing and lifeguarding at that point, and she was dedicated to her hula *halau* and their upcoming performance at the Merrie Monarch Festival. Besides, Nobleen often felt like she was competing with his love of the ocean. "I wasn't too into surfing," she admits, "so Kathy would tell me, 'Oh, you know, Brian Keaulana is famous. . . . He's da *kine;* he's Somebody.'" In local parlance, this was high praise. But Nobleen says, "I wasn't one of those girls who idealized him." Brian went to the Merrie Monarch Festival that year, and seeing her perform in the Miss Aloha Hula Competition, he was taken by her graceful beauty onstage. She, too, was Somebody.

Gradually, the Westside's most eligible bachelor began to realize that Nobleen was the woman for him. After three years of dating, Brian finally asked her to marry him after they took a romantic trip to Maui for Valentine's Day. He says the most frightening moment of his life was when he and Buffalo went to meet Nobleen and her dad so he could ask for her hand in marriage. They were at the Pagoda Restaurant, looking at the koi and other fish in the pond, nervously waiting for Nobleen and her father to show up.

As Brian walked over to welcome them, he heard a splash and Buffalo's voice, screaming something like, "I got 'em! We should fry 'em up!" Brian looked back to see his father lying on his stomach on the side of the pond, holding the tail of this large fish. Brian was mortified that his dad would do such a thing on the most important day of his life. But then he saw Nobleen's father running over to take a look at the fish. It turns out they were both fishermen and they laughed as Buff finally let go of his big catch. Both parents agreed it was a good union, and a date was set in August of '89. But planning for the big event would prove to be a challenge.

When both families put together their list of people to invite, there were more than one thousand names on it. Worried about the rising costs of the wedding, they tried to cut back on the number of invitations. But the list just kept growing, surpassing two thousand guests. Between Brian, Nobleen, and their families, they seemed to know everyone on O'ahu and across the Islands, especially those involved with surfing and hula. The food setup alone was staggering, and Brian decided it was better to have too much than not enough. "We had ten humongous pigs, one thousand pounds of fish, two hundred pounds of *'opihi* [a small mollusk], and a crazy amount of food at the Makaha Resort," Brian says, shaking his head with a laugh. "We had seating in front for one thousand, seating in the tent for one thousand, and seating in the back for one thousand. We had six bars and four humongous food lines." Of course, a reception this size could have bankrupted the bride's family, but Nobleen says, "There was a lot of planning, and everybody helped out. People donated pigs and fish and stuff like that."

The wedding itself took place at Makaha Beach, where they had set up a big tent and a red carpet in the sand. It was a traditional service designed for Hawaiian royalty. The bride and groom each had eight members in their wedding party to represent each island and their different-colored sashes. Mel Pu'u was Brian's best man, and his two brothers were groomsmen. Nobleen's best friend was her maid of honor, and her two sisters were bridesmaids, along with Pua and Kathy. After Nobleen and her father proceeded down the red carpet toward the water, Kahu Kealanahele, a well-known minister from the Big Island, conducted the service and pronounced them man and wife. With the sun setting behind them, the couple and wedding party posed for pictures at Carlton Beal's huge house on the Point. A long white limousine then took the newlyweds up the valley to the Makaha Resort. There they would be honored at one of the biggest parties of the decade. Over three thousand people showed up for the reception at the resort!

The most famous entertainers in Hawai'i appeared onstage that night, including the Makaha Sons, the Brothers Cazimero, and Henry Kapono. "Israel performed, and Rella danced. We had so much top entertainment," Brian recalls. "Everybody donated their time." Henry Kapono came by the wedding table and sang some of the songs Brian and Nobleen had heard at the Shell on their first date, including "Good Times Together" and "Friends." Rell's husband, Frank Shaner, was the emcee, and he made jokes about the size of the crowd. After announcing that Nobleen's *kumu,* Palani Vaughn, and his dancers were going to put on a show, Frank invited Nobleen to do a dance. Watching her perform a hula in her long white dress as she smiled lovingly at her husband, the crowd went wild.

"It was like the biggest May Day Pageant extravaganza you've ever seen, with colors and music and flowers everywhere and tons of people having a good time," Mark Cunningham says. Pops Aikau had made plenty of swipe, and the old-time surfers were passing around jugs of the potent mixture. Old friends like Greg Noll and Henry Preece were there, along with Wally Froiseth and George Downing. "There were a lot of great watermen and surfers from throughout the state there, a lot of legendary old-timers from the Neighbor Islands," Mark adds. The huge gathering was like a who's who in the worlds of surfing, hula, and entertainment. Because of the enormous expenses of the wedding, which had gone way over budget, friends of the couple had put calabashes around the hall, and almost everyone donated. Amazingly, Brian says, the donations covered almost all of their added costs down to the dollar!

After they were married, Nobleen soon realized that Brian's first love was still surfing. He was a dedicated husband, but he was also a die-hard waterman. Though worried about his safety, she knew there no way she could stop him from trying to ride the biggest waves he could find. When winter came around that year, fierce storms in the Aleutian Islands began producing large swells that rolled thousands of miles across the Pacific gathering size and strength before they hit the north and west shores of O'ahu. The bigger the waves, the fewer surfers who could handle their power. Always ready to ride, Brian became part of an elite group of big-wave surfers called the Makaha Point Screamers. This group included legends such as George Downing, Buzzy Trent, and Greg Noll, as well as up-and-comers like the Keaulana brothers, Keoni Watson, and Mel Kinney.

While the biggest north or northwest swells often close down the North Shore, they can produce huge, barreling waves at Makaha Point. Sitting out in the lineup, surfers can see the swells coming toward them like blue, moving mountains. "I never saw a place that put the fear of God in me like Makaha," Greg Noll once said. Only a handful of the best and bravest surfers could ride these mammoth waves, which break hundreds of yards from the shore. Only the most knowledgeable local surfers knew exactly how far to paddle out to find the lineup where the waves break. Big-wave rider Mel Kinney said that Brian taught him to keep paddling until he could see at least two of the three round weather-dome stations at the top of the distant mountains. If it was really big, Mel says, "you gotta see all three balls." Mel might as well have said that you need three balls to surf waves that big.

When Quiksilver sponsored the first big-wave contest at Waimea Bay in honor of Eddie Aikau, it was natural that Brian was invited to the epic event. There had been a holding period of three months because the waves had to have at least thirty-foot faces. On the overcast morning of February 23, 1986, George Downing, the contest director, stared at the massive waves thundering across the Bay and debated whether they were too big and dangerous. Then he announced that the competition would begin in an hour. Brian was nervous but ready.

Thousands gathered to watch the ant-sized surfers paddle

into the giant-sized waves. Brian was in the first heat, and he says, "Everyone is kind of over-amped, and that's when people get hurt." Like Eddie, Brian was a lifeguard first and a competitor second. This meant that he was often more concerned with watching out for the other surfers than doing well in the contest. After paddling into one of the beasts, Brian wiped out and fell almost twenty feet before being slammed against the water. The force of the wave pushed him down against the ocean floor and pinned him beneath tons of churning water. When he finally came up for air, another wave came crashing down on him. It seemed like nobody would be able to save him.

"The first year that we had the 'Eddie' at Waimea, we had lifeguards on rescue paddleboards," Brian remembers. "I was a competitor in this event and took a few really bad waves on the head and got worked to the point where I almost blacked out and gave up. I remember after coming up from taking one on the head and there was Squiddy [Sanchez] on a stand-up Jet Ski right there in the impact zone asking me if I was all right. He couldn't grab me in time with that type of Jet Ski, but amen, he kept a watchful eye. I was so shocked that he was in so close to me. Then at that moment a thought came to my head, and I told myself, 'If I survive this whole nightmare, I am going to look for some kind of Jet Ski and do the research to develop a rescue technique for this type of situation.'" Brian managed to swim in and compete in his second heat, but he was still shaken by his wipeout. In an emotional climax to the contest, Eddie's brother Clyde barely beat Mark Foo and ended up winning the event.

"I did a whole lot of research that night, and the next day I quickly bought a Yamaha Waverunner," Brian recalls. From that day forward, he became a man possessed with ocean safety. Partnering with an older lifeguard named Terry Ahue, Brian began training on the Jet Ski, also known as personal watercraft (PWC). Terry was a Vietnam vet who had worked as a lifeguard with Eddie Aikau at Waimea Bay, where they had saved hundreds of lives. The old-school method on the North Shore was to wait until guys got into serious trouble and then paddle out on a big rescue board to bring in the victims at the last minute—the idea was to teach them a lesson. "Us young guys would say, 'Let's get 'em *before* they get into trouble!'" But the older lifeguards would tell them to wait until the victims yelled for help. "I'm like 'you gotta be kidding me,' but that's the way they did it in those days."

Lifeguards were often hired to help out with safety during surf contests as well. Previously, a gang of local surfers called the Black Shorts had wrestled their way into "keeping order" and providing safety at the big events. But Fred Hemmings resented the group's strong-arm tactics and said that they represented the "thugs and drugs" of the North Shore. So he brought in Brian and Terry to do water patrol. Working with some of these guys, they brought a new level of professionalism and safety to the contests. Brian knew most of the Black Short "bruddahs" and hired these guys to help out during the contests as a peace gesture. He and Terry also began training them how to do Jet Ski rescues.

Just as Buffalo did water patrol during the Duke Contests at Sunset, Brian and Terry began working with Fred to help with the big Triple Crown events on the North Shore like the Pipeline Masters. "Dad used to do the water patrol in a Boston Whaler," Brian says. "That's where we learned the whole theory of water patrolling on a Jet Ski." They worked with Yamaha to refine the engine design so the PWC could go faster and be more reliable. Collaborating with Mel Puʻu and Dennis Gouveia, they designed a rescue sled and attached it to the back of the PWC.

During rescues, one guard would drive and the other would be on the sled ready to pick up the victims. They practiced pickups in the water and tested the weight limit by trying to pull Israel behind the ski. "It was more like one dare because we were close with Israel," Brian says. "He said, 'That thing cannot hold me,' and I said, 'Yeah, it can. Jump in the water.' " The engine strained and they worked hard to get his voluminous body onto the sled, but they were able to carry the Gentle Giant to shore! Another time, they rescued a group of ten Japanese kids, who all fit on the sled.

After testing their equipment and practicing rescues, Terry and Brian felt like they were finally ready for the big waves on the North Shore. When they showed up for the first time on their Jet Ski at the Smirnoff Contest at Sunset Beach, Fred asked them what they were doing. "This is the way we're going to do it," Terry told him. Terry and Brian explained that paddleboards were too slow, that the boats were too big and dangerous because they could be capsized by big waves, and that their propellers could injure someone. But Jet Skis were smaller, quicker, and more maneuverable, and there were no external propellers. During the contest, Brian and Terry demonstrated how the ski could outrun the waves and rescue surfers in a moment's notice. At another event, they raced out between sets and saved a kneeboarder, who had almost died after falling down a huge wave and hitting his head on the reef.

"That's how the whole thing started, and it just took off!" Terry says. That year, he and Brian formed a company called Hawaiian Water Patrol, and they were hired for almost every major event on the North Shore. But the city and county lifeguards weren't using the new technology at all. Brian and Terry talked their supervisor, Ralph Goto, into asking the City Council to buy Jet Skis for each lifeguard district. "So Ralph said, 'Okay, we'll see what we can do and we'll bring the City Council people down there for a little demonstration at 'Ehukai Beach Park [near Pipeline].' "

City and county officials and bureaucrats opposed the use of Jet Skis at first because they were too new and weren't being used anywhere else. Besides, the county had already purchased an expensive fleet of Inflatable Rescue Boats (IRBs), which the Australian lifeguard service had promoted in Hawai'i. Brian and Terry called the IRBs rubber duckies partly because they felt like sitting ducks in the face of large waves. In fact, they took one out in big surf at a place called Avalanche on the North Shore and a large wave just buckled and destroyed the vehicle, whose deflated remains later washed up on the beach.

During the demonstration at 'Ehukai Beach Park, Brian, Terry, Mel, and other lifeguards performed mock rescues in the traditional way, using swim fins, rescue boards, and IRBs, all of which were slow and ineffective in the powerful six- to eight-foot surf. City Council members then watched in amazement as Brian raced his Jet Ski into the impact zone between waves, Terry grabbed the victims and put them on the sled, and they zoomed out of harm's way, all in a matter of seconds. The demonstration by these young lifeguards greatly impressed the City Council members, and their old neighbor John "the Flyin' Hawaiian" DeSoto helped convince the group to support buying a fleet of Jet Skis for lifeguard districts throughout Hawai'i.

After getting the City Council's approval, Brian and Terry then had the more difficult challenge of convincing the state officials who were in charge of boating. In 1988, the state was on the verge of banning Jet Skis in the Hawaiian Islands. According to Jim Howe, "There was an accident out in Hawai'i Kai, where somebody let their six-year-old son ride a Jet Ski and the kid lost control and killed a woman that was paddling a kayak." At the time, many people believed that Jet Skis were just dangerous, loud toys and that thrill-seeking surfers were recklessly using them to tow each other into huge waves. But Brian was convinced that they could greatly improve ocean safety, and he went around the state giving talks and demonstrations.

At one community meeting on Kaua'i, an angry local fisherman took the microphone and started attacking Brian, saying the Jet Skis were dangerous and loud and went against tradition. "He listened to the whole thing, then got up and said that he understood," recalls Jim, who was sitting in the audience with his parents. Brian went on to explain, "We're all a part of the same culture, and to really make our community better, we have to use the technology that's available to us." In his diplomatic way, Brian transformed the hostile situation by saying how lifeguards now combined traditional Hawaiian wisdom with the best modern equipment.

"'We have ancient knowledge, but we're using high-tech weapons these days,'" he said. "It was masterful. Everybody realized that what he was saying was true," Jim recalls. "I was sitting behind Buff and Momi, and I could see tears rolling down his mother's face. Tears of pride. And it had to be Brian. Nobody else could have done it so well." After his talk, the fisherman apologized and the audience applauded the young lifeguard. The attempt to ban Jet Skis was abandoned, and they soon became a crucial piece of equipment in the lifeguard service across the state and eventually around the world.

In the early nineties, Brian, Terry, and the lifeguard team went to New Plymouth, New Zealand, for the World Rescue Boat Championships to demonstrate the use of Jet Skis. At the opening ceremony, Brian gave a brief talk about how effective Jet Skis had been in rescuing people. But the Australians felt threatened by the skis because they had pioneered the use of IRBs. Terry recalls that a group of Aussies challenged them, saying, "Hey, mate, let's race! Let's race my boat against your Jet Ski. We'll race all the way to that flag and then see who can get in first." By the time the boys from Down Under got their "rubber ducky" through the waves, Brian and Terry were already zooming their ski back toward the beach. "All the Aussies are just looking like 'whoa, whoa,' and after that, they're all interested," Terry says with a laugh. In fact, the next morning he and Brian came back and found the Aussies had "hijacked" their Jet Ski and were riding it all over the place!

The Makaha crew did a similar Jet Ski demonstration with Southern California lifeguards and the crew of *Baywatch*. Often referred to as *Babewatch*, the series was the most watched TV show in the world at that point. Created and produced by Greg

Bonann, the show was loosely based on his experience as a Southern California lifeguard, but its success was more likely due to Pamela Anderson's large breasts and skimpy bathing suit rather than her lifeguarding or acting skills. During that time, Brian got to know world champ Kelly Slater, who made guest appearances on the show and began dating Pamela.

In spite of all the Hollywood melodrama on and off the set, the show brought a lot of needed attention and money to a department that was traditionally overlooked and under-funded. Although the Southern California lifeguards had better funding to buy helicopters and rescue speedboats, they couldn't compete with Brian and Terry's Jet Skis. They were just faster and more maneuverable in picking up victims, and soon the Hawaiian guards were teaching the California lifeguards their new rescue techniques.

After getting to know Brian and his crew and seeing how well they performed, Greg Bonann would later resurrect his TV show in the form of *Baywatch Hawaï*. Brian would play a major role in front of the camera and behind, and he had high hopes of using actual Hawaiian watermen to show how real rescues were done in the Islands. But the producers opted instead for more skimpy bathing suits, slim plotlines, and flimsy actors. After two years, it was canceled, but the show brought in a heightened awareness of Hawai'i's lifeguards and needed money for Brian and his growing family.

In 1992, he and Nobleen had a baby girl named Channel and, immediately after her birth, Momi called her friend Kaupena Wong and asked the *kupuna* to help them find a proper Hawaiian middle name. Nobleen wanted the name to reflect her love of hula, but Brian wanted it to signify his love of the ocean. "I wanted some kind of joy or love that ties these two names together," Momi says. "He calls me and says, 'Kai Ha'a Le'a.' That means the 'joyful dancing sea.'" She went by Ha'a for short. Two years later, Nobleen and Brian had a boy whom they named Chad, whose Hawaiian middle name, Keanu Kalani Ku'a Kapu, means "safe and peaceful under the heavens." Nobleen says that like his father, Chad "needs all the safety he can get because he's a daredevil."

Brian and Terry could have patented their use of the Jet Ski and rescue sled and made a lot of money in Hollywood and from lifeguard departments around the world. After all, Surf Lifesaving Australia had charged other lifeguarding groups for the use of the IRBs and other equipment. But the guys decided against it. "That's one thing Brian is real clear about—if you have this knowledge, the best use of it is to share it," says Ralph Goto, the ocean safety administrator. "That's the kind of guy Brian is. I think he's smart enough to see the potential, but his philosophy is to share."

From then on, his and Terry's training programs just took off, and they were invited to do demonstrations across the globe. "We ended up in Taiwan and Hong Kong—the guys would treat us like kings!" Terry says. They taught guards throughout Asia and Europe how to use Jet Skis in their rescues and revolutionized ocean safety in the process. While serving as a lieutenant, Brian had basically been in charge of the Westside. In recognition of his leadership, he was promoted to captain of the Leeward District and later received the Eddie Aikau Waterman Award for his innovative reforms.

Brian was one of the youngest lifeguards ever selected to become a captain, a position usually given to older guards who had gradually risen through the ranks. "But Brian was a pretty obvious choice out there because he's such a part of the community," says Mark Cunningham. "He has unquestionable water skills, and he wanted it. He wanted to take the bull by the horns and make some improvements out there that could still work with the Westside culture." He brought in radical new training techniques like running with rocks underwater. He and the other lifeguards would dive down, pick up a big rock, and run on the bottom for twenty yards. They would then come up for air, go back down, and take the heavy rock a half mile out to sea. To random tourists snorkeling above, it must have looked like these local guards were building an underwater temple.

As captain of the Westside, Brian had to contend with the fact that he was now his father's superior. "It was hard being his boss and his son at the same time," Brian says. But after working as a lifeguard for thirty-four years, Buffalo decided it was time to pass the torch to a new generation. He finally retired in 1995, and there was a huge party in his honor at the Makaha Resort. Hundreds of people attended, including the governor, the mayor, and old friends like Greg Noll and Henry Preece. Seeing all the dignitaries paying homage to Buffalo, Greg says, "Henry and I looked at each other like 'Can you believe how far he has come?' It was like he was an *ali'i*. The respect level was so high it was like he was Duke Kahanamoku."

When he took over, Brian says that many of the lifeguards didn't understand the importance of their work. "They just existed from nine to five, sitting in the lifeguard tower, waiting for their paycheck. They had no sense of value before." So he tried to instill in them a new sense of pride. "When I was captain for this whole district, I wanted to give a sense of value back to the lifeguards, not only in themselves but in the area they are guarding and the people they are guarding."

Along with a new sense of professionalism, Brian wanted lifeguards to be more accountable, alert, and prepared. "It was Brian who initiated the 'morning muster' there at the Poka'i Bay substation," Mark says. Instead of just going directly to your beach as they had done in the past, Brian gathered the guards together several mornings a week to talk about the wave and weather conditions, discuss preventive measures, and design new rescue techniques. "He definitely improved the lifeguard department by what he did out there in District Four."

Craig Davidson was nineteen when he and his friend Jason Patterson became lifeguards out in Makaha. Craig was a handsome Hawaiian kid who wore gold chains around his neck and liked the image of working on the beach, where he could surf, look at girls, and rescue people on occasion. But when he started working under Brian, Craig soon learned how little he knew about what it meant to be a real lifeguard. He was selected to be a Jet Ski operator, and his training suddenly went into high gear.

At the morning muster or on the beach, Brian would challenge the other guards to think about what they would do in every kind of emergency scenario. "He gets you thinking what you're going to do," Craig says. "He's always testing your mind. When he was captain, everybody wanted to work because he would motivate you. That's what Brian taught not only me but all of the lifeguards: just prepare yourself before it happens. . . . When you're a rookie, you don't know what you're doing. . . . The adrenaline is kicking in, and you don't know what to do, you're freezing up. It takes years for it to be routine." Two years after becoming a lifeguard, the young rookie saw Brian in action and discovered the truth of those words.

A complex, paradoxical man, Brian can be both humble and confident, easygoing and ambitious. After becoming captain, he vowed to become "the world's greatest waterman and teacher of ocean survival." He began taking all kinds of ocean-safety and risk-management courses with the military and sharing the lessons he learned with the other guards. During one of his classes, Brian was teaching Craig and a group of rescue operators in a worst-case scenario workshop. "One of the things we talked about was my father's rescue when I was a small kid when he went into the cave." Brian explained how Buffalo had gone into the coral cave to rescue the two kids but was unable to save the father. Brian then asked the class what they would do, and they went over many different rescue scenarios. He even took a group of lifeguards to the spot to practice. But nothing could have prepared him for the bizarre fact that he would perform one of the most challenging rescues of his career in almost the exact same spot.

On January 25, 1993, Brian and Craig were practicing rescue pickups on the Jet Ski in the ten-foot waves at Makaha when they got a call on the radio: "Swimmer in distress near Yokohamas." Seeing the fire engines and police cars racing down the road, they took the ski down the coast to a place called the Moi Hole (named after a type of bottom fish that lives there). They soon learned that a man and his girlfriend had been standing on a sharp-edged cliff taking pictures of the volatile surf when a wave broke over them and swept the man over the side. He was trapped in a coral cave, just like the one Brian had seen the dead man float out of twenty years before. "I was faced with the same situation as my father," he says. Meanwhile, the chief of the lifeguards had called Buffalo to ask him if he should let Brian and the other guards try to swim into the cave. "Tell Brian, 'Don't go into the cave.' They should yell in," Buffalo recalls. "But I had a feeling that he was going to go in, so I just prayed a little bit."

Circling the area on the Jet Ski, Brian looked for signs of the man, but nobody had seen or heard him. "We were thinking it was a body recovery, so we pulled back, not taking any chances because the surf was so extreme. Kaena Point was huge," Brian says. "And just when the biggest set was coming through, we pulled back, the water sucked out, and the guy was in the back, yelling, 'Help me! Help me!' Then, we knew the guy was alive in the back of the cave, which is the worst scenario that we were thinking about."

While trying to rescue the guy, Craig watched in amazement as Brian tried swimming toward the cave. "I was telling him, 'Don't go in there—your dad would freak out!' I was telling him all kinds of shit, but he still went." On one pass through the frothy white water, the Jet Ski slammed into a sharp rock, which pierced the bottom and broke the engine. Craig managed to swim the ski out of the impact zone before the next wave crushed him against the rocks. A helicopter hovering above threw Craig a rope and towed him and the ski to shore. During a lull, Brian swam onto a nearby rock ledge. He then called on his emergency radio for Pua Moku'au, the lifeguard on duty at Makaha, to bring down the backup Jet Ski. She also picked up another lifeguard named Earle Bungo on the way.

Earle didn't know how to operate the ski, so Brian drove and put him on the rescue sled. In between the sets, they tried backing the ski into the mouth of the cave and yelling for the man to try to swim out. Meanwhile, inside the cave, the man could barely hear their shouts over the roar of the waves washing in and out of the dark cavern. Cut, bruised, and barely conscious, he realized that he would probably die if he didn't make one last effort to jump into the churning water. When the man finally crawled out of the cave, Brian and Earle moved in immediately. "I didn't even think but just went," Brian recalls. "We just gassed the ski in, and I said, 'Earle, hang on!' Earle grabbled the victim, and when we punched through the first wave, Earle and the victim slipped off the back of the sled. But we were prepared for that because we had the rescue tube and the rope [tied to them], so all I did was pull them into a safety zone."

The crowds on the cliffs yelled and clapped as Brian and Earle brought the victim to safety. As they tended to the young man's wounds, Brian says, "he had cuts and bruises, and it looked like someone had a bat and slammed him all over the place. But he had no major injuries. It was a miracle that he survived." The man was shivering and still in shock. His girlfriend said that his name was Hugh Alexander and he was a lawyer visiting from San Francisco. The paramedics noticed something clutched in his hand and saw the keys to his rental car. After being washed off the cliff and swept into the coral cave for two hours, Hugh had managed to hold on to his car keys throughout the whole ordeal. The next day, the victim called Brian and Earle and thanked them for saving his life.

The entire rescue was captured on film by a local guy who happened to have his video camera that day. The footage was later edited and put into a TV show called *I Witness,* which aired all across the country. At the end of the video, Brian paid tribute to his dad. "I'm grateful to my dad for teaching me about the ocean," Brian said. "The fact that he went through a similar rescue before and he shared the information with me really helped out tremendously." Later that year in San Diego, Brian was given the U.S. Lifesaving Association's Medal of Honor, their highest award. The Lifeguard Department began using the video as part of their training program for new guards.

❧

Until that rescue, Craig Davidson thought he knew what it meant to be a lifeguard. "I thought I was hot shit. I had the gold chains and gold earrings," he says with a laugh. "When that rescue happened, it was a rude awakening. . . . What that rescue taught me was to ditch all of the gold chains because it made me realize what level of lifeguard I wanted to be. Brian was up at the top with Melvin [Puʻu], and we were these young lifeguards thinking we knew everything. That was a defining moment in my lifeguarding career. I was like, 'Shit, I want to be like them.'" Craig also began working with Brian and Terry on the Hawaiian Water Patrol, helping out with water safety at the big surf contests on the North Shore and on movies being filmed in Hawaiʻi.

"Brian's taken his knowledge, and he's spread it into the movie industry, and he's spread it into the surfing industry," says Jim Howe. "The contribution that he's made is not just to the community of Waiʻanae and the Leeward Coast, but really to the whole world through the sharing of his knowledge, his *manaʻo* [meaning], and his ability to help people—it's a huge contribution."

During his tenure as a lifeguard, Brian helped transform their image from glorified beach boys into respected first responders. He also helped them embrace the best technology, and their equipment went from fins, flotation devices, and bullhorns to Jet Skis, ATVs, and waterproof radios. Yet in spite of his accomplishments, Brian was restless and ready to take on new challenges. After providing water safety for shows like *Baywatch* and films like *Point Break,* he decided to do more film work. That's when he took some time off from lifeguarding and dove into the making of *Waterworld,* the big Hollywood film starring Kevin Costner that began filming on the Big Island in the mid-nineties.

Originally hired to provide water safety for the film, Brian and Terry soon caught the eye of the stunt coordinator, who wanted to see if they had what it takes to be stuntmen. During one training on a barge out in the ocean, the coordinator asked them to take Jet Skis down the ramp, run through an obstacle course, and come back to the barge. After finishing the course, Terry and Brian were zooming back to the barge when they decided to try to jump the Jet Skis up the ramp and land them on the deck! The other guys on the barge shuffled back and stared at these daredevils as they flew through the air and landed perfectly on the barge. The stunt guys gathered and were talking when the coordinator came over and said, "Terry, Brian, why don't you guys go over there and sign a contract. I want you guys to work with us on the stunt team."

Suddenly they were making more in three months as stuntmen than they earned all year as lifeguards. Although *Waterworld* was the most expensive movie ever made at the time, the plot was basically a watered-down adaptation of the apocalyptic *Mad Max* series (the desert being replaced by the ocean, thanks to global warming). The film floundered in theaters, but Brian learned a lot about filmmaking and enjoyed his work as a stuntman. Afterward, he made the difficult decision to leave the Lifeguard Department for a while and build up his company, Hawaiian Water Patrol, so he could pursue work as a stuntman and ocean safety specialist full-time. Although it was a risky move, Brian was eager to expand his knowledge of the ocean and his interest in film.

"Every day you get up, you have a choice," Brian once told Jim Howe. "And the choice is you can write another page in your book and keep growing and keep learning and trying to help people, or you can say you know it all and close the book. The choice is yours every day you get up." Even though he was no longer a captain in the Lifeguard Department, his primary mission was still ocean safety. "For those that have made that choice to go out and share the message, they're making a difference," Jim says. "And really what they're doing is carrying on that same body of knowledge that came from Buffalo and so many others. The *mana'o* comes from the centuries, it comes from everyone that passed before us this way, and the bits and pieces they were willing to share made us all richer and stronger."

CHAPTER 11

☜☞ ☜☞ ☜☞ ☜☞ ☜☞ ☜☞ ☜☞ ☜☞ ☜☞ ☜☞ ☜☞

Makaha Goes International

The journey is the reward.
—Chinese proverb

Ever since she was a young girl at the Makaha International, Rell Sunn had dreamed of traveling to far-off places. "People from all over the world came to Makaha," she says. "There were men telling these great stories, and I swore then that women could tell these same wonderful stories and I would enjoy that same life they lived. I just knew surfing was my life." As a pro surfer, she was now living the dream and competing in contests in Australia, Japan, South Africa, and Brazil. Unable to keep up with the younger, more radical shortboarders, Rell had joined the newly formed longboard tour after her first bout of cancer and had risen through the ranks to become one of the top women in the world.

In 1986, Rell got the chance to be part of the first group of Westerners ever to surf in China. But just prior to leaving, she found another lump in her breast. Unwilling to pass up on the opportunity to go to China, she decided the treatment could wait till after the trip. Unfortunately, she would later say, cancer is "like rust; it never sleeps." Although Rell was able to surf in remote Chinese coastal towns and roller-skate along the Great Wall, the trip took a toll on her health.

Back in Hawai'i with her doctors, she learned that she would have to have a radical mastectomy. "That was pretty rough and traumatic," Frank says. "That whole time was pretty crazy." For such a public figure and someone who practically lived in her bathing suit, the news came down on her like a big wave, and she was wiped out by it. After the operation, she tried wearing falsies while surfing, but they would get waterlogged in the ocean. Then a friend named Marilyn Link found a prosthetic made of rubber that Rell could use in the water. She called Marilyn her bosom buddy and would joke that after a wipeout her prosthetic boob would sometimes slip around inside her bathing suit and end up on her back. Rell tried to laugh about these things because otherwise she would cry.

It helped that she was married to a comedian, and Frank did all he could to keep her laughing. When she lost her long dark hair due to the chemo, he would joke that she still had more hair than he did. He would tease the nurses and ask if they could put any liquor in the IV drips to make the medicine go down smoother. Yet as hard as he tried to take care of her, Frank found himself slipping into his own depression. The woman he loved was in terrible pain, and there was nothing he could do to help her.

After the chemotherapy treatments at the hospital, they would usually go back to his place in town and just stay put, trying to recover from the debilitating drugs. But for a restless soul like Rell's, sitting around doing nothing was like dying. Frank lost his desire to drive out to Makaha and surf, but she was determined to get back on the board. After her surgery and radiation treatments, Rell gradually recovered and resumed training for the next contest season. She would later fly to Australia with Frank to compete in the pro events there. Yet as much as she loved traveling and surfing exotic new spots, she was always eager to get home.

Although Rell looked healthy, the cancer had metastasized and gone into her bone marrow. As part of her treatment, Rell and Frank decided to fly to Houston for treatment at the M. D. Anderson Cancer Center, one of the best oncology hospitals in the country. Her doctors were going to try high-dose chemotherapy with drugs so powerful they wipe out the bone marrow and any trace of cancer. But the treatment would also leave her very vulnerable. After the endless hours of watching the chemo drip into her veins and feeling her strength fade, Rell gradually slipped into a coma. Her sister Val had flown in to be with Rell and stood beside her bed, wondering if she would survive. As Rell struggled to gain consciousness, she says she drifted back to Hawai'i in her mind and had this long, extended dream about surfing.

Rell later told Bruce Jenkins about the dream that saved her life. "When I was in the coma," she said, "I was dreaming that I was trying to catch waves out at Waikiki. I was so frustrated, because I kept paddling and paddling, and I couldn't catch a wave. It seemed like just a session, but actually Val had been with me in the intensive-care unit for a couple of days. Finally, one swell bumped up, it caught me, I stood up, and I was surfing! And I woke up and said, 'Val, did you see that, I finally caught a wave!' And she was just beside herself, you know. 'Rell, we've been here for days, we thought you were gonna die.' But that kept me occupied while I was in a coma. I've always said surfing saved my life."

After her near-death experience, Rell came back to Makaha, where she resumed surfing almost every day, even when she felt terribly ill. She had lost her hair and a lot of weight. "I was completely bald, but I wanted to go surfing; so I put a swimming cap on," Rell recalls about one of her first sessions back in the water. "Then, one of the waves knocked it off and I was so embarrassed I came in, ran home, and cried. I was sitting there crying, but I kept looking out the window, and I could see the sets rolling in. That's when I told myself, 'Forget it; that's where I belong.'"

When she paddled out into the lineup the next day, Brian, Mel, and all the guys were also wearing rubber swimming caps. A few had even shaved their heads so she wouldn't feel self-conscious about her lack of hair. It was touching and funny at the same time. Meanwhile, Rusty, Sunny, and Johnny Boy Gomes prowled the beach like pit bulls making sure no one bothered her or asked why she looked so thin and bald. Eventually, her long dark hair grew back and she resumed her active lifestyle as if nothing had happened.

Rell took comfort in diving and spearfishing, and Frank would sometimes accompany her to bag her catch. He would hang out at the surface and watch her through his mask as she disappeared into the blue. "I've seen her dive deep," Frank says. "Going down, her hair would be flowing and her mermaid body would be going with this Hawaiian sling, holding her breath. I would be up there, holding the surfboard, watching her. She would sneak into these holes and *pap!* That spear would be shaking, and she would pull this big *uhu* out of there."

Yet with each descent into the darkness, he felt like he was losing her. She was a world-class diver and surfer, and he had trouble keeping up with her. Though they had had many good times together, the cancer had also taken its toll on their relationship and they began drifting apart. He was constantly driving back and forth between Honolulu and Makaha, which was more her home than his. "In retrospect, I wasn't even supposed to be out there," Frank says. "It was her world. I was a town guy, and I stumbled into the whole romance of it all."

Eventually, they separated and Rell dove into a new relationship with another DJ named Dukie D. Frank was devastated. He quit his job and moved to a remote town on the Eastside called Ka'a'awa, whose green, lush surroundings were a world away from Makaha. "For three years, I lived out there and was just kind of licking my wounds," he says. When Dukie and Rell eventually broke up, she drove out to Ka'a'awa to see Frank. They surfed and went diving together like old times. Back at the house, they talked, laughed, and cried about the cancer and their breakup. "She made everything *pono* [right]," he says. "She was really a scared little girl in a sense, because she knew time was not on her side."

⚭

Time was not on her friend Israel's side, either. Although he would perform at big parties to raise funds for her cancer treatments, he was not doing well himself. Physically or financially. He was in and out of the hospital nine times in one year, and he kept missing gigs with the band. "He would get sick all of the time, partying too much and not enough rest; and then when it was time to go to work, he wouldn't show up," his wife, Marlene, says. "I was always the one telling him, 'You can't be doing that. You want to see your daughter graduate?'" Iz loved Marlene and Wehe, but he was still a wild and restless teenager beneath all his bulk. He would stay out all night, eating and drinking like he would live forever. But in 1989 his wakeup call came in the form of a mild heart attack. Not ready to join Skippy or repeat his fate, Israel knew the symptoms and called for help in time.

In between the verses of the song "Hawaii '78 Introduction," Israel would share stories about his life and how his brother's death affected him. "He had a massive heart attack. The weight and just the depression. He was real depressed. I was on the same course he was going, and he knew it, too. That's why he came back. . . . He did come back and told me, 'Hey, cuz, don't be scared. There's people here for help you.' It's kinda like telling me if he had them, he would still be here. I still believe that if he had called me he would still be alive. 'Cause he died of one broken heart."

Having just started work as a nurse in the cardiac unit, Marlene had a good idea of what Israel was going through in his recovery. "So it helped me a lot to understand and step back and let the staff do what they gotta do." She and Wehe stayed with Israel at the hospital, where their romance had first begun and where they would spend much of their time together. Friends would come visit to cheer him up.

"Uncle Buff, Frank Shaner, and a bunch of them came to the hospital late one night," Marlene says. "I think they were in town partying or something, and they stopped at the hospital, talked story, and sang some songs with him." In spite of the encouragement from family and friends, Israel's fist-sized heart was barely able to pump enough blood through his enormous body. Even after leaving the hospital, he would have to go on oxygen periodically. He tried dieting and lost two hundred pounds at one point, but he gained the weight back and couldn't seem to lose it. He eventually stopped trying and just returned to his previous lifestyle.

With his morbid obesity, Israel also found comfort in the ocean or in the pool near his apartment in Honolulu. After living with Marlene's parents in Salt Lake for several years, he had rented an apartment in town where he could go after performing his late-night gigs. His new "crash pad" allowed him to stay out all night and sleep all day without Marlene knowing. But after she heard stories about his partying, she and Iz would get into angry arguments about how his wild lifestyle was hurting them, physically and financially. "His prior management would always say it was my fault," Marlene says. "They went to my in-laws and said that they needed to keep me a thousand feet away from Israel before his gigs. And my in-laws turned around and told them, 'If it wasn't for this girl, he would have died a long time ago with all the drugs he's been doing.'" After many disagreements, arguments, and fights, the couple eventually decided to separate for a while.

As the Makaha Sons became bigger and more popular internationally, they began receiving invitations to perform in Tokyo and New York and around the country. Unfortunately, Israel's massive weight and fragile health made it very difficult for him to travel. When the Sons would play on the Neighbor Islands, he would have to fly in a special "big-boy" seat on Hawaiian Airlines that had been made for the King of Tonga. At hotels, he would need to sleep on two reinforced king-sized beds joined together. But traveling to Japan or Europe seemed out of the question for Israel, and this frustrated the other band members.

After releasing a solo album called *Ka 'Ano'i* in 1990, Israel began to get a taste of what it would be like to go on his own one day. Ka 'Ano'i was Israel's middle name, meaning "the beloved." After banning their language, the haole authorities had also discouraged the people from giving their children Hawaiian names. But most families continued to give their sons and daughters Hawaiian middle names, a tradition that continues to this day, even among local and haole families. Iz and Marlene would often call each other by their middle names as a sign of affection. Hers was Ku'upua (my flower).

Just as their names were a mix of English and Hawaiian, Israel's album had a unique blend of Hawaiian music, Jamaican reggae, and pop melodies that he would later develop into a new genre called Jawaiian. Influenced by the music of Bob Marley, Israel was also moved by his message of "one love, one heart," and the new CD reflected a similar spirit. In 1991, he won Male Vocalist of the Year at the annual Na Hoku HanoHano Awards.

Though there was lingering resentment toward Israel, the band reunited to produce what would become their final album the next year. Meanwhile, Israel kept smoking, eating, and drinking too much.

Wanting to check up on his old friend, Rusty Keaulana used to visit Israel at his one-bedroom apartment in town. Rusty would often sneak up behind the resting giant and slip his finger across his throat like a dagger and whisper, *"Supee!"* Surprised by the sneak attack, Iz would snap back, "Oh, you buggah!" He would try to slap the lean Hawaiian surfer, but Rusty was usually too quick for him. *"Supee"* was like *"da kine"* and *"shaka"* in that no one really knew what the words meant, but they became popular Israelisms in Hawai'i. Iz would give the *shaka* sign (a local hand gesture with the thumb and pinky finger extended) and yell, *"Supee!"* at his concerts, and the crowd would roar it back.

Like Iz, Rusty was a rascal, and he loved partying and playing pranks on his friends. After drinking with "da boys at the beach," he would put a coconut behind people's car tires at Makaha. When they backed up over it, he would begin yelping like a wounded dog. Friends would jump out of their cars, terrified that they had run over a local dog. Rusty would just howl with laughter.

Being a practical joker is one thing, but Rusty didn't seem to take anything seriously. He was an incredibly talented surfer, but he didn't know what to do with his life. Buffalo and Brian tried to steer him straight, but he kept veering toward trouble. Rusty began flirting with crime and running with a dangerous crowd. "Right after high school, I started getting in trouble," Rusty says, "getting into crazy things, hanging out with the mafia. Those guys were teaching me how to fight and all *kine* crap."

But after witnessing the violence and seeing guys go to jail, he finally decided to become a lifeguard like his father and brother. Brian was the captain at the time and tried to teach him, but Rusty resented being told what to do. It was also hard trying to follow in the footsteps of his father and older brother because they were already considered legendary lifeguards. Besides, Rusty wanted to pursue his childhood dream of becoming a world champion surfer. "I only worked for like eight months," he says of his brief career as a lifeguard, "and they didn't want me to go out to the contests. I said, 'I ain't staying in this pigeon coop; I'm movin' on in my life.'" Rusty began training for the pro contest circuit.

Much of Rusty's talent and thirst to become a champion surfer came from his competition with his brother, who constantly pushed him to improve. "We were always each other's biggest competitors, and when we compete, we lock horns big time," Brian told journalist Greg Ambrose. "But we're still brothers. We love each other." Although Brian was a more talented shortboarder, Rusty soon realized that he was better on a longboard (generally nine feet or longer). Brian encouraged Rusty to start competing in longboard events because there were fewer competitors and he had a better shot at becoming the best. "My brother said, 'Russ, do the longboard.' He kinda helped me out and guided me, and I started doing my thing."

Ever since Nat Young helped introduce them in 1968, shortboards had dominated the surfing world because they were narrower, faster, and more versatile in big waves. But many of the surfers from the sixties who had helped make surfing one of the country's most popular water sports began longing for the return of longboards. After all, they were easier to paddle and catch smaller waves on, and they harkened back to the roots of soul surfing. Aging baby boomers started surfing again and buying longboards, and soon younger surfers who liked the old style better joined them in droves. This revival created a lucrative new market but also caused a rift between the more mellow longboarders and their aggressive, shortboarding cousins.

Although Rusty had grown up surfing and competing on shortboards, he loved longboarding and thought it was more fun. He had also competed every year in Buffalo's Big Board Classic, which had helped keep the sport alive over the decades. "There were two places where the longboard never died," says surf historian Mark Fragale. "The longboard never stopped being a viable tool at both Malibu and Makaha." And in both places, the more traditional style was revered as an art form.

Surfboard shaper and former pro Dave Parmenter once wrote: "There are only two authentically American art forms: jazz and longboarding." Watching Rusty surf on a longboard was like seeing a jazz master at work, and each ride was like a wild, impromptu performance. He spontaneously integrated the radical maneuvers of shortboarding with the graceful rhythms of longboarding, creating a fluid new style in the process.

In the late eighties, Rusty and his parents flew to Japan, where longboarding was starting to become the hot new trendy sport. Realizing the potential profits to be made in the booming Japanese economy, former world champion Nat Young began putting on a contest there. Ironically, just as Young had pioneered the shortboard revolution of 1968, he was now heralding the return of longboarding and had become the reigning world champion. But Rusty managed to beat him at his own contest, perfecting the switch-stance maneuver that Buffalo had used to win the Makaha International thirty years before. "As a longboarder, Rusty is just frickin' incredible," Mark Cunningham says. "And to this day, I still don't know if he's goofy foot or regular. He's so incredibly ambidextrous."

During his stay, Rusty bonded with the local Japanese surfers and industry folks who were blown away by his surfing skills. It didn't hurt that he was also the son of Buffalo Keaulana, whom they greeted and bowed to as a wise tribal elder. Inspired by his mentor Rell, Rusty organized a beach cleanup after the contest, and the locals started doing cleanups after every event. After that trip, Rusty picked up several corporate sponsors and began traveling to Japan two or three times a year to compete and meet with them. Likewise, when they came to Hawai'i, the

Keaulanas would invite them to Buffalo's Big Board Classic and show them the laid-back Makaha lifestyle.

Competing in contests around the world, Rusty and Brian began climbing through the ranks of the newly organized pro longboard circuit. Starting in 1992, however, the world title was decided by one big contest: the Oxbow World Longboard Championships. The inaugural event was held on the southwest coast of France, near the Spanish border, as part of the first annual Biarritz Surf Festival. Inspired by contests like the Makaha International, a wealthy French surfer by the name of Robert Rabagny created the Festival and modeled aspects of it after the Buffalo Big Board Classic.

Each summer, tens of thousands of Europeans would gather to surf, party, and celebrate Hawaiian culture. Just as Buffalo had learned that surfing was a high-class sport in Peru, he soon realized that his French sponsors were equally well-off. Robert invited a large gathering of Hawaiian surfers and legendary big-wave riders like Greg Noll and Peter Cole to attend the week-long event and helped pay for their flights and accommodations. The group of thirty or so locals from Hawai'i would basically take over their section of the plane during the long flight over, drinking, switching seats, and talking story like it was a big reunion.

After a brief tour of Paris, the group from Hawai'i would be taken by bus to Biarritz, where they felt right at home among the Basque people. "They're like locals, indigenous people, and they're radical, man. They loved us, and we loved them," Boogie Kalama says. "It was like the two cultures just melted together." They would party, play music, and dance all night long. Likewise, in their travels to Australia and Japan for similar surfing festivals, the Hawaiians would form tight bonds with the aboriginal people and those indigenous to Okinawa. This was partly because of their common lot as colonized people. But they also enjoyed being part of an international tribe whose shared love of surfing and the ocean transcended national boundaries and cultural differences. At the welcoming parties, the Europeans rolled out the red carpet with plenty of food and drink and the Hawaiians reciprocated by entertaining them. "Buff got up onstage, and he starts playing 'ukulele, and the boys start dancing the hula," Ants Guerrero recalls. "No matter where we would go in the entire town of Biarritz, they wouldn't accept our money."

The Keaulanas were asked to lead the opening ceremony and form a Hawaiian royal court like they used to do at the Buffalo Big Board Classic. Knowing the eyes of the world would be watching, Auntie Momi and Uncle Buff made sure their sons and all the Makaha boys rehearsed and trained so the event would go off perfectly. During the ceremony, Buffalo, Brian, and the Westside boys wore traditional Hawaiian *malo* and asked all the participants to bring seawater from their home breaks to pour into a big calabash. After sounding the conch shells and reciting Hawaiian chants, the Keaulanas would lead the surfers into the ocean, where they would form a circle on their surfboards and pour out the water from around the world. After an opening blessing, the hula performances and surfing contests began. That first year, a Californian surfer named Joey Hawkins won the world championship over thirty other international competitors, but Rusty was determined to win it the next year in his home territory.

Bonga Perkins was an up-and-coming surfer who was competing against Rusty and Brian in the 1993 Championships at Hale'iwa Beach. Bonga had grown up surfing with the Keaulanas, who he said were two of the best longboarders in Hawai'i at the time. After surfing in smaller waves during the preliminaries, Bonga says the surf doubled in size for the semi-finals. Of the remaining six surfers, he and Rusty were the only two Hawaiians left, and they wanted to win back the title. The two were competing in big, stormy surf when a large wave broke Bonga's board in half, leaving him stranded in the impact zone. Swimming to shore, he saw Brian running down the beach with his board. "Take this out!" he told Bonga. "You're doing good, man; keep it going for the Hawaiian team." Bonga didn't make it to the finals, but he was there on the beach with Brian, Rell, and half of Makaha to cheer on Rusty.

During the final heat, Rusty surfed well in the big, blustery waves, but he was still a few points behind Australian surfer Glen Winton. Glen and another Aussie finalist named Rob Bain were pro surfers who were going for radical maneuvers and rode their longboards like shortboards, while Rusty used more traditional moves like walking to the front of the board and hanging five or ten toes off the nose. Toward the end of the heat, he heard that he needed a score of 8.00 or better to win. With only a minute or so left, Rusty caught a big outside wave, did some impressive cutbacks, and then rode it all the way inside, standing on the nose. It was a solid ride, but he didn't think it was enough to beat Winton.

Heartbroken, Rusty swore at himself for losing in front of his friends and family and the people of Hawai'i. But when the emcee announced that Rusty's final ride received an 8.33, he saw Rell and his girlfriend, Sunny Kanaiaupuni, jumping up and down on the beach. All of the local boys from Makaha came running down to hoist him on their shoulders, and Brian was yelling, "You got 'em; you got 'em!" Rusty Keaulana had won the 1993 Oxbow World Longboard Championships—at the same break where he had won Rell Sunn's Menehune Contest almost fifteen years before!

Bonga was stoked for his friend. "Rusty was so excited at that point. He did his media stuff, got his money, got his trophy, and sped back to Makaha," Bonga says. After the awards ceremony, a big caravan of cars headed back to the Westside, where friends had set up two long tables of Heinekens at the beach for the new champ. A big party ensued, and a photographer from *Longboard Magazine* took a shot of Rusty with his family and a big posse of friends gathered around him. Rusty was on top of the world, and Bonga looked up to him with a mixture of admiration and envy. "From that moment on, I knew I gotta win one," Bonga recalls. "I wanted to be that guy."

During the next eleven months, they both trained hard for the World Championships in Malibu, where they would have to face California's reigning champ, the eighteen-year-old Joel Tudor. When Rusty, Bonga, and another Hawaiian longboarder named Lance Ho'okano flew to LAX to compete in the contest, they sensed some antagonism from a few of the locals. Though a lot less extreme than Makaha, Malibu was also known for its territorialism. Many of the locals resented outsiders coming to surf their breaks, especially when they had to get out of the water for contests. During the semi-finals of the Oxbow Contest in 1994, one knee-boarder refused to leave the lineup. Angered by the man's obstinance, Joel's father and Lance paddled out to talk to the guy and ask him to leave.

According to Bonga, "Tudor's dad initially went out there to say, 'Hey, buddy, the contest is going to start. This is the last day. The swell's going to be bigger tomorrow, and you can have your spot back. Give us like half a day.'" But he and the man got into a fight, and the knee-boarder ended up taking off one of his fins and whacking Joel's father with it. "I don't know who started it, but I just saw this fin flying," Bonga says. "Lance went out to help Joel's dad because Joel's his friend, and that's when the whole thing erupted." Known for his violent temper, Lance ended up beating up the guy fairly badly, and the cops came and arrested him.

Tension was riding high at the contest, but the cops were convinced to wait on the beach and let Lance surf in the finals. The final four contenders included Rusty, Bonga, Lance, and Joel, who was upset about the fight. Joel was also resentful of the fact that he had to surf against the three Hawaiian friends who seemed to be teaming up against the lone Californian. More than a chip, he seemed to have a boulder on his shoulder. Here was this thin eighteen-year-old haole kid who probably felt like he was way over his head, yet he had a cocky air about him and flaunted the fact that he was one of the best and highest-paid longboarders in the world.

According to Bonga, Joel suddenly started yelling at them in the water right before the heat. "We're sitting out there, and he looks at all three of us and says, 'You know what, fuck you Hawaiians! I make more money than all three of you put together!' That's why there was a grudge between California and Hawai'i in the finals," Bonga recalls. "So all the Hawaiians ganged up on Joel." Lance was known to have a short fuse and that comment would have set him off, but the cops were already waiting onshore. Instead of exploding, he just stayed close to Joel, trying to block him so his friends could catch more waves.

As the final minutes ticked down, though, Rusty and Joel had each caught two good waves, so the Makaha champ began pulling out every maneuver from his big bag of tricks. "He would paddle into a wave, bottom-turn, go to the nose, step back, do a big cutback, pop his tail, do another hit [against the lip of the wave], do a helicopter, do a tail three-sixty, walk to the nose, switch-foot step back, walk to the nose," Bonga says breathlessly. Most of the people on the beach that day had never seen some of those moves, nor could they understand what all those terms meant. "I think the judges couldn't even understand him at that point. They couldn't tell how hard it is to do all that because nobody does that!"

With Lance hovering around Joel, Rusty went on to win first place and Bonga came in second. At the awards ceremony, Rusty was given his second world championship trophy. Joel walked away from the ceremony, and this began a long-simmering feud between the young Californian and the more seasoned Hawaiians.

In 1995, the Oxbow World Championships were held on Réunion Island, a remote volcanic isle several hundred miles east of Madagascar in the Indian Ocean. After becoming more serious with his girlfriend, Sunny Kanaiaupuni, Rusty decided to invite her to join him on the long journey toward what he hoped would be his third championship title. A former Miss Hawai'i, Sunny was the pretty, blond-haired daughter of Barry Kanaiaupuni, who was not only a top Hawaiian surfer during the seventies but also one of the best surfboard shapers in the Islands. In fact, BK had competed against Buffalo at the Makaha International. So there was a tight connection between the two families, and Rusty hoped this trip would bring them even closer together.

After flying from Honolulu to Los Angeles to New York to Paris and then finally to Réunion Island, the Hawaiian couple staggered off the plane and onto a land that looked very similar to Hawai'i. They had flown halfway around the world to arrive at a place that looked just like home. With its volcanic mountains, jagged lava fields, and crystal blue waters, Réunion reminded them of the Big Island. Before the contest began, Bonga trained with Rusty and they were both blown away by the beauty of the island and the quality of the surf. They would get up at six in the morning to do stretches, talk about strategy, and study the local surf break. "It's one of the best lefts I've surfed in my whole life," Bonga says. "It's shallow, with fire coral, sharks everywhere, lots of fish—it's awesome."

When Joel Tudor showed up, the Hawaiians acted as if last year's feud had never happened. But the tension lingered just below the surface like the razor-sharp reef just beneath the waves. With his freshly shaved head, Joel looked like a pale young warrior whose only goal was to win. By contrast, Rusty paraded his Westside swagger, long hair, gold chain, and winning smile like the two-time world champ he was. Instead of getting worked up about Joel's comments at the previous year's event, Rusty used humor to get in his head and play with him psychologically.

"Rusty's always been a practical joker, so it's in his nature," Bonga says. "He'd go up to Joel and grab his board and say, 'Oh, this is a nice board!' Joel used to have this whole thing like 'don't touch my board' as he waxed it up. That's his precontest ritual, and Rusty would just screw him up! Joel's vegetarian, and Rusty would go over there with a big hamburger and say, 'I've got a hamburger for you.'" Once the contest began, though, Rusty became more serious and focused. His girlfriend, Sunny, watched from the judge's tower as he caught the biggest waves, made the longest nose rides, and disappeared inside the deepest tubes. It was his contest from start to finish, and that day he won his third world championship title. Joel was eliminated in the quarterfinals, and Bonga placed third behind Rusty and Alex Salazar.

Before going up onstage to receive his trophy, Rusty asked Bonga if he should propose to his girlfriend in front of the large crowd. "It's up to you. She's right there, and we're going to be up onstage in just a second," Bonga told him. "So he did it. We carried him up to the stage, and he got his award. He said, 'This is my girlfriend, and this is the biggest moment of my life!'" After Rusty proposed and Sunny accepted, the crowd on the beach started clapping and whistling. And then Rusty added, "And you guys are invited to Makaha for the wedding!"

That same year, Rusty and all the Keaulanas traveled back to France for the annual Biarritz Surf Festival. But of all the festivals they attended, this was the most memorable because Rell Sunn decided to take a big group of Menehune champion surfers along with her. Somehow, she had managed to raise enough money from her sponsors to pay for twenty local kids to travel all the way to France for the festival. "Ten years ago, she was trying to get stickers for these kids as prizes," says Ron Mizutani, a TV reporter who worked with Rell. "Now, she's taking them to France. Are you kidding me? Talk about a woman who had an incredible vision."

Some of these kids included future pro surfers and big-wave riders such as Melanie Bartels, Jamie O'Brien, Fred Pattachia, and Jamie Sterling. At the time, they were just kids who were thrilled to travel around the world, but only later would they realize what a selfless act it was on Rell's part. Jennifer Lee was another Menehune champion on the trip who had always looked up to Rell and had heard about her cancer but thought it was all gone. "She looked healthy and had long hair," Jenn recalls. "She was just beautiful and glowing as usual."

Even though Rell was still very sick, she insisted on going to France with her Menehunes, whom she referred to as "future legends." While teaching them about French culture, she also gave them hula and 'ukulele lessons so they could share their culture with their hosts. She had also asked them to bring vials of water from the home breaks as part of the opening ceremony. Then Buffalo, Brian, and the other Hawaiians led a procession to the beach, where people from around the world poured their samples of ocean water into a big koa bowl. Then, the Menehunes joined these famous watermen and paddled out into the surf. In the ocean, they formed a big circle and joined hands to form a living lei to bless the festival. "It was really special," Jenn recalls, "like a chicken-skin moment." After their performance, the crowds screamed, whistled, and shouted for more. Rell's Menehunes blushed and smiled with newfound pride.

"When these kids smile, you can feel the Hawaiian sunshine," Rell said. "The French were crazy about the Hawaiians and they stopped and questioned what our culture and history was all about. And the neat thing was to watch these kids share their knowledge and, at the same time, gain knowledge themselves about somebody else's culture." There was one moment that really captured the spirit of the trip in her mind. "T. J. Baron is only nine years old, and he comes up to me and says it was so fun he's going to bring his kid there someday. He's nine years old," Rell recalled. "I knew then that that was worth everything we went through to put it together."

Although the trip to France with the Menehunes was a big success, it took a lot out of Rell, who was exhausted afterward. Fred Hemmings had traveled with her and still couldn't believe she pulled it off. In the documentary *Heart of the Sea* about her life, he said, "You're dying of cancer, you're sick, and you take some twenty-odd kids around the world—my God." That's when

Rell's status as the Queen of Makaha rose even higher in the pantheon of Hawaiian heroes. Back in Makaha, she was happy to stay put for a while.

After traveling around the world with his fiancée, Rusty was also glad to be back home. "I can only imagine how much traveling Rusty has done as a pro surfer," says Mark Cunningham, who had been in Biarritz with him. "It's like you can take the boy out of the country, but you can't take the country out of the boy. He's such a son of Makaha."

Joining together two famous Hawaiian surfing families, Rusty Keaulana later married Sunny Kanaiaupuni. Like Brian and Nobleen, they had an enormous wedding, and the three-time world champ and the former Miss Hawai'i settled down in Makaha. Life was good for Rusty. Sunny's father, Barry Kanaiaupuni, shaped Rusty's boards, and he was sponsored by Quiksilver, one of the largest surf companies in the world. The couple later had a baby boy named Keali'i. His full name came from his grandmother Momi, who called him Keali'i O Ke Kai, or "little chief of the sea." He would inherit his mother's blond hair and good looks and his father's smile and mischievous behavior.

After being sponsored by Quiksilver for many years, Rusty worked with the billion-dollar corporation to open up a new surf shop and design his own line of longboards. Working with his business partner Craig Inouye, Rusty later created the Russ K Makaha store in Honolulu and a distribution outlet in Tokyo. Craig took care of most of the financial matters, and Sunny helped manage the Honolulu store, which was filled with photos of the whole family. There were framed pictures of Buffalo surfing at the Makaha International, of Brian and Rusty surfing big waves at Waimea, and of the Keaulana clan at the beach. After opening his store, Rusty gave his nephews and nieces new boards as gifts that year. "I cried when he did that," Momi told journalist Greg Ambrose. "I thought to myself, 'He understands—he's got that feeling of generosity I've been trying to teach them all.'"

While Craig and Sunny ran the surf shop, Rusty continued

competing around the globe in hopes of capturing his fourth title. In 1996, the Oxbow World Championships were held in Guéthary in southern France near the border with Spain. At the event, Rusty and Bonga began the peacemaking process with Joel Tudor, all of whom had mellowed over the years. At the contest, the skinny haole even posed for a picture with the beefy Hawaiian, holding up three fingers for each world title. "Rusty is by far the best switch-footer ever," Joel later told the media. "I mean, this guy won a world title goofy foot and another one regular foot." At that point, Rusty also realized that his former archrival, Joel, and his best friend, Bonga, were nipping at his heels for the world championship title, and it was only a matter of time before they won it.

"If the waves are small, Joel Tudor is the biggest threat," Rusty told *Longboard Magazine*. "If big, Bonga Perkins is the one to watch out for." That year, the waves in Guéthary were large and threatening. "If someone's gonna beat Rusty, it's going to be me," Bonga says. "I've been competing against this guy since I was ten years old and we were bodyboarding. It's always been him and me, him and me. I'll be the one to take him off his throne."

Sure enough, Bonga fulfilled his promise and beat both Rusty and Joel to win the world title in '96. Two years later, Joel would break the Hawaiians' winning streak when he took the 1998 World Championships in smaller waves at Fuerteventura in the Canary Islands off of southern Spain. After that, the three competitors became better friends. "We were all young and arrogant," Bonga says of the early days when they first started competing. "We all grew up, and we have kids now. Bygones are bygones, and we can laugh about it now."

CHAPTER 12

◑ ◑ ◑ ◑ ◑ ◑ ◑ ◑ ◑ ◑ ◑

Shooting Stars

Remember the past but do not dwell there—
Face the future where all our hopes stand.
—Israel Kamakawiwoʻole

After his first heart attack in 1989, Israel had the first glimpse of his own mortality, but he still didn't change his wild behavior. But following his many subsequent visits to the hospital, he had gradually come to realize that he might not have long to live. It was time for him to grow up and face the future.

This realization began a long process of cleaning up his act, becoming more independent, and eventually leaving the band.

In 1993, Iz landed in the hospital once again. He weighed over seven hundred pounds, and his obesity caused all kinds of problems, such as irregular heart palpitations, chronic cellulitis, shortness of breath, and low blood pressure. Facing a mountain of medical bills and rising debt, he knew something had to change. Then, out of nowhere, two guardian angels appeared before him in the form of Oswald "Oz" Stender and Dwayne Steele. Oz was a board member of the Office of Hawaiian Affairs and Dwayne was a local businessman, and both were fans of Israel's music. Hearing that the popular Hawaiian musician had no insurance and was living on welfare, the two men decided to help him get back on his feet. Using their own money, they gave him a gift of fifty thousand dollars to help pay for his medical bills and finance the new solo album, no strings attached. "It was never a loan, never was a business thing," Stender says in *IZ: Voice of the People.* "We just wanted to do it for Israel."

In spite of his poor health, Israel began to feel better about the future. While lying in two jointly reinforced hospital beds, he called record producer Jon de Mello and told him, "I really want to break away from the Makaha Sons of Ni'ihau and I want to do my own thing. Will you come and see me?" Jon was a fellow musician and the founder of Mountain Apple Records, which had produced many top local bands like the Brothers Cazimero. Jon went to see him at the hospital and found about thirty people in his room, partying and playing music while Israel plucked his 'ukulele in bed. The big man asked everyone to leave, and this began a three-hour meeting with Jon that would eventually lead to the most successful partnership in Hawaiian music history.

Initially, Jon tried to convince him not to leave the Makaha Sons because they were one of the most beloved bands in Hawai'i. But he could see that Israel was adamant about going on his own. Frustrated by a lack of money and creative control, Iz had been dreaming about starting his own band and music company to help support his wife and daughter. That's when he created the Big Boy Record Company and joined forces with Jon.

"He came down to the reality that he had done eleven albums over seventeen years [with the Makaha Sons], and he was still on welfare," de Mello recalls. "He said, 'I've got to take care of my family.'" Knowing he might not have much time, Iz added, "I want to be clear. I want to make the decisions, but I want to make sure my family is taken care of after I'm gone." After talking for another hour about all the details, Jon finally said, "All right, let's go; let's do it!"

Breaking with the band was a difficult decision, though, because they were like family. Israel's sister Lydia was torn apart: she wanted to stand by her brother, but she was loyal to her husband, Moon. The band also felt that Israel's health problems had held them back and kept them from traveling to destinations like Japan.

To add insult to injury, their agent at the time had tried to say that Iz's wife was part of the problem and that she was not loyal to him or the band. Even though Marlene and Iz were separated at the time, she still came to his apartment and took care of him almost every day. Her loyalty was beyond question. So Israel made the break right before their annual Makaha Bash at the Waikiki Shell, and the trio played without him. This caused a rift with Moon, John, and Jerome for years. The separation was painful for all involved because it was like breaking up the family. "When he left," Jerome says, "there was a lot of blame."

Soon after leaving the hospital, Israel joined Jon in his Palehua recording studio at the top of the Wai'anae Mountains to start working on the new album. Iz loved the cool air and the view up in the mountains, where he could see Honolulu to the east and the Wai'anae Coast to the west—town and country, the two sides of his life. Marlene and his daughter, Wehe, were also up there, and on a clear day they could see almost all of the Hawaiian Islands. He and Jon worked together for weeks up at Palehua, staying up late recording Israel's sweet voice and the plaintive melodies of his 'ukulele.

A talented musician, Jon played all the other instruments besides the 'ukulele. Iz nicknamed him Yoda, because he was small and thin, and the two used to tease each other about their respective sizes. Late one night at the end of the recording, Jon played back the new collection of songs for Israel. Toward the end of the first song, "Hawaii '78," he looked up and saw the big Hawaiian musician just shaking with his head down. "I thought, 'Oh my God, he's having a stroke or a heart attack!'" John recalls. "He turns around, and he was just absolutely soaking wet from sobbing. He couldn't believe it." After risking everything to go out on his own, Iz was just so relieved to hear how good the album sounded.

Working together, Israel and Jon co-produced *Facing Future*. Israel's debut album included a remake of the song "Hawaii '78" and a new medley that combined two timeless classics: "Somewhere Over the Rainbow," popularized by Judy Garland, and "What a Wonderful World," most famously performed by Louis Armstrong. That song and three others, including the melodious "White Sandy Beach," had been recorded during a brief late-night session at another studio years before. After performing at a local club, Iz had called a sound engineer named Milan Bertosa at 2:00 A.M. to ask if he could record a few songs. Milan didn't want to do it because it was so late, but he told the singer to come down for a quick session. Thirty minutes later, Iz showed up at the studio.

"I open the studio door, and this house carrying a 'ukulele walks in," Bertosa recalls. "He was the biggest human I had ever seen at that point!" Yet he soon realized that Iz's talent was equally big. Though it was late and he was tired, Bertosa was energized by the poignant power of "Hawaii '78," the timeless beauty of "White Sandy Beach," and the ethereal melody of "Over the Rainbow." He watched in amazement as Israel's sausagelike fingers danced along the strings of his small 'ukulele. "He nailed four songs, and then walked out," says Jon, who worked with Milan to include the songs on the new album. "That was it. One take. Period. Over. Done." In one thirty-minute session, Israel changed the history of Hawaiian music forever.

Along with his unique version of "Over the Rainbow," Israel included the song "Maui Hawaiian Sup'pa Man" on the new album. The playful number was written by his friend and fellow band member Del Beasley about Maui the demigod, whose magical fishhook had raised the Hawaiian Islands out of the sea. Wanting people to realize that Hawai'i had its own cultural superheroes, Iz sang, "Before there was a Clark Kent, there was a Hawaiian Sup'pa Man. . . . Mischievous, marvelous, magical Maui, the hero of this land."

Before the album came out, Israel wanted to thank Oz Stender and Dwayne Steele publicly for their generous support. But in their humble way, both men said that he didn't need to tell anyone about their contribution. So in the liner notes, Iz coyly dedicated the album to "The Wizard of Oz and the Man of Steele." A fitting tribute for an album that would soon transport listeners to a magical land of rainbows and soar to dizzying heights of popularity.

At one of his early performances to promote the album, Israel was onstage with his new band just before the show was about to begin. According to band member Mel Amina, the emcee announced the singer's name and the huge crowd went crazy. In the few moments before the curtain went up and the lights came on, Amina says Iz began strumming his 'ukulele and the band started playing. But he couldn't hear his bassist, Analu "Ants" Aina, so he called out to him in the darkness.

"You all right?" Iz asked.

"No, cuz," Ants whispered.

"What's da matter?"

"I scared, I scared," he confessed.

"Bruddah, no worry," Iz told him in his soothing voice. "Just close your eyes and sing from your heart." The lights then came on, and Israel began crooning. Ants performed most of the concert with his eyes closed and a big smile on his face. Throughout the turmoil of his life, Israel had always found comfort in singing from the heart. Like the ocean, music served as a kind of refuge, where he felt light and free.

Facing Future immediately became a local hit in Hawai'i, but it also began to gain popularity on the mainland. After "Over the Rainbow" and a few other songs were highlighted in an NPR segment about the "Gentle Giant of Hawaiian music," national sales began to skyrocket. "Over the Rainbow" would also be featured in the soundtracks of films such as *Meet Joe Black* and *Finding Forrester* and TV shows like *ER* and countless commercials. *Facing Future* eventually went platinum, selling well over a million copies and becoming the bestselling album ever recorded in Hawai'i.

Beyond all the record sales and commercial tie-ins, however, Israel represented something far more spiritual and powerful for the people in Hawai'i. His lyrics cried out for social justice. His songs gave voice to the Hawaiian people, expressing their sadness and anger over the suppression of their culture and the continuing desecration of the land. But like Bob Marley's reggae protest songs, that message was often lost in the laid-back Island rhythms of Israel's music. Beneath the catchy melodies, there was a growing sense of anger.

When *Facing Future* was released in '93, the Hawaiian sovereignty movement had just exploded. On the one hundredth anniversary of the overthrow of Queen Lili'uokalani, thousands of protestors marched to 'Iolani Palace, chanting and waving signs. Among other things, the marchers demanded that the royal ceded lands taken over by the U.S. government be returned to the Hawaiian people. That same year, President Clinton signed the Apology Resolution, which acknowledged the illegal overthrow of the kingdom of Hawai'i in 1893. While most Hawaiians were fighting for reparations and some form of federal recognition, some extreme groups wanted complete sovereignty from the United States. They carried signs and wore T-shirts that said: "Last Star On, First Star Off."

Later that year, a Native Hawaiian activist and controversial leader named Bumpy Kanahele seized a part of Makapu'u Beach as a form of protest. A descendant of King Kamehameha, Bumpy demanded that he and his band of militant followers be given land for an independent kingdom. Speaking to reporters, he would clutch a copy of President Clinton's Apology Resolution and use it to justify his occupation of Makapu'u and demands for sovereignty. Eventually, a compromise was reached. The protestors moved from the beach in exchange for a parcel of land in Waimanalo, which became a kind of Hawaiian reservation.

Bumpy and his followers had planted the seeds of protest, and young radicals began rising up all over the Islands, demanding that their lands be returned. Yielding to public pressure, the military stopped the bombing of Kaho'olawe and in 1994 the U.S. government handed over the island to the state "for the preservation and practice of all rights customarily and traditionally exercised by Native Hawaiians."

During one concert, Israel dedicated his concert to Bumpy and talked about what it means to be Hawaiian. Israel then ended the evening with one of his favorite laugh lines: "Haoles, it's nice to have you guys here. But when *pau* (finished) with vacation, don't forget—go home!" According to his good friend Betty Stickney, his comments that night and at other performances offended some of his haole fans who felt like he was discriminating against them. Betty had been a longtime friend and loyal supporter and had painted his portrait for the cover of his first solo album. Iz loved her and often introduced her as his "haole mom," and in her motherly way she said he needed to embrace *all* of his fans, haole and Hawaiian.

Israel was sorry about his comments and said he hadn't intended to alienate any of his fans. "He was terribly conscious of people's feelings," Betty says. So at the next concert, he talked about what it means to be Hawaiian, but this time he included all those who were "Hawaiian at heart." Yet deep down, the sumo-sized performer was still wrestling with feelings of anger about the social injustices his people faced, and he sought to numb the pain by drinking and smoking whatever would get him high.

Israel became more overtly political in his next album, calling it *E Ala E*, which is a kind of rallying cry, meaning "to awaken or rise up." In the liner notes, he dedicated the songs to the Hawaiian people, whom he called "the heartbeat of Hawai'i." On the cover, he included an image of his actual EKG, measuring his heart rate. And at each concert, his heart would race as he sang the lyrics from the title song: "We, the voices behind the face, / Of the Hawaiian nation, the Hawaiian race / Rise for justice the day has come / For all our people to stand as one." Among the many issues confronting Native Hawaiians, nothing united and angered the people more than the continued bombing of Makua Valley.

Roland Cazimero was one of Israel's closest friends and remembers how they both witnessed the military's bombing exercises in Makua, where they used to camp and play. "We'd go early in the morning, and we'd hear the choppers coming, low on the water," Roland remembers. "Right over us, they'd start firing. By nighttime, the whole valley would be on fire. . . . It's so sad," Roland tells me with tears in his eyes. "I think Hawai'i and her problems kind of opened up for Iz . . . so all he did was speak her mind. As his life grew shorter, he realized something should be said, something should be done."

Along with urging the military to stop the continued bombing of Makua, Israel wanted his people to be given the land they had been promised. In the song called "Broken Promise," he, Roland, and Cyril Pahinui joined Henry Kapono in singing about one of many Hawaiian Home Lands scandals. It was a sad tribute to an old Hawaiian man who had been waiting for his land for decades. The song won Single of the Year at the Na Hoku Awards. But the social conditions barely changed, and this made Israel angry. He and Roland thought of themselves as warriors, which can be seen in the next verse of Israel's title song, "E Ala E": "We the warriors born to live / On what the land and sea can give / Defend our birthright to be free / Give our children liberty . . . E ala E."

According to Roland, he and Iz felt like they had to fight for their rights as Hawaiians. After three centuries of slumber, the ancient warriors inside them had finally woken up. "It's like the Hulk telling the guy, 'You don't want to upset me,'" Roland says, adding that anger often led their people toward drugs, violence, and prison. When Israel returned to prison to play for the inmates, he encouraged them to let go of their anger and violence.

"In order for you to become a better person, me and Israel both knew that you gotta put that animal away," Roland says of their anger. Seeing how young Hawaiians were joining gangs and doing crystal meth or ICE, Roland and Israel both realized that it was time to change their lives. "Everybody has to grow up and learn to fall in line and be good soldiers—warriors second, soldiers first," Roland adds. "In the meantime, be a good soldier with a higher vision, higher purpose, higher understanding, a higher, better life for *all* of us, not just some of us, *all* of us."

Just as Iz fought for Hawaiian rights, he felt like Hawai'i's famous sumo wrestlers were fighting for Hawaiian pride in a foreign land. In the song "Tengoku Kara Kaminari (Thunder from Heaven)," he honored these "gentle giants from the countryside." Like Israel, they came from local areas like Waimanalo, Nanakuli, and Wai'anae and went on to become hometown heroes in Hawai'i. Relating to their massive weight, Iz admired their warrior spirit and soldierlike discipline and the way they had risen to be the best in their field.

Saleva'a Atisonoe (Konishki) was the first American to achieve celebrity status in sumo, and he was followed by Chad Rowan (Akebono), who became the first non-Japanese *yokozuna* (grand champion) in the two-thousand-year history of the sport.

When Makaha's own Fiamalu Penitani (Musashimaru) went on to become the second grand champion, Israel was proud to sing about these "champions in a foreign land, national heroes, famous idols in Japan—Akebono, Musashimaru and Konishki." All three were revered in Japan, where they became wealthy and were treated like rock stars. Israel was also on his way to becoming the biggest star of Hawaiian music, which was becoming popular around the world.

With the release of his third and final album, *N Dis Life,* Israel continued fighting for Hawaiian rights. Mountain Apple's Leah Bernstein says that Israel was no radical, but he wanted justice. "He understood we were part of the United States, but he also wanted to be recognized as a Hawaiian. He wanted the apologies, he wanted the reparations, because he felt his people had been wronged. He felt very strongly about it." Leah adds, "He became a leader in the movement." After Skippy's death, Israel had gradually become an "accidental activist," stumbling into issues like Hawaiian sovereignty that his brother had been so passionate about. Yet Israel later came to embrace the idea of racial harmony and peace. Toward the last years of his life, Iz wanted people to forgive past wrongs and come together in unconditional love.

Taking his own advice, Israel finally reconciled with Marlene and the family was reunited. "About a year and a half before he died, we finally matured," Marlene says. "We used to cry at night and talk about our daughter." They forgave each other for the pain and arguments that had come between them. Iz also gave up drugs and had a kind of spiritual awakening. In the beginning of their marriage, Marlene had wanted them to go to church, but he had said, "Ku'upua, if you get into church, you gotta go with two feet—you cannot drag the other one."

Now that Israel was ready to dive in, he was baptized again and started attending a congregation called Word of Life. Just as he had put a picture of his baby footprint on the cover of his new album, *N Dis Life,* he seemed to regain a childlike innocence. "For me, the biggest, most exciting moment was just being able to spiritually connect with him," Marlene says. "In the long run, we knew where each other was coming from. . . . We used to laugh and tell each other, 'Why couldn't we be like this when we were younger?' "

In the song "Starting All Over Again," Israel compared the plight of his people to his own personal and spiritual turnaround. "Starting all over again / it's gonna be rough for us / but we're gonna make it," he sings. "We lost what we had / that's what hurt us so bad / it set us back a thousand years / but we're gonna make it up / though it's gonna be tough / to erase the hurt and fears." On one level, he was singing about his reconciliation with Marlene, but the *kaona,* or hidden message, is about how the Hawaiian people were starting to rebuild their culture after losing their kingdom and most of their land.

"Remember the past, but do not dwell there," Iz would say. "Face the future, where all our hopes stand." But facing the future also meant dealing with his own imminent death, and this gave him a clearer vision of life and made him appreciate his friends and family even more. That was partly why he loved Rell and related to her so well, because she, too, was living day to day, moment to moment.

Whenever Iz and Marlene would drive out to Makaha, they would stop by Rell's house. "Those two would encourage each other," says Marlene. "They would be down-and-out also. They kept in touch with each other and they used to go back and forth: 'I'm not going first!' 'I'm not going first, either!' Enough already. Going first in terms of going to heaven. They freely talked. They were going through something that other people weren't going through. He was fighting his battle with his weight, his heart disease. And then Rell with her cancer. It was unreal. They couldn't control it, but they could make temporary choices, and it was to live for each day. The two of them were living life each and every day to the fullest."

In the midst of his suffering, though, Israel found new life and happiness with his wife and daughter, and it showed in his music. His new album, *N Dis Life,* hit the top of the charts and received critical acclaim and huge sales. In the back of his mind, though, Iz was still sad about his breakup with the Makaha Sons because they had never really reconciled. But he would soon get his chance to make things right.

At the Na Hoku Awards in 1996, Israel was the headlining performer of the event. Wearing wraparound sunglasses to mute the glaring lights, he was dressed all in black except for his white shell necklace and trademark fishhook pendant. The biggest star at the awards ceremony, he had swept most of the top honors for his first two albums, *Facing Future* and *E Ala E.* But on that May evening, Iz looked frail up onstage. Tubes from an oxygen tank fed him his every breath. His huge bulk overflowed the steel-reinforced chair, and he could barely move.

Before Israel's performance, the emcee that night announced his presence onstage by referring to one of his songs: "Look up on the stage. It's a bird, it's a plane, it's the Hawaiian Sup'pa Man." Iz smiled and waved to the crowd, but he clearly had things on his mind that he wanted to share with the audience. Saddened by what he saw happening to his culture, he said, "I'd like to send a message out there to all the Hawaiians and all the Hawaiians at heart: Take responsibility for all our *kuleana* [rights]. 'Cuz our culture is suffering." Yet in spite of his failing health and heavy heart, he seemed to come alive soon after plucking the first chords on his 'ukulele.

Out of his entire repertoire, Israel chose to perform Moon Kauakahi's moving song "Kaleohano." Strumming his 'ukulele and singing with his eyes closed, Iz began to hear the voices of his former band members, hovering above him. "I didn't know what was going on," Iz would say later. "I heard Moon's voice, and I opened my eyes and looked to the side, and there he was." Inspired by the sound of Iz's voice, Moon, Jerome, and John had spontaneously walked up onstage and just began singing with him.

"It was almost like [he was] just calling us to be together on-stage," Jerome would say later. "There was something in his voice that just said that he needed us guys to be up there." The crowd stood up and cheered as the Makaha Sons reunited once again. At the end of the song, the three men gathered around Iz, hugged him, and cried. "I love you, bruddah," they said to each other as the audience watched in tears. In that one moment, all was forgiven. "There was a lotta emotion, a lotta feeling of love," Israel would say later, "an awesome feeling of aloha."

Over the next year, though, his health declined rapidly. On the evening of May 20, 1997, Israel's album *N Dis Life* was nom-inated for several awards at the twentieth annual Na Hoku Awards Ceremony. But he was forced to watch the event on tel-evision in his hospital room, where he was hooked up to all kinds of medical equipment. Lying in bed with oxygen tubes, IVs, and heart monitors, Iz watched the ceremony with Marlene and their daughter, Wehe, beside him. He won four Hoku awards that night, including Favorite Entertainer by popular vote, and Jon de Mello went up to receive each of them in Iz's place. He was excited, but he could barely speak. His heart was giving out, he had diabetes, and his extreme weight was making it hard to breathe.

In the introduction to his song "Starting All Over Again," Is-rael had said, "I not scared myself for dying 'cause I believe all this is just temporary. This is just one shell, because we Hawai-ians, we live in both worlds, we live on both sides." He did his best to console Marlene that he would see her and Wehe on the other side. "One day we going to meet. . . . I'm going to be wait-ing for you at that golden gate," he told Marlene during his final days. "But you know what, I'm not going to look the same; I'm going to be skinny." That comment touched her deeply. For his funeral, he said he wanted people not to mourn his death but to celebrate his life. "Israel told his friends before, 'Brah, when I pass away, no cry; I no like no tears. Just bust all the fireworks.'"

During his last days at the hospital, Israel went in and out of consciousness and said all kinds of things like he was going to live forever. "He used to talk in Hawaiian, calling his grandfather's name, his mom's, his dad's, his sister's, his brother's," Marlene recalls. "He was calling out colors and telling us he's flying." He asked for water but wouldn't drink anything. Marlene finally realized that he was referring to the ocean. As she bathed him with saltwater that had been brought to him from the beach, he spoke like an excited child.

"Look, Ma, I shining, I shining!" he said, as if his soul had already left his body. When his heart finally stopped, the doctor, nurses, and even security guards tried to resuscitate him, but there was barely a pulse. "I told him I loved him and that I would be at the end of the bed and I could go with him all the way to the light," Marlene says through her tears. "I saw his shadow come up by the monitor. All I heard him say was, 'I love you, Kuʻupua!' And I just told him, 'I love you, too, Kaʻanoʻi!" And then he was gone. The "flower" had lost her "beloved."

Israel Ka ʻanoʻi Kamakawiwoʻole died on June 26, 1997, at the age of thirty-eight. The news of his death hit the people of Hawaiʻi hard, and his fans around the state mourned his passing. Radio stations played his songs around the clock, and tributes appeared in all of the papers and on nightly news programs. National Public Radio played "Over the Rainbow" and announced his passing to the rest of the nation. "The Gentle Giant of Hawaiian song has died," announcer Robert Siegel said. "Israel Kamakawiwoʻole maintained a respect and reverence for traditional Hawaiian music, while integrating it into popular songs. He died early this morning of respiratory failure." Condolences began pouring in from fans across the country and around the world.

Marlene and the family talked to Governor Ben Cayetano about having a public funeral service at the State Capitol. Although this kind of ceremony had only been done two times before (for Governor John Burns and U.S. Senator Spark Matsunaga), officials agreed to honor the popular Hawaiian singer at the Capitol courtyard, where he would lie in state. His body was placed in a huge koa coffin beneath a fifty-foot Hawaiian flag and a large picture from his first album of Marlene combing his hair.

Marlene and Wehe sat next to his coffin during the service and watched in tears as more than ten thousand people came to pay their respects to this mountain of a man. It was like they were mourning for a king. As Rick Carroll wrote, "People who had never once set foot in the State Capitol and might never go there again came to honor a young Hawaiian who stood for self-determination, revival of Hawaiʻi's culture and sovereign rights."

After the funeral, Israel's body was cremated and a final memorial service was organized at his beloved Makua Beach. Marlene worked with Brian and Buffalo to plan the service. Israel had always wanted to sail on the voyaging canoe *Hokuleʻa*, and on the morning of his memorial service he finally got his wish. Nainoa Thompson sailed the double-hulled canoe down to Makua, where thousands of friends and fans waited at the beach. Before the memorial service, a long convoy of eighteen-wheelers were blowing their horns along the coast. The horns sounded like the conch shell that Hawaiians of old used to blow at the birth and passing of Hawaiian royalty. Cazimero said it sounded like "the Island was crying, like it was grieving for a lost son."

Holding the large, wooden urn that Bunky Bakutis had carved for them, Marlene, Wehe, and Uncle Mo Keale poured Israel's ashes into the sea—in the exact spot where they had spread Skippy's ashes fifteen years before. The Kamakawiwoʻole brothers were reunited at last.

Standing on the deck of the *Hokuleʻa*, the mother, daughter, and other relatives then dove into the water, where Israel used to swim and play with his family. Bands performed musical tributes as families just sat on the beach and enjoyed the beautiful summer day and their memories of Israel. On the sail of one of the canoes, the words "IZ LIVES" were painted in big red letters. Those two words turned out to be a prophecy.

Shortly after his death, the Honolulu Symphony played at the

Waikiki Shell and dedicated its concert to Israel Kamakawiwoʻole. Sitting under the stars, his family and friends watched as the symphony performed with a local band called Na Leo Pilimehana. They opened the show with a song called "Flying with Angels," in memory of Iz. Later in the show, the emcee asked Marlene to perform the hula to one of her husband's songs. As she moved across the stage, it was like seeing her dance once again at Hank's during the first year of their relationship. After her performance, fans looked up to see a shooting star streaking across the sky. It was a magical moment. Three days later, on July 4, the sky exploded with fireworks celebrating Independence Day. Receiving his final wish, Israel had gone out with a bang.

CHAPTER 13

❧

Healing Waters

The cure for anything is salt water—sweat, tears, or the sea.
—Isak Dinesen

If Iz embodied the soul of Hawaiian culture, Rell was its beating heart. Saddened by Israel's death yet inspired by his fierce spirit and playful personality, Rell was determined to fight for her own survival. Even though her doctors had told her that her cancer was incurable, she had refused to believe it. "I've heard stories of people being terminal for twenty years," she said. "It's how you make your body fight and tell your body it's not going to die. That's why I never think of my cancer as terminal. It would take a lot more than that to finish me off."

Her friends admired her positive attitude, though some probably wondered if she was in denial. But Rell was fully aware of what she was going through and actively worked with other cancer victims at the Wai'anae Cancer Research Center to help them cope with the ravaging effects of the disease and the debilitating side effects of the chemo and radiation treatments. Along with being a "surfragette" and pioneer in women's professional surfing, Rell had also become a leader in breast cancer awareness. As a counselor, she promoted mammograms and helped many young women deal with their cancer.

Henry Kapono's ex-wife, Pam Ka'aihue, used to visit Rell with her two daughters, whom she treated like her own. Rell had so many friends and visitors that Pam was just glad to have a chance to be with her. "Whatever time you got with her you were just blessed to get and thankful for it. She made a big impact on me and my children." The women used to go to swap meets together and collect glass fishing balls, Hawaiian tikis, and rattan furniture. At night, they would watch rental movies or play board games.

"She had a lot of energy," Pam says. "Last one to bed and first one up. You know, who wants to waste time sleeping? They say when your time is measured, you make the most of every minute, which she did!" She would get up before dawn each morning, ride her bike to Makaha to check out the surf, and then call in the surf report. She would then lead a breast cancer counseling session in the morning and later on hold a geriatric exercise class in the afternoon. She seemed to have love and energy for everyone, from the young kids at the beach to the older folks at the senior center. "They meant a lot to her," Pam says. "She just did things to help so many people in so many different ways."

After 1995, Rell had lost faith in most of the invasive medical treatments, saying, "I'm not treatable now because they consider me terminal. There's nothing more they can do." From that point on, she took the process of healing into her own hands. She received herbal remedies from Momi Keaulana, using the traditional Hawaiian practice of *lapa'au*. And she surfed almost every day. "Surfing frees everything up," she told *Surfer*. "It's just the best soul fix. Life should be stress-free, and that's what surfing is all about."

Watching her glide down the face of wave after wave, her closest friends wanted to believe that Rell had beaten her cancer—at least for a while. With the return of her long, flowing hair, she looked like a vision of health as she gracefully danced across the water with a big smile on her face. Rell believed that surfing and being in the ocean healed her. "Some call it salt water," Momi Keaulana likes to say, "but we call it holy water."

Friends continued throwing fund-raisers of all kinds to help pay for Rell's lingering medical expenses from all the previous treatments. Surfers in California and Hawai'i held longboard contests and donated all the proceeds to her medical fund. Pro surfers dedicated a portion of their winnings to her. Musicians performed at benefit concerts for her, and afterward they would all line up to present her with lei till she was almost drowning in flowers. At one benefit luncheon for her at Compadres Restaurant, Rell had tears in her eyes as she thanked her extended 'ohana of friends. "There isn't a moment of a day where love isn't made visible. It's love like this that makes you go on."

At another benefit, she said, "Take it from me, love and prayers really do work." Her friends were astonished at how strong and loving she was in the face of such an insidious disease. "She has had a hard life, but nothing gets her down," Momi said. "She has a zest for life. She helps everyone. What's keeping her alive is fight. She's fighting this thing; she's a real scrapper." But the illness had taken a toll on her relationship with her daughter, Jan, who had moved to San Diego under pressure from Rell.

"When you're from here, you don't want to go anywhere else; you just want to stay here," Jan says about Makaha. But Rell insisted that Jan move away for a while to see other places and cultures. "I was so pissed she wanted me to go. She was miserable. She goes, 'Look, I love it here—this is where I live; this is my heart; this is where I want to be. I want to live and die in Makaha. But if it takes me to pack up and move all my things to California just so you can get a taste of the world, I'll do it; I'll do it for you!' I'll never forget that argument. She was crying."

Although Jan didn't want to leave Hawai'i, she took Rell's advice and moved to the West Coast. She hated being away from home at first, but gradually she grew to love Southern California and understood why her mom wanted her to travel. Now that she's a mother as well, Jan says, "You want to show the children that there's more out there."

Even though she had cancer, Rell was still a vibrant woman with a healthy case of wanderlust. In 1994, she had been offered the chance to travel to Christmas Island, a low-lying coral atoll located some twenty-two hundred miles south of Hawai'i. Patagonia founder Yvon Chouinard organized and sponsored the "surfari" and knew Rell was tough enough to hang with five guys on a remote atoll in the middle of the Pacific. The other surfers were Sam George, Bernie Baker, Yvon's assistant, and Dave Parmenter. There were only three rooms in the small compound, so everyone had to double up. Rell ended up in the same room as Dave, and the two immediately hit it off. Although she was ten years older and they came from different worlds, their shared love of the ocean and surfing created a close bond between them.

Dave had grown up surfing in the crowded breaks of Southern California and then moved with his mother to the central coast. A self-described outsider who loved Mark Twain and Jack London, Dave enjoyed surfing by himself in California's frigid waters, where often his only companions were seagulls and an occasional seal. Dave started competing in his late teens, and by his early twenties, he was one of California's best surfers. He also began shaping surfboards and writing acerbic articles about the sport. In a series of jeremiads for different magazines, he became the outspoken surf prophet who criticized both the xenophobic tribal mentality of many local surfers and the trendy, commercial mind-set of Southern California's surf industry.

After several years on the pro tour, Dave burned out on what he considered the soulless and mercenary contest scene. Dropping out of the tour, he focused on shaping surfboards for a living and would occasionally write travel articles about his surf trips around the world. Though somewhat of a loner, he still longed to find a partner who understood his passion for the purity of surfing. And on Christmas Island in 1994, he found that Rell Sunn was more than just a soul surfer—she seemed to be the soul mate he had always been looking for.

Dave was impressed with Rell's extensive knowledge of surfing history and her incredible talent in the waves as well. During one session, she broke her board in the warm, head-high surf. So Dave lent her his longboard. Watching from the shore with *Surfer* editor Sam George, Dave was amazed by the fluid and stylish way she wove the board down the wave as if dancing hula. "And when she did a drop-knee cutback," Sam said later, "you could see it right then. Dave was gone." Even knowing she had terminal cancer, he couldn't help but fall for her.

"We're so alike, we recognized it instantly," Dave said. Though usually tight-lipped and quiet, the lean California surfer became animated with praise for the beautiful Hawaiian waterwoman. "I've never come across anyone as passionate as I am about surfing and all the romantic aspects about it. There's nobody like Rell. There never has been. She's like a female Duke Kahanamoku. The differences in age, culture, where we lived, things like that are inconsequential when you compare them to eternity."

In spite of their intense connection, neither of them spoke about their deep feelings for each other until after the trip. They began talking on the phone and became close, but both were aware of the distance between them. With Dave in California and Rell in Hawai'i, they lived an ocean apart, yet it was their love of the sea that would bring them together. One day while diving in

Makaha, Rell found an old, crusty surfboard fin on the reef. After scraping off the debris, she saw these words: "Shaped by Dave Parmenter."

"That was like a bolt of lightning from heaven," Dave told journalist Bruce Jenkins later. "I mean, I don't have many boards in Hawai'i, and none on the Westside as far as I knew. That was too much. I booked a flight over, and I've been here ever since." Dave moved into Rell's cottage near the beach, and they began surfing, diving, and fishing together. Makaha can be an intimidating place to move into, especially if you're a haole. But as Rell's new boyfriend and an established surfer and shaper, Dave was welcomed into the community. He had always admired Brian and was stoked to become good friends with him and the Keaulanas. Seeing how happy Dave made Rell, their extended 'ohana practically adopted him as a hanai son.

"They're the most extraordinary people—they're kind of like my only family," Dave says of the Keaulanas. "I've learned more from them than anybody in my life, not just about surfing but about everything, just about family, what it is, and that it's unconditional. . . . I've always been an outsider everywhere I've lived, so this is the first place where I didn't feel that way." As Rell used to say about the influx of people to Makaha, "No one moves out—they just move over."

In the process of falling for Rell, Dave also fell in love with her culture. He enjoyed the laid-back lifestyle in Makaha and the way their lives revolved around the natural rhythms of family, friends, and the ocean. "Growing up on the mainland, families split up and disintegrate and people move every two years and go thousands of miles apart," Dave says. "When people come here, they see that there's no hiding. Everybody has gone to school together. There's three or four generations in the water, and everybody knows each other from grade school. . . . It's a sense of solidarity. There might be people squabbling or there might be discord, but they always pull together."

Seeing the Makaha community through his eyes, Rell began

looking at her hometown in a new light. Calling him a "young curmudgeon but with a wonderful innocence to him," Rell said, "he taught me to admire and respect the people I play with every day. He's given me a reason to really love living."

When Dave decided to propose to Rell, he wanted to do it in a way that she would always remember. So one day while diving together, they went out to her favorite spot: a fishing hole about forty to fifty feet deep where she had caught many *ulua*. Knowing she liked to collect beautiful shells and coral rocks, Dave came up from a dive and told her that he saw a heart-shaped rock that was too deep for him to reach. Even with her cancer, Rell was still an impressive diver, and she volunteered to go get it for him. "So she took one breath, dove down, and grabbed the rock," Brian says with a smile. "When she looked down, the rock was engraved with 'Will you marry me?'" As she swam back up to the surface, she could see Dave silhouetted in the sunlight and knew that he was the one. She came up crying with joy and breathlessly said, "Yes!"

Rell and Dave decided to have a small, intimate wedding with just one or two friends and the minister. They planned to get married on the ocean in outrigger canoes, but as the small group paddled out, the lifeguards noticed something was up. "It's so hard to make things private because everybody knows everybody's business—the 'coconut wireless' is big down here," Brian says. "By the time she reached the shore, it was on the radio and on the TV that she was getting married at Makaha Beach. It spread that fast around the whole Island." After all, she was a well-known and beloved media figure, TV reporter, radio DJ, and community activist. People had seen articles and TV shows about her struggle with cancer, and they were happy to hear she had found love amid her suffering.

For a short yet blissful time, the couple surfed, fished, and dove together like kids in an ocean playground, as if unaware of the dark forces lurking beneath them. Like the tiger shark that once attacked her prize *ulua*, Rell's cancer returned with a vengeance. As strong and healthy as she looked on the outside, the disease was attacking her insides. Rell and Dave had to fly to Chicago to visit one of the nation's leading oncology centers. During her last treatment, her doctor was amazed by what a healthy attitude she had in the face of so much cancer. Lying in a hospital bed, she and Dave strummed 'ukulele and sang Hawaiian songs.

"Most physicians wouldn't have given her a couple of months to live," says Dr. Keith Block. "Rell had not only been pretreated, having gone through three chemotherapies and a bone marrow transplant, but she was also suffering from skin involvement, bone metastases, and liver metastases at the same time. Really an extraordinary amount of disease. In the midst of all that, believe it or not, she was still surfing almost every day." But now that the cancer had metastasized throughout her body, she and her doctor knew her time in this world was coming to an end.

"If I'm ever getting sick where you're worried about me, you have to promise me that you'll get me home in order that I can be in Makaha at the time that I die," she told her doctors. Yet even close friends like Kathy Terada, who worked with cancer patients on a daily basis, wanted to believe that Rell could still beat it. "She fooled us enough times where we thought she was going to outlive us all."

The wakeup call came when Rell's close friend Pua Moku'au found out that she, too, had breast cancer. A pure Hawaiian woman, Pua had been Rell's fellow lifeguard, waterwoman, and hula sister. Both had made Makaha their home, yet there seemed to be something in the land or the sea that was making them sick. The community was shocked when they heard about her cancer because she seemed to be a model of fitness and health. Yet as Rell would tell her fellow cancer patients, the Westside has some of the highest rates of breast cancer in the country and even the healthiest women get sick.

As close as Pua and Rell were, they dealt with their diseases in completely different ways. Rell had sought the most cutting-edge medical technology to treat her cancer and fought hard to prolong her life, but Pua barely sought any modern medical treatment at all and seemed to be at peace with the prospect of death. Focusing on traditional Hawaiian healing methods, nutrition, and fitness, Pua found comfort in studying her culture and deepening her faith. "Rell never talked too much about the spirituality of everything. Pua did a lot," Kathy says. "Rell was more of this world, this earth—*this* life is what was important. And Pua was more like 'what comes next,' which became real important for her. It was two different things, but you learned from them both."

While Pua's health seemed to improve for a while, Rell's took a downturn. She had trouble surfing and couldn't travel, not even to her daughter's wedding. While living in California, Jan had fallen in love with a local boy from Hawai'i named Tony Carreira, and they had recently become engaged. They were going to be married in the spring of 1997 in Southern California at their new house. Rell planned on being there, of course, but Dave and her doctor were saying that she shouldn't travel because she could get infected on the flight over. "If she gets sick, that's it; she's done," Jan says. "But others were telling my mom, 'It's your only daughter—you need to go.' So she was torn and totally conflicted."

In the end, Dave and her doctor decided that she shouldn't go because it was too risky. Rell was heartsick because she had once traveled all over the world, but now she couldn't even fly to California for her daughter's wedding. Yet Rell took some comfort in the fact that her mom and sisters went over in her place. The family all chipped in to decorate Jan's new house to make it look like Rell's cottage, her old home. Jan and her husband would later open up a popular store in Laguna Hills called Rell's Motel, where they would sell the kind of Hawaiian-style furniture and decorations that Jan's mom always loved.

On top of missing her only daughter's wedding, Rell lost her best friend, Pua, a month later. "She wanted to be there for Pua, and she reached out to her," Jan says. "But Pua chose another route, and she passed." Pua died suddenly, and her ashes were spread at Makaha, where she and Rell had surfed and worked as the first female lifeguards. "My mom was just crushed," Jan says, "and she lost herself for quite a long time."

Although her parents and grandparents were Catholic, Rell "did her own spiritual thing." According to Jan, she believed that her ancestors lived on as 'aumakua, or spiritual guardians, taking the forms of sea turtles or sharks or any aspect of nature. "All of our forefathers, all of our uncles, and everyone who had passed away were in the ocean," Rell once said, "so there was nothing to fear." Yet toward the end, she did start thinking about what the afterlife might be like. "She just felt like she'd be surfing; she'd be with Israel; she was not afraid of it," Jan says. "There were other family members waiting for her; Pua was there; she was ready."

During her last few months, Rell fought the hardest to stay alive and leave a legacy. Although she was dying, she agreed to take part in an independent documentary about her life that would create greater awareness about the dangers of breast cancer and the joys of surfing. In the film, called *Heart of the Sea,* Rell still looks healthy and beautiful, though her hair is short and her body thin from all the chemotherapy.

In the film, Rell talks candidly about how she may have contracted her cancer as an adolescent when they used to spray DDT in the area to get rid of mosquitoes and she would breathe in the toxic chemical. She also suspected that other possible causes for the extraordinarily high levels of cancer in the area could be the military's dumping of chemical munitions off the coast and hog farmers' dumping their animals' waste into the streams that flowed down into the ocean. In her subtle way, Rell made the connection that this kind of modern pollution was like a cancer infecting the land and ocean.

Rell never wanted to be remembered just for her cancer, and

in the film she talks more about the power of surfing, the beauty of Hawaiian culture, and the importance of protecting the environment. One of the Menehunes remembers how Rell used to hold beach cleanups after her contest and always used to tell the kids, "If you're gonna use this beach, you gotta take care of it, too. One of the Hawaiian values is *malama 'aina,* to care for the land, and *malama ke kai,* to care for the ocean." In the film, she says, "We don't want plastic in the ocean because of the turtles [who mistake it for jellyfish and often get sick and die after eating it]. That turtle could be somebody's ancestor who was protecting us."

Toward the end of 1997, Rell's health rapidly declined. In the documentary, the normally stoic lifeguard confesses through tears that her cancer had entered her lungs, making it hard to breathe and impossible to dive or surf. "You're like a basket case, and you're crying all the time," she says, "and you just think, 'God, this is not me.'"

In the most poignant moment of the film, Rell talks about how she loved taking local kids on Easter egg hunts on the reef and showing them the wonders of nature. "When we go in that tide pool out there on the reef, that's one of the first things that should catch a child's attention. Just flip that rock over and look at the life that's under it—that's the life in the ocean where we surf," Rell says with tears in her eyes. "And the beauty of surfing or being a kayaker or a canoer is the magic that Isak Dinesen wrote about in *Out of Africa,* when she says, 'Wherever I am in the world, I'll always wonder if it's raining in the Nayong Hills.' I'll always wonder if there's a trade wind or how big the swells are in the Kaiwi Channel. . . . We'll always have that in our hearts; we'll always wonder."

Knowing the end was near, Jan flew home for the last few months to help Dave and Rell's sisters take care of her. With her athletic build and six-foot frame, Jan towered over her mother, who looked so skinny and frail. "It was so hard," Jan says, especially "when you grow up with a mom who's been a lifeguard, a pro surfer, a diver." As Rell still wanted to be in the water, Dave and Brian would take her out and push her into the waves on a bodyboard. Just being in the ocean gave her joy, and watching her ride one last wave made her friends and family both happy and sad at the same time.

Friends started coming by her cottage to say their final good-byes. "The last time I saw her," her friend Pam Kaʻaihue says with tears in her eyes, "she was waving good-bye to me at the gate. And she gave me that look, kind of like 'it's the end.' I think that was the time she showed me the lesions all over her body—it looked like a map of the world."

During the last month, Jennifer Lee begged her parents to drive her out to Makaha to see Rell. After traveling to Biarritz with Rell, Jen had become like one of her children. "I just had to see her, but they wouldn't take me," Jen says. "I knew she was sick, and I was like 'Let me go. Take me. I need to see her.' But my parents were like 'She's sick. You shouldn't see her like that. Just remember her like the last time you saw her when she looked healthy.'"

After making it through Christmas, Rell vowed to hang on till New Year's. That year, Brian and the Keaulana boys paddled into the surf on New Year's Eve at 11:45 P.M. and caught the last wave of the old year and the first wave of the new one in honor of Rell. Coming in and out of consciousness, she could hear the fireworks in the distance, and she lived to see the dawn of a new year. But on the evening of January 2, 1998, at the age of forty-seven, Rell Kapoliokaʻehukai Sunn finally took her last breath and passed from this world to the next.

That same night, Jen had tossed and turned in bed, crying and worrying about Rell. "I get up in the morning and call the house, and someone says, 'Hello?'" she recalls. "And I said, 'Auntie Rell?!'" She sounded like her old self, young and healthy, and for a moment Jen thought that Rell might have recovered. "'Oh no, this is Nell, her sister. . . . I'm so sorry, but Auntie Rell passed away last night.'" Jen cried and felt sick for days, as if one of her own parents had died. "I dreamt about her like crazy when she passed away. This one dream I had was of her in Waikiki. I was walking in Waikiki, and I saw this lady in a red *mu'umu'u* [a flowered Hawaiian dress], and she was passing out flyers by the Duke statue. I was like 'Auntie Rell!' and she kept looking at me and looking away. 'Auntie Rell, Auntie Rell!' I'm crying and trying to make her look at me. She just looked at me and said, 'I'm okay; just go on.' And she gave me a hug, and I walked away. I woke up crying."

Two weeks later, on January 17, Rell's memorial service was held at Makaha. That morning, a cool mist hung over the green mountains and gray clouds covered the sky. The intermittent rain was considered a blessing in Hawaiian lore, marking the passing of an *ali'i*. Friends and family had set up a big tent on the beach and had been working hard all week to decorate it with pictures of Rell from different times in her life. There were photos of her surfing, diving, fishing, dancing hula, paddling canoes, working with the elderly, and playing with the Menehunes. Her surfboard, fishing spear, throw nets, and mementos were placed all around the tent. In the center, her ashes lay in a glass fishing ball, which had been carved with images of fish, waves, and an octopus, along with the words "Aloha, Queen of Makaha."

When Rell was just a girl, she had found a glass ball washed up on the beach at Mahaka and asked her father what it was. He had explained that it used to be tied to a fishing net, probably from Japan, and had floated all the way across the ocean. Years later, Rell would remember his words and wonder if he was telling her what her life would be like. "She symbolized herself as the floating glass ball," Jan says, "fragile yet strong, surfing the best spots but always coming home." And now, she was going back to the sea.

Thousands of people from the Westside, across the Islands, and all over the world began arriving for the service, filing into the tent to pay their last respects. The sound of the conch shell filled the air, signaling the beginning of the service. The Brothers Cazimero played some of her favorite songs, like "The Sound of the Sea Surrounds Me," and prayers and chants were said in her memory while hula sisters danced in her honor. Local reporter Ron Mizutani gave the eulogy, but he and others kept breaking into tears during their tributes.

At the end of the formal service, Brian Keaulana organized a ceremony where people could bring seawater and sand from their local beaches and mix them in a big wooden bowl on the beach. People brought sand and water from all of the Hawaiian Islands and from places as far away as Australia and Fiji. "Because Rell has touched so many people, she also touched many shores and many oceans," Brian said. "This is a way of giving back . . . like an ocean community around the world."

For the scattering of her ashes, Rell had asked Brian months before to take charge of the ceremony. They were surfing one day at Makaha, and she looked at him and said, "You know, it's not if, but when I pass away. Brian, just remember, this is where I want to be." It was a specific area right near the Blowhole, which was her favorite takeoff spot when she was surfing. Brian made sure that no one was in the water at the time. "The only person who is going to be surfing will be Rell Sunn. We're putting her to rest at the Makaha Blowhole."

Steering from the back of the outrigger canoe, Brian paddled with her daughter, Jan, her brother, Eric, and her husband, Dave, into the four- to six-foot waves. After almost being swamped by a large set of waves, Brian says he was trying to find the exact spot where the Blowhole was when he received a sign. "All of a sudden, the boil just erupted right there in front of us. It was like she was playing games with us, hide and go seek. When Dave poured her ashes out, it was like this big bloom of ash—she got her wish." They caught a wave in the canoe and rode it to shore, and then friends were invited to paddle out and catch a last wave in honor of Rell.

Eleven months later, on New Year's Eve 1998, Brian, his

brothers, and several friends paddled out into the black water for their annual midnight surf session. The last year and a half had been difficult for Brian and the entire Makaha community after losing Israel and Rell. Both friends were weighing heavily on Brian's mind as he glided through the liquid darkness, waiting to catch the final wave of the old year and the first wave of the new one.

Sitting on his surfboard, looking up at the sky, Brian saw fireworks exploding above. Watching them streak across the sky, he thought about Rell and Iz. Like shooting stars, their lives had burned out all too soon. But both friends had left behind an enduring legacy of light and love. Their ashes had become one with the healing waters all around him, and their memories would live on in the hearts of his people. Comforted by their presence, Brian caught a wave in the darkness and rode it toward the lights on the shore.

CHAPTER 14

⊃⊂ ⊃⊂ ⊃⊂ ⊃⊂ ⊃⊂ ⊃⊂ ⊃⊂ ⊃⊂ ⊃⊂ ⊃⊂ ⊃⊂

Aloha Means "Love"

He ʻohu ke aloha; ʻaʻohe kauhiwi kau ʻole.
Love is like mist; there is no mountaintop that it does not settle upon.

—Hawaiian proverb

(translated by Mary Kawena Pukui)

With the passing of Israel and Rell, Brian began to see traces of their legacies everywhere he looked. A chubby boy playing his ʻukulele on the beach, an athletic girl riding the waves at Makaha. Having witnessed Israel's and Rell's years of suffering,

Brian was inspired by their courage, love, and commitment to their community, even in the face of death.

Barely able to take more than a few steps without stopping to rest, Iz had still struggled to walk onstage and put on one last benefit concert. When he could no longer perform, he sang in his hospital bed. Riddled with cancer, Rell had still managed to take twenty-odd kids to the Biarritz Surf Festival and put on her annual Menehune Contest. Although they had died relatively young, both friends had made the most of their talents and captured a bit of eternity in the process. Though Rell and Iz never got to meet their grandchildren, not long after they passed away both Jan and Wehe had their first babies.

Israel's music would continue to skyrocket in popularity, and his posthumous release *Alone in IZ World* rose to the top of the charts. His 'ukulele version of "Somewhere over the Rainbow / What a Wonderful World" would eventually become one of the most popular and downloaded songs in the world. Singing with a childlike innocence, the Gentle Giant gave new life to the old lyrics: "I hear babies cry and I watch them grow / They'll learn more than we'll ever know / And I think to myself, What a wonderful world." Adopted by producers and advertisers, the song has appeared in more than seventeen Hollywood films, on thirty-two TV shows, and in scores of commercials, from Italy to Australia. But his wife, Marlene, says his most enduring legacy was "the love that he had for his culture. . . . I think he showed a lot of them how to love unconditionally."

For Rell's Menehune Contest the following year, Jan flew in from California to help Brian and the others run the event. His daughter, Ha'a, and son, Chad, would compete in the contest with scores of other kids as large crowds of friends and families gathered on the beach to watch. Sitting in the lifeguard tower where he used to work, Brian looked out over the ocean and remembered his friend. "Emotionally, it is hard," he said. "All of us are trying to deal with it. But the bright side is that Rell was always focused on our future, the kids . . . I feel her essence here in the waves and the water. But also in each kid she touched. I see her in each smile or in their fluidness on the waves."

The contest would continue to grow in size and popularity each year, and now Quiksilver is helping to organize a Triple Lei of Menehune Contests in California, Hawai'i, and Tahiti. Jan and her husband, Tony, have created the Rell Sunn Educational Fund to help promote breast cancer awareness and work with local hospitals to provide treatment and find a cure. Like waves moving across the ocean, Rell's legacy seems to keep traveling to distant shores. When the film about her life called *Heart of the Sea* aired on national television, it was one of the highest rated documentaries shown on PBS. A bronze bust of Iz was erected in Wai'anae, and Jan is working to raise funds to create a statue of Rell as well.

Inspired by Rell and Iz, Brian decided to pursue his passions for traveling, big-wave riding, and filmmaking. As much as he loved his life in Makaha, Brian became increasingly restless and eager to explore more of the world. "Even when I was a small kid, all I thought about was traveling, getting away from here," he says. Ever since the days when he sat in the lifeguard tower reading comic books, Brian had dreamed about being in the movies, in front of the camera and behind. After working as a stuntman on *Waterworld,* he was hooked. Brian eventually had to leave the lifeguard service because he was getting more gigs with the Hawaiian Water Patrol as a stuntman and water safety specialist. Besides, the film industry paid ten times as much as the city and county and gave him more creative freedom to travel and do the things he loved.

After his first gig with *Baywatch* in the late eighties, Brian went on to work on the sequel, *Baywatch Hawai'i,* in the late nineties. He was not only in charge of water safety behind the scenes, but he also starred in several episodes as the wise local lifeguard. By 1998, he was so well established in the film business and the surf world that he was basically asked to play himself in an upcoming movie called *In God's Hands*.

Although the film suffered from a choppy plot and inconsistent acting, *In God's Hands* allowed Brian's talents to shine on the big screen. One of the unique aspects of the movie is that it was one of the first Hollywood feature films to showcase tow-in surfing and actors who actually surfed, including newcomers like Shane Dorian and Matty Liu and legends like Gerry Lopez and Shaun Tomson. After Brian pioneered the use of Jet Skis in rescue techniques, tow-in surfing quickly became the cutting edge of extreme sports. Laird Hamilton, Dave Kalama, Buzzy Kerbox, and a few hard-core watermen on Maui were now using the skis to tow surfers into huge swells at the outer reef called Jaws, where the waves were too big and fast to paddle into. Photos of Laird and friends riding sixty- to seventy-foot monsters began appearing in the surf magazines and in the mainstream media. Images of these men riding mountains of water blew people away.

In order to capture the excitement of this new extreme sport, Zalman King, the director of *In God's Hands,* worked with surfer-writer-actor Matt George to concoct a story that would follow a group of hard-core big-wave surfers trying to ride the biggest waves in the world. In the movie, Brian is portrayed as a fearless big-wave rider and yet a cautious lifeguard as well. He is training them how to do tow-in surfing in the biggest swells ever ridden, yet he wants to make sure nobody dies in the process. Behind the scenes, he was also hired as the water stunt coordinator, which was a big promotion and a risky venture. In pursuing the ultimate tow-in surfing scenes at Jaws, Brian often had to put himself and his friends in the most dangerous waves and ride the line between life and death.

"There are two types of surfers that we have to be concerned with in surfing waves that can kill you," Brian says in the film as the other surfers huddle around and listen intently. "One is the gung-ho surfer. This guy does not consider the risks, and the other guy is gun-shy—he does not want to accept the risks. In this gauge right here, gung-ho and gun-shy, one focuses on his abilities and the other focuses on his limitations. . . . Another thing you have to understand is that we can augment our own abilities through the technology we have. But technology isn't everything." Although he originally pioneered the use of Jet Skis to save people, he was now using them to sling his fellow surfers into tsunami-sized waves.

Brian's lines came straight out of his playbook on ocean safety, and in the scene he's deadly serious because he knows just how dangerous filming these scenes can be. Even with life-guards on Jet Skis racing around and medics in helicopters hovering above, there is always the chance a big wave can snuff out even the most experienced surfer's life. In fact, the big-wave surfer Mark Foo had died in giant waves at a Northern California break called Maverick's in Half Moon Bay in 1995. His lethal slow-motion wipeout was caught on film, and the image haunted the surfing world.

A year before *In God's Hands* was released, Todd Chesser, the stunt double for Matt George's character in the film, also drowned while surfing big waves at an outer reef break called Alligator Rock. Todd's mother, Jeannie, was good friends with Rell, and their two kids had grown up together. Within one year Jeannie lost both her son and her best friend, and a decade later she, too, was diagnosed with cancer. But like Rell, Jeannie is a fighter and a strong waterwoman, and the surfing community rallied together to help her.

Working in such a dangerous environment, Brian and the others knew what was at stake. "As we all know when we surf big waves, you can be held under for more than one wave," Brian tells the surfers in one scene, perhaps recalling the time years before when he was held underwater at the Eddie Contest for several waves at Waimea Bay. "We understand the risks involved. We know exactly what we're up against. We know exactly what our bodies are able to do. We practice extreme safety when we're doing extreme things." South African surfer Shaun Tomson plays the wise tribal elder of the group, and he questions whether such extremes are worth risking their lives. "At what price?" he asks. "When only the most skilled stand a chance to survive, to ride waves this big is to put yourself in God's hands." These lines would resonate deeply with every surfer who ever put their life on the line in huge surf.

Laird Hamilton and Dave Kalama were the original Jedi masters at Jaws, and they had perfected the art of tow-in surfing at this remote outer reef. But when the director and his film crew suddenly converged on the scene with all of their boats, helicopters, and camera equipment, Laird and Dave wondered if these slick Hollywood types were dangerously out of their element. But both men knew Brian was the man to have on board when it came to driving Jet Skis, filming massive waves, and providing safety for surfers and cinematographers.

"Brian is where the past meets the present in Hawaiian culture," says Laird Hamilton. "He's like an ancient warrior, but he's armed with all the modern amenities and knows how to use them." In one scene, he trains the younger surfers by having them dive down twenty feet and run along the seafloor with heavy rocks—just like he did with his former lifeguards. It looks like an ancient ritual performed in slow motion underwater, and it's a striking contrast with the fast-paced scenes of modern Jet Skis whipping the surfers into giant waves.

While working on the liquid set of *In God's Hands* at Jaws, Brian wanted to test the rescue teams and his own endurance in the crushing waves. Before risking anyone else's life, he had to experience the full force and fury of Jaws to measure the danger and see if he could survive. So he took off on a monster thirty-foot swell and wiped out on purpose right in the impact zone! Brian must have felt like someone going over Niagara Falls, as walls of white water three stories high pummeled him and slammed him against the coral reef seafloor. When he finally surfaced, he waved off two Jet Ski operators and took two more white-water avalanches on the head before he let the third ski pick him up.

"The difference with tow-in surfing is that it's not about surfing," Brian says. "It's about surviving." He knew that he always had to be ready for anything. "You train for the worst, you hope for the best, and you expect the unexpected."

"Brian's one of those people who gives you more confidence by his presence alone," Dave Kalama says. "If you know he's there, it helps you surf better." During one of their most epic sessions at Jaws during the filming, Dave adds, "I towed him into a wave that really jacked up. I knew he was really deep. I couldn't see it because I'd driven out the back, but Mark Angulo was right on the shoulder, watching the whole thing." Sitting in the channel, Mark says he saw Brian disappear into the roaring maw of the beast and thought for sure he had been devoured by it. "Two or three times, I thought he was gone. But the thing held open; he weaved a perfect line and came out. Unbelievable moment!" Brian's epic tube ride was captured on film during one of the most dramatic scenes of *In God's Hands*. For a full five or six seconds, he stood in the eye of that churning hurricane of water. "Probably the highlight of my life," Brian says. "The biggest, best, deepest barrel I've ever had."

Throughout the film, the surfer-actors argue about the merits of using modern Jet Skis to tow them into the waves as opposed to the traditional method of paddling into the waves. This same argument would divide much of the surfing world, and it later came to a head during the Quiksilver in Memory of Eddie Aikau Contest. On the morning of January 7, 2002, Brian and other big-wave riders were forced to decide whether to compete in "the Eddie" on Oʻahu or fly over to Maui for the first annual Tow-in World Cup, which was being held on the same day. Did they want to paddle into the big surf at Waimea Bay or be towed into massive waves at Jaws? It was a classic choice between man versus machine, tradition versus technology. While some surfers chose to compete in the Tow-in World Cup, Brian and most of the other invitees decided to stay for the Eddie contest. The prevailing feeling that day at Waimea Bay was that "Eddie Wouldn't Tow."

The swells were huge, and Brian and Rusty caught some great rides. But world champion Kelly Slater won the event by catching the biggest and longest waves of the day.

Though he enjoys the thrill of tow-in surfing and riding the world's biggest waves, Brian's loyalties still lie with the Eddie Contest. "For me, the whole competition and the money are secondary. It's really important to represent who Eddie was and what he did." Brian and Rusty competed against each other in the next Quiksilver event that was held at Waimea Bay on December 15, 2004. "Me and my brother, we're real competitive with each other," Brian says. "There's always that feeling of 'Okay, let's charge, do good, and don't get hurt.' It's that brotherly rivalry, as well as that love also." World champ Andy Irons was also competing against his brother Bruce in the contest. Bruce won the event after catching one of the biggest outside waves of the day and riding it all the way into the massive shorebreak. Just before disappearing into a bone-crunching, close-out tube, he raised up his arms in a victory salute. When he emerged uninjured in the shallows a few seconds later, the crowds on the beach roared.

Brian continued doing stunt work on several big-budget Hollywood films, but the biggest was the blockbuster movie *Pearl Harbor* in 2001. Working in the world's largest water tank in Rosarito, Mexico (where they filmed much of *Titanic*), Brian and his partner Terry Ahue had to stand on the decks of these big model battleships and be set on fire during the explosions. "They rolled the ship and blew everything up," Terry says. "It was like the *Arizona* sinking. We had like forty of us stunt guys running around on deck. They built this gimbo boat, and it went completely over." Scene after scene, they had to be lit on fire and then fall some thirty feet into the water as the ships rolled over. It was a physically demanding and punishing job, but Brian and Terry knew the importance of reenacting one of the most crucial scenes in American history. In honor of his stunt work, Brian was asked to join an elite international group called Stunts Unlimited, which includes only forty members around the world.

The following year, he and Terry worked on the film *Blue Crush,* filming on the North Shore and on the Westside. The movie reflected the growing influence of women in surfing, thanks in part to the enduring legacy of pioneering pro surfers like Rell Sunn. Again, the film's story line was not the strongest, but Brian worked with the director to make the surfing scenes look real and the wipeouts painful. Even though his title was co–stunt coordinator, Brian was basically the second-unit director in charge of filming most of the surfing scenes. "They give me the storyboards and say, 'Oh, can you do this?' So I do 'em, and I'm actually doing it for them," Brian says, "but they're getting all the credit." But more than credits, Brian focused on the safety of the surfers and the successful completion of each shot.

"The one thing about Brian that's really great is that he's such a team player," says cinematographer Don King, who worked with him on *In God's Hands.* "He doesn't need to be the guy getting the credit. He's just really working to make sure it's a successful production. . . . He's really got a lot of creative ideas." His wife, Nobleen, once asked him where he came up with the ideas to translate the storyboards into actual scenes, and he told her, "Believe it or not, it's from reading the comics." Although she used to tease him about his large comic book collection, Nobleen laughed and said, "Really? That paid off!" Along with doing work on the hit show *Lost,* Brian later became a second-unit director and even helped produce a cable TV series about surfing called *Beyond the Break,* which was filmed in Makaha.

Building on his credentials as a water safety specialist, stunt coordinator, and second-unit director, Brian continued to get bigger and better job offers as his reputation and salary rose in the film industry. He had access to some of the biggest names in Hollywood and was often at the beach talking to some producer on his cell phone. With his dark glasses, cool demeanor, and smooth voice, he looked and sounded like some movie mogul living in

Makaha. Some locals couldn't help but be jealous of his success, but most realized how hard he had worked to achieve it. His gnawed fingernails and tired eyes couldn't hide the stress and fatigue he often felt. "He started from the bottom," Nobleen says. "People forget all our sacrifices."

Brian's tandem partner and good friend Kathy Terada recalls that as a lifeguard captain he always tried to share his success with others. "He would see their strengths and bring that out in them, and I always admired that," Kathy says. "He could have just stayed on the beach as a lifeguard and been like everybody else, and he would have done well at it. But he took the chance of leaving the department and going out on his own, and he did it! And now, he's trying to bring other people into the business with him. To me, he's such a self-made person."

Along with training younger lifeguards like Craig Davidson to do water safety and stunt work, Brian and Terry helped countless friends like Mel Puʻu get into the film business. Recognizing Brian's contributions to the industry, the Hawaiʻi International Film Festival gave him and his partners the 2004 Film in Hawaiʻi Award during their closing ceremony. "In my mind, Brian is a modern-day Duke Kahanamoku," said film commissioner Donne Dawson. "He has quickly become an ambassador for Hawaiʻi and our film industry."

Along with being an Olympic athlete and the father of modern surfing, Duke was the original "Ambassador of Aloha." On the back of his business cards, the silver-haired surfer had once written: "In Hawaiʻi, we greet friends, loved ones and strangers with aloha, which means love." Following in his wake and inspired by his example, Buffalo had helped rally his people together around Hawaiian cultural values and fun community events at his Big Board Classic. Now Brian was helping to carry that flame forward by developing Hawaiʻi's film industry, which celebrates the Islands' unique culture and landscape without damaging the environment. As Greg Noll once said, "Buff took the torch from the Duke, and Brian will take the torch from Buffalo."

In one of his earliest recollections, Brian remembers when Duke Kahanamoku came down to the Westside in the mid-sixties and was so warm to his family. Buffalo and Momi knew the legendary waterman and Olympic athlete during their days working in Waikiki, and they were proud to introduce him to their first son. "One of my favorite memories is of sitting in the Duke's lap as a young boy," Brian says. "He was already of an old age at that time, and I recall him coming out to Makaha in his white tuxedo suit as a guest of the Makaha International. He influenced so many people in his prime and throughout his lifetime. When I think of Duke Kahanamoku, I think of someone who willingly shared his knowledge, his abilities, and his aloha in a way that represents the heart of Hawai'i and what it means to truly be a waterman."

In honor of Duke's legacy, a bronze statue of him was erected in the heart of Waikiki. Standing in front of his tall surfboard with his arms open wide, this larger-than-life figure still welcomes people each year to Duke's OceanFest, which is celebrated during the week of his birthday on August 24. When Brian returned to Waikiki for the OceanFest competitions in 2006, he was the leading contender in the tandem surfing event. Standing on the beach with the thousands of tourists and locals, Brian couldn't help but think of how Duke and generations of beach boys like Uncle George Downing and Buffalo had helped pioneer so many different aspects of surfing. Now Brian and his generation were continuing to shape the modern evolution of the sport.

Back in his day, Duke had been one of the first surfers to perform the art of tandem surfing when he hoisted visiting female tourists on his shoulders and had them pose for the cameras and crowds in Waikiki. (In old Hawai'i, men and women used to surf together on the same board, including King Kamehameha and his wife Ka'ahumanu, but they didn't do the acrobatic moves associated with the sport.) Duke was also one of the first to do stand-up paddle (SUP) surfing, using a long canoe paddle to paddle around on his board.

Both water sports enjoyed periodic bursts of popularity during the sixties and seventies when two beach boys and brothers named Leroy and Bobby Ah Choy became masters of tandem and SUP surfing. Partnering with an acrobatic young haole girl named Blanche Benson, Leroy had won a couple of tandem surfing events at the Makaha International. As a photographer, Bobby had really developed SUP surfing so he could take better pictures of tourists surfing. Brian remembers seeing Leroy hoist Blanche up in the air and compete in his backyard at the International while Bobby paddled around like a modern gondolier, snapping shots of tourists.

Tandem surfing's popularity declined after the demise of the Makaha International in the early seventies, but the sport began to thrive again at the Buffalo Big Board Classic, the Biarritz Surf Festival, and other contests around the world. Surfing with his partner Kathy Terada, Brian had led the pair to many victories in Hawai'i, California, and France over the years. Although ten years older, Kathy was still in perfect shape, and she and Brian worked well together. But as tandem surfing enjoyed an international revival in the nineties, the competition grew tougher. Even though Brian had injured his back a week before, he and Kathy were competing in the OceanFest in 2006 against a former French decathlete and his partner and a number of talented younger pairs from Hawai'i, Australia, and California. Some of the women were trained gymnasts and acrobatic artists from Cirque du Soleil.

During the finals, Brian paddled into the waves and gently lifted up Kathy as she performed a series of balletlike maneuvers, including the One-Knee Stand, the Helicopter, and the High Swan. Tandem surfing is very similar to ice skating, and there are almost fifty poses, which are incredibly difficult to perform on such a shifting surface. The crowds were astonished Brian and Kathy could pull off such strenuous acrobatic poses on a liquid stage, while gracefully riding their board across the waves. During the awards ceremony, the judges announced that Brian and Kathy had won the contest and a new world title.

Brian also helped bring about the revival of SUP. Although Bobby Ah Choy inspired a number of beach boys to try stand-up paddle surfing in the sixties, the sport was virtually unknown until Laird Hamilton resurrected it in the late nineties. Laird began pushing the limits of the sport, originally conceived as a fun thing to do when the waves were flat, and demonstrating what a great form of core exercise it was. Gradually, he and his buddy Dave Kalama started taking it around the world, paddling their boards down the rapids of the Colorado River, across the English Channel, and into giant waves at Tahiti's Teahopu. After picking it up from Laird in Tahiti, Brian became hooked on the sport and brought it back to Makaha.

"I brought that home, and I was the only guy on the Westside paddling around and catching waves," Brian says. Following his lead, locals like Bunky Bakutis and Bruce DeSoto took up stand-up paddle surfing. Most of them used their big tandem boards for stand-up surfing and referred to them as their "standem" boards. Brian then introduced SUP surfing to his dad's contest, and the sport jumped up in popularity like a young surfer catching his biggest wave. "So the first stand-up contest in the world was at Makaha," Brian says proudly. In 2006, he decided to compete in the first SUP contest in Waikiki.

During the competition, Brian found himself going head-to-head with young world champions like Bonga Perkins and older beach boys like Bobby Ah Choy, who was still an active and talented waterman. The waves were small but fun, and Brian was able to paddle his board into some of the best waves of the day. He would swing around his SUP board like a shortboard, while wielding the paddle like a martial arts weapon as he flew across the waves. In the finals, he barely managed to beat Bonga

Perkins to win the contest. But when they announced that Brian had won, he took his trophy and gave it to Bobby Ah Choy in honor of all that the older beach boy had done for the sport. It was a spontaneous and heartfelt gesture, and the fans at the ceremony were moved by Brian's tribute.

Seeing the growing popularity of SUP surfing, Brian joined two partners to form C4 Waterman, a company that makes and sells SUP boards and paddles. His friend Dave Parmenter designed and shaped many of the boards. Because SUP surfing is such a good workout and can be done on any body of water, the sport began to take off in Hawai'i, on the mainland, and across the world. But Brian was more focused on perpetuating a certain lifestyle than making a lot of money. "I wanted to get into the sport not just to start our own business but also to drive the sport in the direction where it started from in the beginning with the watermen and the Hawai'i beach boys, people who had etiquette and respect," he says. "A lot of this is driven by our strong values—respect the environment, respect other people."

Brian says his company's name, C4 Waterman, stands for the four core values that define what it means to be a waterman: Balance, Endurance, Strength, and Tradition (BEST). But these values go beyond physical skills to include emotional, mental, spiritual, and cultural dimensions. Brian wears many different hats and has to balance his roles as husband, father, athlete, and businessman. "In everyday life, you're always playing this balancing game," he says, but his work often took him away from home. Whether promoting stand-up surfing in Japan, filming in California, or competing in a tandem competition in Spain, Brian found himself constantly traveling on the road or in the air. But after being away so much, Brian began spending more time in Makaha so he could be with his family and give back to his community.

SUP surfing requires incredible balance, but Brian likes to say that surfing is just a metaphor for the balance that we have to maintain in our personal and professional lives as well. Knowing the Westside has the highest rates of poverty, crime, and addiction in Hawai'i, Brian says he and many of his friends were saved from these pitfalls by water sports and the ocean's healing touch. In order to give back to the community where he grew up, he and his partners worked with Red Bull to put on the new Quiksilver Ku Ikaika (Stand Strong) Challenge. This is the world's first big-wave SUP surfing event, bringing together twenty-four of the world's best competitors at Makaha. But unlike other big contests, all the prize money would go to local organizations trying to help the community.

Like the Quiksilver in Memory of Eddie Contest at Waimea, the Ku Ikaika Challenge has a minimum wave height and a holding period during January and February. When a big swell finally hit Makaha Beach on February 14, 2008, it looked like it might be another Valentine's Day Massacre as surfers tried to paddle their big boards through the heaving eight- to twelve-foot sets. But the competitors caught some spectacular rides and had a great time. Aaron Napoleon won the event and Brian's nephew Keoni placed second, and their prize money went to the Westside Junior Lifeguard Association and other charities on the Wai'anae Coast. "What we're trying to do is heal this side, give back to this side," Brian says. "It's more about giving."

While Brian built up his new company, C4 Waterman, and worked in the film industry, Rusty continued to surf for Quiksilver in longboard competitions around the world. For almost eight years, he and his wife, Sunny, managed the Russ K Makaha store in Honolulu. But the couple eventually separated, and they sold their share in the store to their partner, Craig Inouye. After leaving Quiksilver, Rusty then developed a partnership with a Japanese surf company called Russ K Makaha Crimson, with whom he signed a ten-year contract that allows him to surf and compete across the globe.

Buffalo, Brian, and the rest of the Keaulana clan also formed a partnership with the Bandai Corporation, which sponsored the line of surf products called Real B Voice. The *B* stands for

"Buffalo," who is revered like a tribal chief in Japan. As the second-largest toy manufacturer in the world, the Bandai Corporation has more money than God. But the executives didn't create the company just to make more money; they were motivated more by a love of Hawai'i and surfing. They formed the company after coming to the Buffalo Big Board Classic one year and competing in the heats reserved for the international visitors. Wanting to hold a similar event in Japan, they had formed a partnership with the Keaulanas to manufacture surf clothing and hold the Buffalo Classic in Japan.

Tony "Ants" Guerrero says that Buffalo is more well-known outside of the United States than he is in his own country or even in Hawai'i. In Japan, he is a living legend. In fact, the Japanese corporation that owns Real B Voice pays to fly out the entire Keaulana family and their extended 'ohana of friends to Japan each year. In 2005, the corporation hosted twenty-three members of the family and paid for all their expenses during their two-week stay. "Buffalo is like a sumo wrestler over there," Ants laughs. "Every place we went, there were lines. Buff is sitting down and signing autographs for three or four hours straight. They're bringing him gifts. He is truly an ambassador for Hawai'i."

Great Hawaiian watermen often have to pass into the big ocean beyond before being recognized for all of their accomplishments. But not Richard "Buffalo" Keaulana, who is still surfing and having fun in his seventies. The recipient of many awards, he lets the honors roll off his back like water. In fact, 2005 might as well have been the Year of the Buffalo. He was inducted into the Surfing Hall of Fame in Huntington Beach, joining the ranks of beloved legends like Duke and Rell.

That same year, Buffalo was also selected as one of the "Honolulu 100," a list of leaders "who have made a significant contribution to the city, its life and culture" over the last century. Israel Kamakawiwo'ole was among the one hundred honorees, and his widow, Marlene, joined the huge entourage of Keaulanas to celebrate at the Royal Hawaiian Hotel. "They've got a great big *'ohana,* and they are blessed and fortunate to have that," Marlene says. "It's wonderful for them to be able to enjoy this time of life."

In spite of his advancing age and white hair, Buffalo still acts like a *kolohe* kid with a sneaky sense of humor. "He's seventy-one going on seventeen," Brian once joked. Hearing of Buffalo's close relationship to nature, an admiring fan approached the elder surfer and asked if he could really tell time just by looking at the sky. He said he could and told the man to hold out his hand to measure the distance of the sun from the horizon. Rubbing his chin, Buffalo then told him the exact time, down to the minute. The man was blown away and asked Buffalo to perform the same feat several days in a row. When the man finally asked how Buffalo did it, the wise Native Hawaiian said that he pointed to the horizon, measured the distance of the sun, and then looked at the man's wristwatch!

Another time, a young local surfer was bragging to Uncle Buff about how good the surf had been the day before, saying, "You should have been here yesterday." Nodding his head, Buffalo just looked at the boy and said, "You should have been here forty years ago." When offered a role as a tribal chief in the movie *In God's Hands,* Buffalo supposedly walked up to the director, raised his hand, and said, "How," like a movie Native American. Then, he lowered his hand with his palm out and said, "How much?" If Hollywood wanted Buffalo, they would have to pay.

Looking back over his life, Buffalo could trace his own success to the growth of Makaha. Born and raised in the mean streets of the wild Westside, Buffalo grew up fighting against grinding poverty and prejudice. But he was able to find food and comfort in the ocean and make lifelong friends with strange haole watermen such Greg "Da Bull" Noll, who came to surf each year. With the advent of the Makaha International Surfing Championships in the mid-fifties, Buffalo's sleepy beach village was suddenly swarmed with thousands of people from Hawai'i and across the globe. The annual migration put Makaha on the map and offered a window to the world for local boys like Buffalo.

After venturing out to Waikiki, Buffalo found a wife, moved back to Makaha, and began raising a family. Although the surfing world forgot about Makaha for a decade or so, he helped bring the community together with the Buffalo Big Board Classic, which was based on "fun and good sportsmanship." As surf historian Mark Fragale put it, "Where the old Makaha International Championships left off is where Buffalo's contest took off and ran. It's now become basically a celebration of surfing that supercedes the competition itself." His contest helped resurrect the lost arts of tandem surfing, longboarding, and SUP surfing. As Brian's business partner Todd Bradley once put it, "We're watermen—no one piece of equipment defines who we are."

Once referred to as "Buffalo's Soldiers," his sons have gone on to become champions in each of these fields. Rusty and Jimmy have the name "KEAULANA" proudly tattooed across their backs, and Brian has it carved in wrought iron on his truck. "All the boys are part of the father," Uncle Ants says. "When it comes down to leadership and people following him around, Brian's the man. Rusty's the star. And Jimmy's the blue-collar man who's always working."

Jimmy is a talented waterman in his own right, but he likes doing construction and staying out of the limelight. He says being Buff's son is a "heavy load to carry, but my brothers take care of the water part, and I'm there to fix things." He laughs about the time when Brian's bathroom plumbing broke down and he cut the first pipe he could find, sending water everywhere. Like his mother, Momi, Jimmy is a natural with plumbing and mechanical repairs, and he had to come save Brian from flooding his entire home.

No matter what struggles and conflicts the family has endured, Buffalo and Momi have always been there to pick up the pieces and help raise their kids and grandchildren. "It's tough, but they've done a great job," Ants says. Even during the darkest times, Momi has been a source of light and strength not only for her entire family but for the community as well. The late surfing legend Tiger Espere once said, "Momi is like a lighthouse that beckons to me. . . . No matter how far you are from her, you can still see the light."

Each year, all the extended Keaulana clan still gathers at the Buffalo Big Board Classic. According to Brian, watching his father's meet is like seeing the essence of old Makaha and what it means to be a real waterman. "In just a couple of days, you see our whole lifetime—canoe surfing, bodysurfing, *paipo* boards, team surfing, you name it." Along with showing off their skills, competitors perform funny surf poses like the Headstand, the Coffin (lying on your back, arms folded across your chest), and the Boogie Bird maneuver (standing on one leg, spouting water out of your mouth), which was named after Boogie Kalama. Yet in the tandem competitions, Brian and Kathy and the other pairs perform incredibly beautiful and balletlike poses like the Big Arrow, where he holds her above his head with one hand as if she were flying above the waves. From the silly to the sublime, the Buffalo Classic has it all.

During the contest, most of Makaha's major clans set up their tents and camp out on the beach to take part in the different events and cheer on family members. Though usually friendly, the rivalries between the Keaulanas, the DeSotos, and the Rapozas can be intense at times. "It's like the McCoys and the Hatfields out there," says Quiksilver representative Glen Moncata, whose company helps sponsor the Rell Sunn Menehune Contest and the Makahiki Festival in Makaha. "But if push comes to shove, they're all brothers out there. If you're from that side, they've got your back."

They also love to play games on each other. One year during the longboard contest, Rusty paddled out with a big grin on his face and a bottle of baby oil in his shorts. "He paddles out into his heat and starts squirting oil on everyone's boards so no one can stand up. Everybody's falling off," Glen says with a laugh. "They're just hilarious."

"Buff's contest is the best surfing contest in the world, period," says longtime lifeguard Mark Cunningham. "It's bitchin'. It's like a big-ass family reunion." While Rusty and Mel play tricks on each other, Brian does his best to make sure everything runs smoothly. "You watch him at Buff's contest," Mark says, "and he will be competing, dealing with sponsors, coordinating water patrol, going out in heats, watching his kids and the neighborhood kids in the shore break . . . He does it all in such a quiet, dignified way."

Locals, pro surfers, and international guests come each year to take part in the contest. When asked what draws so many people to Buffalo and his contest, Mark says, "It's like paying homage to a Buddha in the Orient. . . . Oh, this is what the magic is all about, and it's not just because he has a big ʻopu (belly). He just kind of radiates a real Zen happiness in his life." Driving out to the wild Westside, people love watching the legendary Buffalo ride again. It's like taking a trip back to Hawaiʻi's past, where the culture still holds firm to its roots.

According to his old friend Greg Noll, Buffalo may not be rich, but he's happy. "I've often thought to myself, 'What is success?' Is it the haole version of how much stuff you own, how much money you've got in the bank, and how thick your portfolio is?" Greg says. "Hawaiians measure success by how many friends you have, how big your family is, and how much you get to surf—things like that. It's a whole different yardstick." Along with his talented children and loving wife, Greg adds that Buffalo has "so goddamn many grandkids that I don't think he can remember all of their names! Success is measured in different ways, and I think Buffalo is one of the most successful people I know."

Hawaiians also measure success by how generous they can be, and historically, this also led to their being taken advantage of. "I talked to Rell Sunn one time, and she said that the best way to describe Hawaiians is that they give and they give until there's nothing left to give," Greg says with tears in his eyes. "And look at the history—they gave their land away; they gave everything away." Although many Hawaiians still wrestle with resentment against haoles, Momi says that they all must live together.

"You can't condemn a whole race—that's not fair. . . . All the races are good, but you have people who are very greedy, and they use the law to get your land. And that's what they're doing to us." With more wealthy people moving to Makaha and driving up home prices and taxes, Buffalo says that more and more Hawaiians are being forced to move away to the mainland, where the land is cheaper. "How can you go to a place and call it Hawai'i when there's no Hawaiians there?" he asks. "Somebody should write a book called *Strangers in Our Own Land,*" Momi adds.

Having served in the army, Buffalo is proud to be American. But many Native Hawaiians resent the military's continued desecration of the land. Just as the island of Kaho'olawe was returned to the Hawaiian people in the late nineties, they believe that the military should stop bombing Makua and return it as well. Like Israel, they just want justice for their people. Buffalo's fighting days are over, and now he just wants to focus on his family and bring his community closer together, no matter what their background. "Buff is not an activist. He's a mainstream Hawaiian who believes that people should be treated fairly," Uncle Ants Guerrero says. "Buff takes people not by color but by who they are. It's about having a Hawaiian heart."

When Kathy Terada first moved to the Westside, she knew hardly anyone. Yet she recalls how Rell and the Keaulanas just took in her and showed her the best of their culture. "I feel so lucky to have made the choice to move to Wai'anae and become a part of that community," Kathy says. "There are very few places in Hawai'i left like that, where people still take care of each other. It's still a community and a family out there, and I don't think you find that hardly anymore . . . I'm not Hawaiian, my husband's not Hawaiian, but people say that we have a Hawaiian heart, and I try to live that way." Yet she feels like many tourists and outsiders misunderstand the culture of Makaha because of its tough reputation.

"There's people that come and they just don't see the beauty of the place—they only see the negative parts," Kathy says. It's like they miss the graceful beauty of the ocean because they can only see the fierce power of the waves. Although anger and violence flare up on occasion, Kathy believes it's just a self-defense mechanism. "I think there's a fierceness, but if you go beyond that, there's a real gentleness, too," Kathy says. "Maybe on the outside, they need to do that for their protection, but there's a lot of gentleness underneath. That's how it is, like how Buff can be intimidating, but then you see him with his grandkids, and all you're going to see is a gentle love there." On the weekends, Uncle Buff often takes the grandkids to the beach in his truck and spends all day playing with them in the ocean.

Although the Westside still wrestles with poverty, drugs, and crime, Makaha has a rich cultural heritage. And nowhere is that more evident than at the Buffalo Big Board Classic, where everyone is welcome. "It doesn't matter whether you're black, yellow, green, or whatever color," Brian says. "If you come here with one Hawaiian heart and learn the Hawaiian way, then you become Hawaiian. . . . Makaha kind of is the heart of Hawai'i, because everybody from around the world comes here when they really want to find the true essence of what Hawai'i is. It really comes down to here, right on this beach, from these people, the surf, the waters, the ocean, the mountains."

In his version of the famous John Denver song, Israel once sang, "Country roads, take me home / to the place where I belong / West Makaha, Mount Ka'ala, take me home, oh country road." Throughout his life, Brian has traveled far from Makaha and shared his culture and lifesaving skills with people around the world, but he always comes back home. Driving down the two-lane country road through the Westside, he is moved by memories of good friends like Bruddah Iz and Sistah Rell, whose spirits hover over the land like the mists upon the Wai'anae Mountains.

"I thought I was going to move and find a better place," he says. "I traveled all over the world, went to Japan, Peru, France, Ecuador, Colombia, New Zealand, everywhere." But no matter how far he flew, he was reeled back in by memories of Makaha. "People come and go, but they always come back," Brian concludes. "I just found that the greatest treasure was here at home."

Acknowledgments

🙂

A'ohe hana nui ka alu'ia.
No task is too big when done together.
—Mary Kawena Pukui, *Olelo Noe'au*

During the four-year odyssey of writing this book, there were times when I thought I might not be able to finish it, but I was helped and encouraged by many people along the way. The experience has taken me to places and introduced me to people who will always be in my heart. While the book is my own independent view of the world of Makaha, I was inspired to write it by the many wonderful people who took me into their homes and shared their stories.

In particular, I want to thank the Keaulana family, especially Uncle Buffalo and Auntie Momi, Brian and Nobleen, Rusty, and Jimmy. I also want to thank Jan Sunn-Carreira, Marlene Kamakawiwo'ole, Jon de Mello, Leah Bernstein, Lisa Soong, and the folks at Mountain Apple Record Company, who have all helped perpetuate the legacies of Rell and Iz. Many *mahalos* to the extended *'ohana* (family) in Makaha who were so generous with their time and stories: Bunky Bakutis, Craig Davidson, Tony Ants Guerrero, Frenchy DeSoto, Bruce DeSoto, Puanani Burgess, Dave Parmenter, Melvin and Momi Pu'u, Kathy Terada, Sunny Garcia and Mike, Sarah, and Keoni Watson.

I also want to thank the legendary watermen who helped shape the sport of surfing and told me wild stories about their glory days: Wally Froiseth, George Downing, Russ Takaki, Greg Noll, Henry Preece,

Kimo Hollinger, Peter Cole, and Ricky Grigg; Fred Hemmings and Randy Rarick, who introduced professional surfing; and the "Bustin' Down the Door" crew who took the pro circuit to the next level, including Rabbit Bartholomew, Shaun Tomson, and Pete Townend. *Mahalo* to the leaders of the Polynesian Voyaging Society and the crew members of the *Hokule'a*: Ben Finney, Herb Kane, Nainoa Thompson, Mel Kinney, John Kruse, and Kimo Hugho. And many thanks to the lifeguards who shared harrowing stories of incredible rescues: Craig Davidson, Ralph Goto, Jim Howe, Mark Cunningham, and Terry Ahue.

Much of *Fierce Heart* is based on personal interviews, so I am grateful to all those mentioned above and all those listed below who shared their memories of the Keaulana, Sunn, and Kamakawiwo'ole families: Greg Ambrose, Bernie Baker, Kelly Beal, Leah Bernstein, Roland Cazimero, Jeanie Chesser, Jon de Mello, Jeff Divine, Mark Fragale, Laird Hamilton, Pam Ka'aihue, Boogie Kalama, Dave Kalama, Don King, Jennifer Lee Koki, Glen Moncata, Bonga Perkins, and Frank B. Shaner. I also want to give a shout-out to those writers whose work helped inform the story: Greg Ambrose, Bunky Bakutis, Steve Barilotti, Rick Carroll, Ben Finney, Jerry Hopkins, Bruce Jenkins, Drew Kampion, Bob Krauss, and Matt Warshaw.

Thanks also to the photographers whose photos help capture glimpses of the larger-than-life personalities of Makaha: Bernie Baker, Doug Behrens, Art Brewer, Lono Goo, Pam Ka'aihue, Minako Kent, Jim Russi, Betty Stickney, and Gary Terrell. Other photos came from the collections of Tony and Jan Sunn-Carreira, Fred Hemmings, and the folks at Mountain Apple Records, who also helped me secure permission to use song lyrics by Leo A. Akana, Del Beazley, Chucky Boy Chock, Mickey Ione, Philip Mitchell, John Denver, Bill and Taffy Danoff, E.Y. Harburg, and Harold Arlen.

This book would have been impossible to write without the help and support of my friends, family, and fellow writers like Sandy Hall, Andrew O'Reardon, David Helvarg, Jesse Kornbluth, and John Morgan. Thanks also to my loyal editor, Daniela Rapp, my helpful agent, Kevan Lyon, and wise counselors Heather Florence and Diana Frost. And a final *mahalo* to all the Hawaiians and "Hawaiians at heart" who shared their aloha (love) and culture with me, as well as my fellow Surfriders and all those dedicated to preserving our oceans, beaches, and coastlines.

Glossary of Hawaiian Words

❦

The Hawaiian language is rich with nuance, and many words have several meanings. The translations below are based on Mary Kawena Pukui and Samuel H. Elbert's *New Pocket Hawaiian Dictionary* (Honolulu: University of Hawaii Press, 1992) and reflect the meanings of the words as they are used in the book.

ahupua'a: Hawaiian land division extending from the uplands to the sea
'aina: land
akamai: smart, clever
Akua: God
ali'i: chief
aloha: love
'anae: mullet
'aumakua: spiritual guardians
e ala e: to awaken, rise up
ha: breath, to breathe
ha'aha'a: low, humble, meek
halau: longhouse for canoe or hula training
hale: house
hana hou: to do again, repeat

hanai: adopted
haole: white person or foreigner
hapa: of mixed blood
he'e nalu: wave-sliding, surfing
heiau: temple
hoku: star
ho'okupu: ceremonial gift offering
hui: group
hukilau: a seine, to fish with a large net
kahili: feather standards, symbolic of royalty
kahu: guardian, pastor
kahuna: priest, minister, expert in any profession
kai: sea
kalo: taro, staple of Hawaiian diet

kama'aina: native-born; land child

kanaka maole: Native Hawaiians

Kanaloa: Hawaiian god of the sea

Kane: Hawaiian god of the sun and sky

kane: male, husband

kaona: hidden meaning in Hawaiian verse

kapu: taboo

kaumaha: heavy; sad, depressed

keiki: children

ki ho'alu: slack key (style of guitar playing)

kolohe: mischievous

Ku: Hawaiian god of war

ku: to stand

kuleana: right, responsibility

Kumulipo: origin, source of life, name of Hawaiian creation chant

kupuna: grandparent, ancestor

lapa'au: to treat with medicine, heal with herbs, cure

Lono: Hawaiian god of Makahiki harvest festivities and agriculture and fertility

lu'au: Hawaiian feast

luna: boss, overseer

maka: eye, face

makaha: fierce, savage

Makahiki: year; ancient festival that begins around August, with four months of sports, festivities, and a taboo on war

makai: toward the ocean

makua: parent

malama: to care for

malo: loincloth

mana: supernatural or divine power

mana'o: meaning

mauka: toward the mountains

mele: song

Menehune: legendary race of small people who worked at night, building fishponds, roads, and temples

moana: ocean

mo'i: King

nalu: waves

'ohana: family

'opu: belly, stomach

pakalolo: marijuana

paniolo: Hawaiian cowboy

pau: finished

pilikia: trouble

poke: sliced raw fish

poli: heart

pono: moral, proper, just

pua: flower

wai: water

Bibliography

Ambrose, Greg. 1996. "Free Your Mind and Your Board Will Follow." *Longboard* 4, no. 1, p. 36.

———.1994. "Heart of the Sea." *Honolulu Star-Bulletin*, March 12.

———. 1989. "An Ocean of Aloha for Sunn, the Queen of Makaha Surfing." *Honolulu Star-Bulletin*, July 18.

———. 1991. *The Surfer's Guide to Hawai'i*. Honolulu: Bess Press.

Bakutis, Bunky. 1979. "West Side Story." *Surfer* 20, no. 9, p. 72.

Barilotti, Steve. 1991. "Makaha: The Forgotten Wave." *Surfer* 32, no. 4, p. 45.

Bartholomew, Wayne "Rabbit," and Tim Baker. 1997. *Bustin' Down the Door*. Queensland, Australia: Harper Sports.

Brody, Bill. 1994. "Russ Never Sleeps." *Longboard* 2, no. 1, p. 20.

Carroll, Nick, and Tim Baker. 1991. "Sons of Makaha." *Surfing* 27, no. 5, p. 99.

Carroll, Rick. 2006. *IZ: Voice of the People*. Honolulu: Bess Press.

Clark, John R. K. 2005. *Beaches of O'ahu*. Honolulu: University of Hawaii Press.

Coleman, Stuart H. 2007. "Beachwise: Brian Keaulana's Heavy Mettle," *Surfer's Journal* 16, no. 1.

———. 2006. "Buffalo Rides Again," *Honolulu Weekly*, March 8.

———. 2004. *Eddie Would Go*. New York: St. Martin's Press.

———. 2008. "IZ Lives," *Hawaii Magazine* 25, no. 1, January/February.

———. 2005. "Waterman," *Spirit of Aloha* 30, no. 4, July/August.

Daws, Gavan. 1968. *Shoal of Time: A History of the Hawaiian Islands.* Honolulu: University of Hawaii Press.

Doyle, David. 2000. *Rescue in Paradise.* Honolulu: Honolulu Island Heritage.

Enomoto, Catherine Kekoa. 1996. "IZ." *Honolulu Star-Bulletin,* May 20.

Finney, Ben. 1979. *Hokule'a: The Way to Tahiti.* New York: Dodd, Mead and Company.

———. 2003. *Sailing in the Wake of the Ancestors.* Honolulu: Bishop Museum Press.

———. 1994. *Voyage of Rediscovery.* Berkeley: University of California Press.

Finney, Ben, and James Huston. *Surfing: A History of the Ancient Sport.* San Francisco: Pomegranate Art Books.

Fornander, Abraham. 1996. *Ancient History of the Hawaiian People to the Times of Kamehameha I.* Honolulu: Mutual Publishing.

Gabbard, Andrea. 2000. *Girl in the Curl: A Century of Women in Surfing.* Seattle: Seal Press.

Grigg, Ricky. 1998. *Big Surf, Deep Dives and the Islands: My Life in the Ocean.* Honolulu: Editions Limited.

———. 2005. "The King of Beasts." *Surfer's Journal* 14, no. 1.

Hall, Sandra K., and Greg Ambrose. 1995. *Memories of Duke.* Honolulu: Bess Press.

Hartwell, Jay. 1981. "Music from the Land." *Honolulu Advertiser,* September 4.

Hawk, Steve. 1994. "Nose First." *Surfer* 35, no. 4, p. 78.

Heart of the Sea. 2002. Swell Cinema. Documentary.

Hemmings, Fred. 1997. *The Soul of Surfing Is Hawaiian.* Honolulu: Sports Enterprises.

Hopkins, Jerry. "Skippy Kamakawiwo'ole: Bigger than Life." Unpublished article.

Hulet, Scott. 1994. "Oxbow World Longboard Championship." *Longboard* 2, no. 5, p. 46.

———. 1995. "Oxbow World Longboard Championship." *Longboard* 3, no. 4, p. 92.

In God's Hands. 1998. TriStar Pictures. Feature film.

IZ: The Man Behind the Music. 2004. Phil Arnone, Prod. Documentary.

Jenkins, Bruce. 1999. "Buffalo's Soldiers: Meet the Greatest Surfing Family of All Time." *Surfer* 39, no. 10, p. 240.

———. 1998. "Catch One for Rell." *San Francisco Chronicle,* January 15.

———. 1999. *The North Shore Chronicles.* Berkeley: Frog, Ltd.

Kamakau, Samuel. 1992. *The Ruling Chiefs of Hawaii.* Honolulu: Kamehameha Schools Press.

Kampion, Drew. 2001. "Clockwork Blue." *Surfer's Journal* 10, no. 2, p. 60.

———. 2007. *Greg Noll: The Art of the Surfboard.* Salt Lake City: Gibbs Smith.

———. 2003. *Stoked: A History of Surf Culture.* Salt Lake City: Gibbs Smith.

Kanahele, George H. S. 1986. *Ku Kanaka: Stand Tall.* Honolulu: University of Hawaii Press.

Kane, Herb K. 1976. *Voyage: The Discovery of Hawaii.* Honolulu: Island Heritage.

Kirch, Patrick V. 1996. *Legacy of the Landscape.* Honolulu: University of Hawaii Press.

Krauss, Bob. 1989. "Surfer Rell Sunn: A Profile in Courage." *Honolulu Advertiser,* February 13.

Kyselka, Will. 1987. *An Ocean in Mind.* Honolulu: University of Hawaii Press.

Marcus, Ben. 1996. "Exer-Psychos." *Surfer* 37, no. 3, p. 74.

McGrath, Edward J. Jr., Kenneth M. Brewer, and Bob Krauss. 1973. *Historic Wai'anae: "A Place of Kings."* Norfolk Island: Island Heritage.

Morinaga, Dayton. 1993. "For Sunn, Surfing Is the Perfect Prescription." *Honolulu Advertiser,* August 20.

Noll, Greg, and Andrew Gabbard. 1989. *Da Bull: Life over the Edge.* Berkeley: North Atlantic Books.

Otaguro, Janice. 1989. "Rell Sunn." *Honolulu,* December.

Paniccia, Patti. 2003. "Seventies Pro Genesis." *Surfer's Journal* 12, no. 2.

Parmenter, Dave. 1999. "Coyote Lines: Buffalo's Waltz." *Surfer* 40, no. 7, p. 108.

———. 2000. "Coyote Lines: The Over-the-Hill Gang." *Surfer* 41, no. 7, p. 106.

Pukui, Mary K., ed. 1983. *Nana I Ke Kumu: Look to the Source,* vol. 2. Honolulu: Bishop Museum Press.

———. 1993. *Olelo No'eau: Hawaiian Proverbs and Poetical Sayings.* Honolulu: Bishop Museum Press.

Sunn, Rell. 1981. "Makaha, Station 47, Bravo." *Surfer* 22, no. 9, p. 76.

———. 1998. "A Young Woman and the Sea." *Honolulu Star-Bulletin,* January 12.

Timmons, Grady. 1989. *Waikiki Beachboy.* Honolulu: Editions Limited.

Warshaw, Matt. 2003. *The Encyclopedia of Surfing.* New York: Harcourt.

Wood, Ben. 1981. "Makaha Sons of Ni'ihau." *Honolulu Star-Bulletin,* February 17.

www.iz.honoluluadvertiser.com

www.mountainapplecompany.com

www.rellsunn.com

Index